MODERN CONDITIONS, POSTMODERN CONTROVERSIES

Modern Conditions, Postmodern Controversies presents an authoritative, wide-ranging and revealing discussion of the complex processes and practices which are reshaping social life today. It provides a clear and detailed analysis of reactions and responses to the problems and possibilities identified with prevailing 'modern' and emerging 'postmodern' forms of life.

Barry Smart explores specific political issues and analytical themes, looking in detail at the effect of information technology on social life, transformations in the capitalist mode of production, ideas about possible alternative 'post-industrial' social futures, and the impact of modern media and communications on forms of human sensibility. The unifying theme and central focus of his discussion is modernity and its consequences, especially the growing anxiety about 'the project of modernity' and the emergence of postmodern conditions. Barry Smart demonstrates the critical and radical potential of postmodern ideas, embodied in new cultural and political forms, intellectual practices, and experiences of space and time. He explores the connections and the tensions between Marxism and postmodernism, and examines the theoretical responses from social thinkers like Talcott Parsons, Daniel Bell, Alvin Toffler, André Gorz, Marshall McLuhan, Walter Benjamin, Jean Baudrillard, Jurgen Habermas, Marshall Berman, Jean François Lyotard, Frederic Jameson and David Harvey.

This balanced and informative account of what we mean by 'modernity' and 'postmodernity' is an invaluable guide to the central intellectual debate of the 1980s and 1990s. It will be of special interest to students of sociology, cultural studies and politics.

ROUTLEDGE SOCIAL FUTURES SERIES
General Editor: Barry Smart

Title in preparation

Ecology, Culture and Politics
Anna Bramwell

MODERN CONDITIONS, POSTMODERN CONTROVERSIES

Barry Smart

London and New York

First published in 1992
by Routledge
11 New Fetter Lane, London EC4P 4EE

Simultaneously published in the USA and Canada
by Routledge
a division of Routledge, Chapman and Hall Inc.
29 West 35th Street, New York, NY 10001

Typeset in Bembo by LaserScript Limited, Mitcham, Surrey
Printed and bound in Great Britain by
Mackays of Chatham PLC, Chatham, Kent

British Library Cataloguing in Publication Data
Smart, Barry *1946–*
Modern conditions, postmodern controversies.
– (Social futures v. 1)
1. Sociology
I. Title II. Series
301

Library of Congress Cataloging in Publication Data
Smart, Barry
Modern conditions: postmodern controversies/Barry Smart.
p.   cm. – (Social futures)
Includes bibliographical references and index.
1. Social change. 2. Postmodernism – Social aspects.
3. Technology and civilization. 4. Information technology
– Social aspects. I. Title. II. Series.
HM101.S62   1992
303.4 – dc20   91-12946
                                           CIP

ISBN 0–415–02902–3
0–415–06952–1 (pbk)

'. . . the First Industrial Revolution devalued muscle
work, then the second one devalued routine mental
work . . .'
'Do you suppose there'll be a Third Industrial Revolution?'
'A third one? What would that be like?'
'I don't know exactly. The first and second ones must have
been sort of inconceivable at one time.'
'. . . I guess the third one's been going on for some time,
if you mean thinking machines. That would be the third
revolution, I guess — machines that devaluate human
thinking.'
Kurt Vonnegut *Player Piano*

I had always thought that doubting was a scientific duty,
but now I came to distrust the very masters who had
taught me to doubt.
Umberto Eco *Foucault's Pendulum*

CONTENTS

ACKNOWLEDGEMENTS

Various versions of the arguments developed in this book have been presented at conferences held in America, Australia, England, and Spain, and in seminars organised at the Universities of Auckland, Complutense, Monash, and Salamanca.

I would like to thank participants for their helpful and encouraging comments, their suggestions, and their criticisms.

An earlier, abbreviated version of chapter 5, presented at the *American Sociological Association* annual conference in August 1989 in San Francisco, has been published in *Theories of Modernity and Postmodernity* edited by Bryan S. Turner (Sage 1990).

I would also like to thank Chris Rojek, Senior Editor at Routledge, for his invaluable advice and assistance, both with this book and the series as a whole, and last, but by no means least, Kym Fullerton for her meticulous preparation of the manuscript.

1

REFLECTIONS ON CHANGE

Change constitutes an increasingly prominent aspect of modern life. Indeed it might be regarded as the defining feature, for modern times are generally held to be changing times. Certainly the prospect of change now seems to be perpetually present, as both promise and threat. And if the possibility and the expectation of change has become virtually a routine feature of everyday life, a commonplace, the reality of change is no less evident. Extensive and intensive processes of social, cultural, economic, and political change, and the impact of such transformations upon experiences of everyday life, make it increasingly difficult to dispute the view that the world seems to be changing in fundamental ways. But it is precisely in such circumstances that it becomes necessary to proceed with a degree of caution, to recall that radical forms of change are by no means confined to the present, and to remember that although change increasingly constitutes the focus of our attention it may nevertheless be 'not the rule but the exception in social life' (Heilbroner 1961, p. 195). In short, as Touraine has observed, 'social life cannot be reduced to change' (1982, p. 233).

A number of analysts and commentators seem, however, to be in little doubt that the present era constitutes a significant moment in history, a turning point, a time of transition and radical change. Ideas abound concerning the 'end of history' (Fukuyama), the 'end of the social' (Baudrillard), as well as the end of industrial society and the promise of the Enlightenment (Touraine). Signs of significant forms of change have been identified in a number of different areas, in scientific knowledge and technology; culture and communications; work, industry, and economic life; political organisations and movements; and social relationships and forms of subjectivity. For example, it has been argued that the increasing internationalisation of

1

economic and cultural life is impinging upon the sovereignty of nation states and eroding the fragile unity of their constituted societies (Touraine 1989). In many instances the changes identified are believed to derive from transformations in the capitalist mode of production. Capitalism, once again responding to its inescapable and recurring crisis tendency, is held to be in transition, this time from 'Fordism' to a more flexible and global form of accumulation. But whilst the current crisis appears to be containable, to be manageable, there are signs that the 'cracks in the reflecting mirrors of economic performance' (Harvey 1989, p. 357) are growing. The perpetually promised prospect of an end to capitalism may, once more, have been deferred, but the contradictions remain, indeed they seem to be accumulating. In short the problems of contemporary capitalism have not disappeared (Heilbroner 1976; Gorz 1982) although actually existing socialist alternatives appear to be doing so at an accelerating rate. Poland, Hungary, Bulgaria, Czechoslovakia, the Soviet Union, and what was, before reunification, the German Democratic Republic, have each embarked upon programmes of social, economic, and political reform, which signify radical departures from the canons of Marxist–Leninist orthodoxy, and an abandonment of what has come to be known as 'actually existing socialism'. What will emerge from the various programmes of reform, from the different twists and turns made towards multi-party political systems and away from centralised state regulation of economic activity in the societies of formerly existing socialism is a matter of speculation. Contrary to one much publicised version of 'the end of history' thesis, the changes and reforms under way do not necessarily signify either that 'the West' has won, or that there is no further scope for viable alternatives to prevailing forms of economic and political organisation (viz. 'free market' and 'liberal democratic'). The disarticulation of Comecon and the collapse of repressive totalitarian political regimes in Eastern Europe demonstrate the economic ineffectiveness and political unacceptability of a particular (per)version of socialism. It does not necessarily constitute a vindication of either 'the West' or capitalism. The radical transformation of the societies of actually existing socialism need not mean the end either of the idea of socialism, or of the possibility of a future post-capitalist social formation. However, if the idea of socialism is to continue to survive as a form of 'radical imaginary' it will be necessary to 'transcend the current mood of . . . "left melancholy"' (Jay 1988, p. 2). Likewise, the possibility of realising a post-capitalist form of life will depend to a substantial degree upon the ability to 'envisage alternative futures whose very propagation might help them be realised' (Giddens 1990, p. 154).

Although it may be argued that 'advanced industrial' capitalism has been responsible for generating 'the highest material standard of living for large masses of people in human history' (Berger 1987, p. 43), that standard has not been achieved without problems or costs, the most serious of which we are only of late, let us hope not too late, beginning fully to appreciate. It is important not to be overawed by unquestioned quantitative indices of increases in standards of living, nor seduced by unexamined qualitative signs of improvement in life-styles. The much vaunted advances in standards of living and styles of life have precipitated new problems and difficulties. If increases in material standards of living have been shared by large masses of people, the shares have been inequitably distributed, and the distribution is, if anything, becoming more, rather than less, unequal. Furthermore, a substantial majority of the world's population have been excluded from a shareholding in most, if not all, of the benefits.

Capitalism continues to generate unacceptable forms of inequality and exploitation, to stimulate individual or private interest to the detriment of public or community provision, and to contribute to the disorganisation of communities and damage of the environment. The material prosperity enjoyed by substantial sections of the population in the geo-political unities of 'the West', 'the North', and the 'developed World' is paid for, in part, by the socially and economically disenfranchised and impoverished inhabitants marginalised within those very same unities, but most of all the cost is born in the other hemisphere, in 'the South', in the societies, spaces, and territories which have provided the raw materials, crops, cheap labour, and sufficiently distant 'safe' locations in which to site potentially dangerous forms of commodity production and to dump toxic waste. 'Actually existing socialism' has failed, and not before time. But the escalating international debt crisis, the increasing volatility of industrial and commercial life, the growing risk of financial failure and bankruptcy, the continuing waste of resources, the degradation of the meaning and place of work in the lives of the majority of people, and the prospect of an accelerating ecological crisis, signify that the profit and growth oriented international capitalist economic system of production is also, in fundamental respects, failing the majority of people, and delivering, at best, a semblance or a simulation of success only to those completely seduced by the promise of increasing consumption, or consumed with the prospect of further seduction (Baudrillard 1990).

The development of industrial capitalism as a mode of economic production has been closely articulated with the formation of the modern nation-state. With the accumulation of administrative power, achieved through an extension of surveillance capacity, the state has become less dependent 'upon control of the means of violence as a medium of rule of its subject population' (Giddens 1985, p. 201) and more reliant upon the participation of the governed in the processes and practices of government. Within the West, liberal democracy has been promoted as the most appropriate vehicle for ensuring that governments are sufficiently responsive to the interests and preferences of their citizens. However, it is becoming increasingly evident that all is not well with liberal democracy. Low levels of participation in the democratic political process suggest a growing disaffection with or cynicism towards democratic politics. Along with increasing fears and insecurities arising from modern forms of life (e.g. rising levels of crime, violence, drug use, and the rapid growth of numerous stress-related conditions) and problems with the funding, organisation, and operation of key social institutions (viz. education, health, and welfare) the West begins to look far from a model of the best.

In addition to the aggravation of a diverse range of 'local' difficulties we now encounter a series of complex global problems. Population growth, the increasing depletion of natural resources, the proliferation of nuclear and chemical weapons, growing environmental pollution, and the prospect of dramatic global climatic changes threaten our survival. We have become acutely aware that 'rationally organised social arrangements are not necessarily a means of increased freedom – for the individual or for the society' (Wright Mills 1970, p. 187). The increasing power of multinational organisations and enterprises, and anonymous bureaucracies equipped with sophisticated surveillance technologies threatens the justice of our social institutions. And not infrequently our attempted solutions add to, rather than diminish, our difficulties. If this summary appears bleak our prospects need not be so. But to proceed more effectively requires a willingness to reconsider the present and its complex possibilities, something more than a nostalgic retrieval of fast fading forms of life, a thoughtless endorsement of the prevailing technicist paradigm of progress, or panic stricken response to the imminent prospect, and

4

potentially problematic impact of future forms of life. And something less than a resurrection of those grand designs which have served to keep us in the dark. What is now necessary is 'neither a return to the alleged virtues of the past nor a simple revival of the approaches of the present, . . . but a change in perspective, in the frame of mind with which we approach things' (Dahrendorf 1975, p. 70). The implication of this is not that we should abandon utopian forms of thought for a 'cynical pragmatism', but rather that the alternative futures we envisage need to balance utopian ideals with realism (Giddens 1990). In brief it might be argued that there is a pressing need to reconstitute utopian thought, both to counter despair and disappointment (Williams 1985) and to overcome notions of historical 'spontaneity' and 'objective' economic laws (Bahro 1978). But more importantly it is needed because the future is constituted, in part at least, through the visions of alternative possibilities informing the actions of agents in the present. Because 'anticipations of the future become part of the present, thereby rebounding upon how the future actually develops' (Giddens 1990, p. 178). In sum the task becomes to analyse the present, to explore existing patterns of social life, as well as potential alternatives, with a view to constructing imaginative conceptions of possible futures. It is not a matter of extrapolating from prevailing trends, but rather of constituting a radical imaginary through which existing social institutions, practices, and experiences may be rendered problematic, or radically relativised, and alternative 'realistic' possibilities promoted (Laclau and Mouffe 1985).

But at the same time we need to exercise appropriate caution in our analysis and assessment of forms of change. In particular it is necessary to consider the extent of our vulnerability to the assumption that our own time is somehow special or different, a turning point, a moment radically disrupted by forms of social, cultural, economic, and political change. The idea that the present is distinctive or unique may well owe something to the proximity of the end of the millennium. Aware as we might be of both the arbitrariness of the dating scheme introduced by Dionysius Exiguus and the range of potential alternative schemes for measuring or ordering time (viz. Jewish, Chinese, and Muslim calendars), the 'millenarian spirit' (Williams 1985) continues to exert a potent and seductive influence upon our understanding. Towards the end of the first millennium Western civilisation was beset by fears about the end of the world, the eruption of 'legions of the Devil' out of the East, and the prospect that epidemics would wipe out humankind (Focillon 1970; Chatwin

1987). As the end of the second millennium approaches it is evident that we are bedevilled by a not incomparable 'modern' set of fears and anxieties. The implication is not that history is simply repeating itself, rather that it is necessary to be mindful of the tendency to exaggerate the distinctiveness or uniqueness of our own time. As one analyst has cautioned:

> Here, I think, we are touching on . . . one of the most harmful habits in contemporary thought, in modern thought even . . . the analysis of the present as being precisely, in history, a present of rupture, or of high point, or of completion or of a returning dawn . . . I think we should have the modesty to say to ourselves that, on the one hand, the time we live in is not *the* unique or fundamental or irruptive point in history where everything is completed and begun again. We must also have the modesty to say, on the other hand, that . . . the time we live in is very interesting; it needs to be analyzed and broken down, and that we would do well to ask ourselves, 'What is the nature of our present?' . . . With the proviso that we do not allow ourselves the facile, rather theatrical declaration that this moment in which we exist is one of total perdition, in the abyss of darkness, or a triumphant daybreak, etc. It is a time like any other, or rather, a time which is never quite like any other.
>
> (Foucault 1983, p. 206)

CONCEPTIONS AND ANALYSES OF SOCIAL CHANGE

Within sociological inquiry conceptions and analyses of change have occupied a central position. The construction of a theory of social change has been a prominent and longstanding objective, but it has proven to be an elusive goal. Ironically in a context where an understanding of the present more than ever requires an understanding of processes of change, the way in which change has tended to be conceptualised and analysed is being increasingly subject to question. The conventional focus of modern sociology upon 'society', the reality of which has tended to be the geo-political form of the nation-state, and the corollary, a preoccupation with *societal* change, is now considered to be difficult to sustain (Touraine 1989). The implication is that as the world has become increasingly 'globalised' so existing sociological understandings of change, drawn predominantly from the works of the master thinkers of the nineteenth century, have become simultaneously less appropriate and more problematic (Robertson and Lechner 1985; Giddens 1987). One proposal arising from the above is that it has now become necessary to deconstruct a wide range of theories of social change, an important consequence of which is 'to deny that some of the most cherished ambitions of social theory – including those of "historical materialism" – can be realised' (Giddens 1984, p. 227). To make sense of such criticisms it is necessary to consider briefly the conceptions and analyses of social change that have tended to inform and influence our understandings of social life.

It is worth recalling that the possibility of a scientific analysis of both the organisation of social life and processes of social change began to be explicitly articulated in a particular historical and cultural context, notably in Western Europe during the course of the eighteenth and nineteenth centuries. In short, sociology emerged with modernity, its epistemological and institutional conditions of existence being synonymous with the development of modern forms of life (Smart 1982). Furthermore, the substantive concerns and methodological preoccupations which shaped the early development of sociology have continued to exert an influence upon contemporary analyses and understandings, and it is aspects of this legacy, and in some cases the legacy itself as a whole, that are now being subject to challenge and criticism. As modernity has become a matter of contention, so sociology, 'bound up with the "project of modernity"' (Giddens 1987, p. 26) has found itself in something of a double-bind. Put another way, it might be argued that the magic associated with 'the mystery of modernity – that great adventure of the north-western tip of the European peninsula' (Bauman 1987, p. 81) has become more than a little tarnished as modernity has become the object of its own powerful 'heretical imperative' (Berger 1979). It is here, in this controversial context, that consideration has turned to the implications for sociological inquiry of a possible transformation of modernity following the apparent development of conditions provisionally and somewhat ambiguously designated *post-modern* (Bauman 1988a: 1988b; Smart 1990).

Scientific analyses of social life and processes of social change are incontrovertibly constitutive features of the modern era. The analytic origins of social scientific forms of inquiry have been carefully traced back to the writings of a diverse group of Enlightenment philosophers in France (e.g. Montesquieu; Rousseau; Condorcet), Italy (e.g. Vico), Scotland (e.g. Hume; Ferguson; Millar) and, to a somewhat lesser

7

extent, Germany and America. It is in the texts of the various Enlightenment *philosophes* that key elements of modern thought concerning the value of science, the power of reason, the irresistible progress or advance of humanity, and the prospect of freedom from oppression first receive systematic articulation and endorsement. As for the institutional conditions of emergence, the conventional wisdom is that the social, economic, and political consequences of the French and Industrial Revolutions provided the appropriate context within which sociological forms of analysis could find their *raison d'être* (Bierstedt 1979; Nisbet 1980; Badham 1986). However, it would be a mistake to believe that the whole story commences with the Enlightenment. Whilst there might be few serious objections to the conventional association of modernity with the conjuncture identified as the Enlightenment, it is indisputable that other events and additional moments have contributed to the inauguration of critical differences constitutive of the modern era. The riddle of modernity is not so easily resolved.

The modern idea of social change, which has grown in the wake of the development of scientific knowledge and technology since the Enlightenment, has its roots in the doctrines of classical antiquity and early Christian thought. Themes present in early Greek and Hebrew thought concerning the progressive advance of humanity subsequently were articulated in Christian theology in a theory of social development (Nisbet 1980). History was effectively constituted as a process of change through which humanity was moving to a divine and preordained end. For example, in *The City of God* Augustine (1931) preserves the Aristotelian conception of reality as one of orderly and purposeful change, developing stage by stage to a preordained end, but invokes in addition the divine will of God as the motor of historical development. In short, history is synonymous with God working his purpose out. A comparable conception of historical development, but assuming a secular form, has continued to exercise an influence over ideas about modern forms of change. The significant difference is that we no longer seem to be quite so sure what the purpose is, or should be, or for that matter how it ought to be worked out. Hopes for modernity may not have been entirely lost, it is true, but there seems to have been a marked shift of emphasis, as the twentieth century has unfolded, to the risks and difficulties arising from the complex forms of change engendered by the process of modernisation (Giddens 1990). The long complex process of erosion of traditional institutions and practices and its corollary, the diffusion of modern forms of life, once seemed to promise the prospect of increasing progress and control, and in consequence was regarded positively, with enthusiasm and optimism. Now the process is viewed more soberly, as a mixed blessing, offering new forms of security, yet simultaneously an increase in risks and dangers.

The characteristic features of modern conceptions and theories of social change began to crystallise in the course of the seventeenth century, in disputes over the respective merits of the works of classical antiquity and an emerging modern Europe. The view of the 'moderns', that knowledge had accumulated over time, and that therefore the human mind might be considered to have evolved to a higher stage or form, ultimately achieved ascendancy over the position articulated by those, the 'ancients', who argued for the superiority of a former 'golden age' (Bock 1979). Such a conception of the necessary historical growth of knowledge prepared the way for the philosophers of the Enlightenment to argue that there existed a more general process of human development to which cultures and civilisations were positively inclined. This was a process of movement and change whose truth the application of reason and scientific techniques of observation would ultimately uncover, thereby opening up the prospect of a rational regulation or progressive (re)ordering of social life. One key implication of this was that progressive change might be considered an intrinsic feature of modern social life and associated forms of human existence.

The eighteenth-century philosophers of the Enlightenment brought together and effectively synthesised two elements of philosophical and intellectual thought which had been a central feature of seventeenth century inquiry, namely 'rational' and 'empirical' philosophy. An understanding or knowledge of natural and social reality was deemed to depend upon a unity of reason and observation, made possible by the practice of scientific methods of inquiry. Through a rigorous investigation of phenomena it was assumed that there would emerge not only an understanding of the prevailing order of things, but also of the potentialities dormant, waiting to be realised, in existing forms. There would emerge a knowledge of both existing and possible future forms of life, as well as the social technologies necessary to achieve a managed transcendence from an existing order to a 'higher', more advanced form of life. Such assumptions, and criticisms of them, contributed to the foundation of later intellectual developments, notably the emergence of the modern social sciences, and sociological forms of inquiry in particular (Kumar 1978). The idea that scientific reasoning and analysis provides an appropriately 'rational' basis upon which social life can be reorganised and social problems and conflicts reduced, if not resolved, remains a feature of contemporary social and political thought. But it is an idea that continues to be a matter of discussion and debate, in particular because of the problematic moral and political consequences which have also been identified with the rationalisation process of modernity (Bauman 1987: 1989). The question of the appropriateness, desirability, and impact, or effect, of particular forms of analysis upon social life and human conduct remains a matter of contention. It is a question which has received a further controversial twist within the debate over the possible emergence of a 'postmodern condition' of knowledge (Lyotard 1986; Lyotard and Thébaud 1985).

As I have implied, it would be wrong to infer that Enlightenment philosophy has exercised an unchallenged influence upon either the formation of the social and human sciences in the course of the nineteenth century, or their subsequent development during the twentieth century. For there have been significant critical reactions to the idea of a progressive, rational reconstitution of society. In direct contrast to the Enlightenment conception of progress through reason, eighteenth-century romantic and conservative thinkers expressed criticism of both the possibility and the potential effects of rationally engineered attempts to engender new or higher forms of social life. Critical reaction to the principles of Enlightenment philosophy was articulated in various ways. But the abiding preoccupation was with the virtues of social order and stability, the problems rather than the benefits following from the transformations associated with the advent of revolutionary democracy and industrialism, transformations which had precipitated a shift from the *ancien régime* to a 'more individualistic, impersonal and contractual' kind of society (Nisbet 1979). In consequence, it was not preservation of the status quo, but rather a restoration of the status quo ante, that constituted the predominant theme of criticisms. For critics such as Bonald and de Maistre the processes of social change unleashed by the forces of Protestant religious activity, capitalist economic practice, and scientific forms of knowledge and investigation were believed to have weakened the fabric of social life. To that extent the emerging 'modern' era, lacking in stability and order, was considered to be intrinsically regressive (Kumar 1987). It was the identification of prevailing forms of social disorganisation and political instability with modernity *per se* which led anti-Enlightenment thinkers to call nostalgically for a return to pre-modern forms of life, to promote the idea of a reconstruction of the medieval European social order.

The idea that modernity has a dark side is a familiar theme. As histories of sociological thought have demonstrated, the difficulties created by the scope, pace, and character of the transformations synonymous with the emergence of modern forms of life have been regularly acknowledged. However, if there has been a general willingness to face up to the problems generated by modernity, there has been a marked variation in diagnoses of the scale of the difficulties encountered, remedies proposed, and future prospects identified. The most common response has been to portray modernity as essentially progressive and, in consequence, the associated instabilities, forms of disorganisation, risks and dangers, what might be described as the crisis tendencies, have been regarded as temporary or transitional dysfunctions or contradictions, which by implication are remedial. In brief the problems of modernity have been conceived to be open to remedy through a powerful combination of increasing scientific knowledge about social life and related forms of sociopolitical intervention orientated to the constitution of a new, more highly evolved or progressive social order. Although articulated at times in radically different terms the general outline of such a response is evident in the respective writings of classical figures such as Saint-Simon, Comte, Marx, and Durkheim, as well as in the works of more contemporary analysts who have returned to, and developed, evolutionary conceptions of social change, the most obvious example here being Talcott Parsons (Kumar 1978; Bock 1979; Nisbet 1980; Giddens 1984). It is a response which represents an endorsement of the idea of progress derived from the work of the eighteenth-century *philosophes*. Generalising from a specific period in Western history, a powerful 'picture of, on the whole, continuous and sustained and mainly endogenous upward growth, morally, intellectually, technologically, is inescapably and gratifyingly suggested' (Gellner 1964, p. 12). This is the 'world growth story', a Eurocentric narrative which filters everything 'through the West and its values' (Nisbet 1980, p. 150).

It is a story which has projected a specific history of Western civilisation as the history of human civilisation in general, a narrative which has assumed that the social, economic, and political development of Western societies exemplifies a universal evolutionary process of 'modernisation'. But it is not the whole story.

There have been other responses, other analyses which have revealed the problems of modernity to be far more substantial, and in so far as they are a corollary of indispensable features of modern forms of life, possibly insurmountable. Consider, for example, Weber's fateful prognosis for the future development of the 'modern Occident', namely that the growth of formal or technical rationality, indispensable to modern industrial capitalist society, simultaneously threatens to undermine fundamental Western values (e.g. autonomy, creativity, and democracy); Tocqueville's critical prophecies concerning the effects which modern democratic forms of equality might have on Western civilisation; Schopenhauer's scepticism about the possibility of historical progress; and Nietzsche's conception of the increasing decadence of Western society. Such concerns have received a further elaboration in the writings of twentieth-century social analysts preoccupied with the alleged detrimental effects of the emergence of 'mass society' or 'mass culture', increasing industrialisation, the continuing growth and diffusion of the capitalist mode of production, and the accelerating rate of associated forms of social change. Notwithstanding such criticisms it is the idea of progress that has predominated within Western civilisation, the idea that humanity 'has advanced in the past . . . is now advancing, and will continue to advance through the foreseeable future' (Nisbet 1980, pp. 4–5).

CHANGE, EVOLUTION, AND PROGRESS

The modern idea of progress was forged during the seventeenth-century quarrel between the 'ancients' and the 'moderns' (Bock 1979). It was essentially a dispute about the relative merits of the civilisations of classical antiquity and modern Europe, from which emerged the theory, articulated by Fontenelle, 'of the indefinite progress of knowledge' (Bury 1921, p. 110). The identification of an increase in knowledge between the two civilisations was conceived to be symptomatic of a progressive process of human development. In the course of the eighteenth century the idea of progress, and the associated notion of a natural evolutionary process of human development, was extended from the sphere of knowledge to the more general social and material conditions governing human existence. These two strands, of a cumulative improvement in knowledge and social, moral, and material advance, have been central to nineteenth- and twentieth-century analyses of modern social life, processes of social change, and visions proffered of potential social futures.

12

From the works of Saint-Simon (1760–1825) and Comte (1798–1857) down to the analyses of modern social theorists such as Talcott Parsons (1902–79) sociological discussion has continually returned to questions of evolution and progress, the present and likely future development of Western societies, the contribution of scientific forms of knowledge and associated technological innovations to the regulation of processes of social change, and the measures necessary to ensure or establish orderly forms of social life. In the respective works of Saint-Simon and Comte there is a conception of civilisation progressing through an evolutionary process of social change interrupted by periods of turmoil as transitional difficulties are encountered and resolved. They each regarded their own age as witnessing the emergence of a new organic form of civilisation, the development of a modern industrial social order, and argued that the organisation and administration of the new order would be based upon science. Both were concerned about the forms of social disorder and disorganisation accompanying the emergence of modern industrial forms of life and proposed similar remedies. To counter the disarray arising from the collapse of the old medieval order Saint-Simon advocated a combination of the administration of social life by a scientific–artistic–industrial estate and the cultivation of a renewed sense of moral unity through a 'New Christianity', charged

> to achieve the triumph of the principles of universal morality in the struggle which is going on with the forces aiming at the individual instead of public interests . . . [and] called upon to link together the scientists, artists, and industrialists and to make them the managing directors of the human race, as well as of the particular interests of each individual people.
>
> (Saint-Simon 1964, p. 105)

Many of the concerns articulated by Saint-Simon are repeated in the work of Comte. For example, the idea of the evolutionary development of human civilisation is endorsed, as is the proposal that the problems of social instability arising from the Industrial and French Revolutions may be alleviated, if not resolved, by a combination of 'positive' philosophy, or sociology, and moral reorganisation (Fletcher 1974). Comte's response to the trials and tribulations identified with the erosion of 'traditional' forms of life and emergence of an industrial social order anticipates a late twentieth-century reaction to an alleged 'crisis' of modernity associated with the development of 'postindustrial' capitalist forms of life (Bell 1973: 1976).

Evolutionary conceptions of change and associated assumptions concerning progress have also been identified in the respective works of Durkheim and Marx. Although their respective conceptions of the mechanism, temper, and tempo of change differ significantly, it has been argued that "'endogenous" or "unfolding" models of change' (Giddens 1984, p. 229) are clearly present in their analyses. In Durkheim's work social changes derive from a process of increasing structural differentiation, and the pace of change is represented as necessarily slow (Smith 1973). Social change for Marx is closely articulated with transformations in the mode of production, with 'the expansion of the forces of production within a given type of society' (Giddens 1984). The temper is uneven and the tempo variable, but it is almost inevitable, in Marx's view, that at some point change will become conflictual, if not violent, and rapid in form. There is also a strong sense of change being progressive as it creates the material preconditions for a promised future realisation of human potential. If it is 'difficult to place the work of Karl Marx in the history of the idea of progress' (Bock 1979, p. 68) it is also necessary, for Marxist analyses have undoubtedly made a major contribution to the 'world growth story'. In a number of texts Marx and Engels outline a conception of historical stages of development which implies an endorsement of the idea of progress. *The German Ideology* (1976) describes human development in terms of the evolution of forms of ownership (tribal, ancient, feudal, and capitalist). Similar arguments are presented in *The Communist Manifesto* (Marx and Engels 1968), the 'Preface' to *A Contribution to the Critique of Political Economy* (Marx 1976), and in more detail, in *Pre-Capitalist Economic Formations* (Marx 1964). Whilst the focus of Marx's analysis is, for the most part, confined to Western Europe, or to be more precise, the capitalist mode of production in England, it is clear that its relevance was assumed to extend beyond those shores. In brief the future of the industrially 'less developed' society is mirrored in the 'more developed' (Marx 1974, p. 19).

The attribution of an evolutionary conception of change and associated assumptions concerning progress is not only controversial in relation to Marx's work, it may also be a matter of dispute in respect of Durkheim's project. Although Durkheim has frequently been represented as the classical theorist most responsible for the articulation of a theory of evolution in terms of a process of increasing structural differentiation, there are one or two jarring notes to which I will briefly refer before proceeding to a simpler case. As is well known, Durkheim argues in *The Division of Labour in Society* (1984) that a distinction may be drawn between 'higher', or more complex, societies and 'lower', or simpler, societies on the basis of their respective forms of social solidarity or cohesion, namely 'organic' and 'mechanical'. The latter, a form of cohesion based upon resemblance, becomes 'progressively enfeebled' as the division of labour advances, producing specialisation, individual differences, and a 'more humane' and 'more rational' morality. The description of the process of a growing division of labour as 'a fact of a very general nature' to which all societies must conform, suggests that Durkheim was indeed influenced by ideas of evolution and progress (Bock 1979). But a number of qualifications are appropriate, if not necessary.

To begin with, Durkheim rejects the view outlined by Comte that the progress of human development may be conceived as a linear evolutionary process. As Durkheim comments,

> if one single social species exists, individual societies can differ among themselves only in degree . . . If on the contrary social types exist qualitatively distinct from one another . . . then they cannot be joined like the identical sections of a straight line in geometry. Historical development thus loses the ideal and simple continuity attributed to it.
>
> (Durkheim 1964, p. 78)

Durkheim's preference was for a classification of societies in terms of 'social species', not historical phases, it being argued that there are as many social types, or species, as there are ways for the most basic or simple social segments to combine to form new societies, and for these in their turn to combine amongst themselves. Elaborating on this alternative schema Durkheim observes that:

> Since its origin, France has passed through very different forms of civilisation; it began by being agricultural, passed to craft industry and to small commerce, then to manufacturing and finally to large-scale industry. Now, it is impossible to admit that the same collective individuality can change its species three or four times. A species must define itself by more constant characteristics. The economic state, technological state etc, present phenomena too unstable and complex to furnish the basis of a classification. It is even very probable that the same industrial, scientific, and artistic civilisation can be found in societies where hereditary constitution is very different. Japan may in the future borrow our arts, our industry, even our

political organisation; it will not cease to belong to a different species from France and Germany.

(Durkheim 1964, p. 88, n. 10)

In turn, the idea that a given stage of development of a civilisation may be considered to predetermine future progress is questionable. All that may be observed is a series of changes with no evident causal link. In other words we are able 'to say that certain conditions have succeeded one another up to the present, but not in what order they will henceforth succeed one another, since the cause on which they are supposed to depend is not scientifically determined or determinable' (Durkheim 1964, p. 118). And turning to the respective analyses of Comte and Spencer, Durkheim argues that although the scientific–industrial stage has been presented as both the definitive state of humanity and the appropriate social milieu for maximising happiness, we do not know, indeed cannot know, 'whether another stage will not emerge . . . in the future . . . or that, in epochs to follow, we shall not seek happiness elsewhere' (Durkheim 1964, p. 119).

Whilst it may be argued that there are aspects of the work of both Marx and Durkheim that sit uneasily with categories of evolutionary change and progress, the same is not true of Parsons's work, which has been described as breathing 'fresh life into evolutionary theory' (Giddens 1984, p. 263). Parsons initially approached the question of social change in terms of an analysis of structural changes *within* social systems. At this stage it was argued that 'a general theory of the processes of change of social systems is not possible' (Parsons 1951, p. 486). Subsequently Parsons changed his opinion, turned to the question of general trends in historical development, to ideas about stages of social evolution, and argued that social change was directional, and progressive (Rocher 1974). In brief Parsons became the foremost exponent of a neo-evolutionary conception of social development.[1]

In later work on the evolution of societies Parsons endorsed the classical sociological view that the industrial revolution in Britain and the democratic revolution in France had initiated a major transformation in Western Europe which led to the formation of modern societies, that is, societies characterised by an 'advanced' or high degree of social differentiation. Where the industrial revolution differentiated the economy from the 'societal community', the democratic revolution likewise differentiated the polity. Both processes of differentiation are considered by Parsons to have led to the need for a regeneration of forms of social integration. The identification of 'integration' as the central problem of modern societies in turn leads Parsons to explore areas in which a resolution might be obtained, and integration restored.[2] But if there are clear continuities with the classical sociological viewpoint there are also differences worthy of note.

The industrial and democratic revolutions may have emerged first in Western Europe but, Parsons argues, they were 'more intimately' combined in America. Indeed it is suggested that the new type of societal community found in the United States of America 'justifies assigning it the lead in the latest phase of modernisation' (Parsons 1977, p. 207). The emergence of 'modernity' is associated with the weakening and gradual displacement of an 'ascriptive framework of monarchy, aristocracy, established churches, and an economy circumscribed by kinship and localism' (Parsons 1977, p. 182) by a 'universalistic legal system and secular culture', a range of political developments (e.g. nationalism, citizenship, and representative government), and a number of economic transformations (e.g. the growth of differentiated markets for factors of production, especially labour, and the structural differentiation of occupational services from households, etc.).

The clear implication is that whilst modernity began in Europe it developed most rapidly in America, within a particularly conducive cultural configuration.[3] The existence of religious pluralism, secular public education, a relative absence of forms of social class consciousness, and an associated 'openness' of the class structure, as well as other marked shifts from 'ascription' to 'achievement', are described as facilitating the development of a modern societal community, one in which citizens hold 'primarily consensual relations to its normative order and to the authority of its leadership' (Parsons 1977, p. 180). It is also argued that within American society there is a clear trend towards 'egalitarianism' and 'voluntariness', and that a core value system exists which emphasises 'activism' and 'universalism'. Elaborating on the 'virtues' of American society Parsons comments that,

> Universalism, which had its purest modern expression in the ethics of ascetic Protestantism, has exerted continuing value pressure toward inclusion – now reaching the whole Judeo-Christian religious community and beginning to extend beyond it. The inclusion of this component *alone* could lead to a static

universalistic tolerance. It is complemented by an activist commitment to building a good society in accordance with Divine Will that underlies the drive toward mastery of the social environment through expansion in territory, economic productivity and knowledge. The *combination* of these two components contributes to the associational emphasis in modern social structure – political and social democracy being conspicuously associational.

(Parsons 1977, p. 187)

The presence of an 'associational pattern' of development in the United States of America is argued to have provided a favourable context for an 'early initiation of the educational revolution and its extension farther than in any other society' (Parsons 1977, p. 191). This represents a third revolution, as central a feature of modernity as the industrial and democratic revolutions, because it constitutes the vital mechanism through which the stratification and occupational systems are opened up and the associational pattern is strengthened.

Modernity may have its origins in Europe but now it encompasses societies throughout the world, and it is the United States of America that constitutes the model for societal development, according to Parsons.[4] Although recognition is given to differences between various 'modern societies', including the Soviet Union, the 'New Europe', and Japan, they are each considered to display important common characteristics, and to belong, in a technological, economic, and sociocultural sense, to one world. As Parsons remarks:

There is a convergence of sociocultural development such that nearly all societies reflect to varying degrees the industrial revolution, the democratic revolution, and the educational revolution. It is therefore only a slight exaggeration to say that all contemporary societies are more or less modern. We should not make too much of the fact that the United States and the Soviet Union have had ideologies varying from older Western European patterns . . . The value content of these ideologies should be regarded as specifications of the more general Western value pattern of instrumental activism rather than as departures from it. The same can be said of the ideologies of social criticism and revolt.

(Parsons 1977, p. 229)

The conclusion at which Parsons arrives, and to which his analysis clearly points, is that the 'development of Western society in the modern era is of universal significance in human history' (Parsons 1977, p. 236). Furthermore, far from the trend of modern development having come to a close there is a suggestion that 'the twenty-first century will discern probably as many factors of continuity with the past as we can discern with the nineteenth century and those previous to it' (Parsons 1977, pp. 239–40). To respond effectively it is necessary to know precisely what 'factors of continuity' are implied and how much significance is to be attached to them. Parsons gives little away on that score. However, it is worth adding that, in the relatively short time that has elapsed since Parsons completed his study of the evolution of societies, at least one of the 'factors' which conventionally has been assumed to connect the present with the nineteenth century has become the subject of analysis and criticism. The future of modernity is now in doubt, uncertain, the desirability of the 'project of modernity' in question. As will become clear below, contrary to the oblique closing assertion offered by Parsons, that the idea of the 'postmodern . . . is premature' (Parsons 1977, p. 241), a number of analysts now argue that it is timely, if not overdue.

OBJECTIONS AND CRITICISMS

Conceptions of social change in terms of evolution and progress undoubtedly have had an 'enormous and almost irresistible appeal' (Gellner 1964, p. 12), and there are signs that such conceptions continue to be influential. Evolutionary theories of social change are marked by a number of common characteristics, for example a tendency to imply or assume 'conceptual continuity with biological evolution'; specification of a mechanism responsible for change – the prime candidate here being 'adaptation'; identification of sequential stages of social development; a frequent conflation of the notion of progression up an evolutionary scale with the idea of 'progress as judged in terms of moral criteria'; and finally the generation of an explanation deemed to be applicable 'across the whole spectrum of human history' (Giddens 1984, pp. 231–3). Such conceptions are also vulnerable to criticism on a number of counts.

A series of logical, moral, and factual flaws associated with evolutionary conceptions of social change have been identified by

Gellner. To begin with, locating a social order in a developmental sequence does not constitute an explanation unless a single causal mechanism can be specified and Gellner comments that it is no longer possible to subscribe to the idea that 'the same kind of force . . . is responsible for the upward propulsion at each stage' (Gellner 1964, p. 16). In a parallel set of criticisms, Giddens argues that the mechanism of social change which predominates in evolutionary theories, namely the concept of adaptation, is 'vague in meaning', 'implicated in a specious and logically deficient claim to functionalist explanation', and, finally, lacking in explanatory force, if not 'demonstrably false' (Giddens 1984, pp. 233–6). The second objection advanced by Gellner is that evolutionism is a moral doctrine and 'in the end [it is] morally unacceptable because we do not wish to prostrate ourselves before the "march of history", "nature", or what not' (Gellner 1964, p. 26). This constitutes an understandable and justifiable objection, but one that detracts attention from a more substantial and telling criticism. What we do, or do not wish is not beside the point, but certainly a secondary matter here, for as Marx enigmatically reminds us, although we make our history, the conditions under which we do so are not of our own choosing. To be more precise, it is necessary to recognise that,

> Human beings make their history in cognizance of that history, that is, as reflexive beings cognitively appropriating time rather than merely 'living' it. . . [and] the reflexive nature of human social life subverts the explication of social change in terms of any simple and sovereign set of causal mechanisms. Getting to know what goes on 'in' history becomes not only an inherent part of what 'history' is but also a means of transforming 'history'.
>
> (Giddens 1984, p. 237)

The final 'factual' objection raised by Gellner seems straightforward enough – 'the world no longer looks as if progress were either continuous or endogenous' (Gellner 1964, p. 28). What this actually means is that it is no longer possible to subscribe to the 'world growth story'. It does not necessarily mean that the idea of progress has to be abandoned, its potential 'reality' denied, rather that the notion needs to be retrieved from evolutionary conceptions of change and reconstituted. There are two observations I would like to make here. First, it is not difficult to agree with Gellner that there are clear signs of a shift in the analysis and explanation of change to accommodate exogenous factors. It is now recognised that contemporary forms of social change cannot be satisfactorily accounted for in terms of 'evolutionist philosophy, as the fulfilment of an inner destiny' (Gellner 1964, p. 28). Increasingly the analysis of complex forms of social change is approached in terms of the diffusion of techniques, methods, practices, and effects associated with processes of (post) industrialisation and (post)modernisation, as well as through a consideration of aspects of what is termed a process of 'globalisation' (Robertson 1990). Second, although evolutionary conceptions of change and associated assumptions about progress constitute a sign of a 'kind of European parochialism', and must be regarded as inappropriate and inapplicable to the experiences of the majority of people, to those marginalised as the 'other', there continues to be a substantial belief in progress. In effect it appears that,

> we both do and yet do not 'believe in progress'. Notoriously, the classical philosophies of progress are out of fashion and seem irrelevant: but equally and most emphatically life *is* lived 'on a slope', there is a general demand of sustained improvement, based on the belief that this is possible, and somehow a human prerogative.
>
> (Gellner 1964, p. 45)

Gellner's response is to outline an alternative to castigated doctrines which invoke a conception of a 'strand of progress' and/or a determinate (moral) destination for processes of change. An alternative 'neo-episodic' conception of progress which does not fall into the trap of representing social life as 'always much of a muchness'; avoids an unnecessary pessimism; and asserts that 'for the great majority . . . current politics is a transition from the certainty of poverty, short life, insecurity and brutality, and the strong likelihood of tyranny, to a condition containing the near-certainty of affluence and at least the reasonable possibility of security and liberty' (Gellner 1964, p. 46). But Gellner's confident assertion is itself highly controversial, for it suggests that elements of 'the world growth story' have infiltrated his narrative. Can we continue to uphold the idea that 'the great majority' of humanity is in transition to the 'near-certainty of affluence' and has a reasonable prospect of achieving 'security and liberty'? If by 'affluence' we are to understand a 'kind of consummation of industrial production and application of science to life, the adequate and general provision of the means of a life free from poverty and disease' (Gellner 1964, p. 114), then the expression of doubt is justified and the presence of a pronounced sense of unease understandable. Qualms about the feasibility of Gellner's proposition do not necessarily reflect 'pessimism', as much as a sense that there are now few, if any, near-certainties, no guarantees, and that 'affluence' has become a questionable goal. Any doubts we might have about the prospects for a positive transition to be enjoyed by 'the great majority' are symptomatic of a widely shared sense of unease precipitated by the 'tough' line on modernity taken by Gellner.[5]

In a series of wide-ranging critical observations Giddens argues that a number of mistakes have been made about the 'types of account of social change that are possible'. Specifically it is not possible to provide a 'general account of structural determination', or to outline 'universal laws governing social change' (1984, p. 228). Within the category of explanations which have sought to delineate structural principles of change it is evolutionary conceptions that have predominated, and these are deemed to be inappropriate, if not harmful. Three reasons are advanced by Giddens in support of the contention that an 'evolutionary "shape"' . . . is an inappropriate metaphor by which to analyse human society' (Giddens 1984, p. 237). To begin with there is the idea, already considered above, that human beings make their history as reflexive beings, a characteristic which effectively undermines conceptions of sovereign causal mechanisms. Then there is the absence of any discrete 'unit of evolution' and the inapplicability of associated notions of change through mutation. What we know of human history does not fit the script of the 'world growth story'. Rather than a continuous evolutionary ascent of civilisation we find, Giddens suggests, something closer to Toynbee's conception of a 'rise and fall' pattern, one which is brought to a close 'by the rise to global preeminence of the West, a phenomenon which gives to "history" quite a different stamp from anything that has gone before' (Giddens 1984, p. 239).

Alongside the reasons for regarding an evolutionary conception of change as inappropriate for an understanding of human history Giddens notes four associated dangers to which evolutionary thought within the social and human sciences continues to be vulnerable. These are (i) a tendency to compress 'general into specific evolution'; (ii) an assumption of 'homology between stages of social evolution and the development of the individual personality'; (iii) a predisposition to equate 'superior power, economic, political, or military, with moral superiority on an evolutionary scale'; and (iv) an inclination to 'presume that "history" can be written only as social change' (Giddens

1984, pp. 239–42). The archetypal modern 'Occidental' evolutionary conception of social change – the 'world growth story' – displays each of these dangers. Modernisation is equated with the specific processes of development of Western industrial capitalist societies, the condition of 'modernity' with the forms of social, economic, political and cultural life conceived to be typical of such societies. In consequence a quite specific and contingent combination of elements are universalised, and attention is diverted 'from the very real possibility that modernisation may never arrive at modernity, so that terms like "development" or "transition" are misnomers when applied to societies whose future condition may not be markedly different from the present' (Bendix 1967, p. 316). Modern Western societies are typically conceived to be 'more mature', 'higher', more 'complex' and 'advanced' in comparison with either earlier, pre-modern or ancient societies, exemplifying 'immature social conditions', an 'immature stage' of development, or the 'historical childhood of humanity' (Marx 1976, pp. 44–5), or concurrent 'oral cultures', depicted as 'primitive', less 'complex', and relatively lacking in 'civilisation'. Furthermore, might is frequently conflated with right, and history confused with development and change, forewarnings on both counts being conveyed in Nietzsche's critical reflections on European modernity, in comments that anticipate current ruminations on the 'project of modernity' and the possible emergence of 'postmodern' conditions. Nietzsche remarks that 'it is characteristic of every "progress" that the strengthened elements are reinterpreted as "good"' (1968, p. 76), and that we should not allow ourselves to be deceived by ideas of progress. 'Time marches forward; we'd like to believe that everything that is in it also marches forward – that the development is one that moves forward. The most level-headed are led astray by this illusion' (Nietzsche 1968, p. 55). Whilst such cautionary observations continue to be of relevance they leave room for the 'not-so-level-headed' to jump to inappropriate conclusions, namely fatalism, resignation, and the abandonment of any prospect of forward movement. A more sober and positive response to the question of modernity and its consequences is both necessary and possible.

The conclusion reached by Giddens on the question of evolutionary theories of social change is that it is not possible to repair their shortcomings, hence the need to deconstruct them. But it does not follow that generalisations about social change are inadmissible.[6] Rather it means, as Foucault argues, that 'changes should be examined more closely, without being reduced, in the name of continuity, in either abruptness or scope . . . it would be better to respect . . . differences, and even to try to grasp them in their specificity' (1973, p. xii). Or as Giddens explains in broadly comparable terms:

If all social life is contingent, all social change is conjunctural. That is to say, it depends upon conjunctions of circumstances and events that may differ in nature according to variations of context.

(Giddens 1984, p. 245)

The focus of analytic interest falls, in both cases, upon modernity, upon a conjuncture of circumstances and events associated with modern forms of life. But matters cannot be left there. Given an interest in the analysis of modernity it has now become necessary to offer a considered response to the idea that we are in the midst of a transition, 'living in the interregnum', perhaps encountering the emergence of a condition of 'postmodernity'.[7]

AFTER PROGRESS

The idea that past, present, and future are connected through a process of unfolding progress has a long history extending from the philosophical discourses of classical antiquity to the institutes of 'futurology' which emerged with what has been termed the 'post-industrial age' (Nisbet 1980; Kumar 1978: 1987). The forecasts, predictions, and extrapolations of trends which emerged from the 'think tanks', institutes, and speculations of 'futurists' from the late 1950s onwards were presented in a form which implied the legitimacy and the security of science. As Kumar observes, 'futurologists were convinced of the imminent realisation of their expectations, and saw the task as one of scientific analysis and policy prescription rather than of utopian picturing' (Kumar 1987, p. 390). But like the nineteenth-century social theorists 'futurologists' were not successful in their attempts to disassociate their projections from a 'utopian impulse'. Whilst they availed themselves of all the hardware and software of computer technology, in practice futurologists were continuing to operate like the prophets 'were when their gaze was toward the future . . . seizing upon some seemingly dominant aspect of the present and then projecting it into the future' (Nisbet 1980, p. 309). Where the nineteenth-century social theorists sought both to understand the processes of social transformation associated with the development of modern industrial society and present a programme for the realisation of its progressive potential, 'the theorists of the post-industrial society . . . felt compelled to project present social tendencies to a future end-point where the shape of a whole new society can be discerned' (Kumar 1978, p. 191). In both cases science was accorded a central role in society. Projections seemingly predicated upon scientific knowledge and ostensibly devoid of any hidden value agenda or utopian impulse were considered to provide a secure and valid basis for social planning, policy initiatives, and social development. Scientific knowledge and associated technological innovations and interventions seemingly offered the prospect of control over what Giddens has aptly termed the 'juggernaut of modernity'.

Confronted by increasing problems, dangers, and 'dis-economies', the dark side of modernity, the price to be paid for its benefits, both the present and the prospects for the future begin to look somewhat different. Exercising tight control or regulation over modernity no longer seems to be a feasible option. It never was a realistic possibility, but we promised ourselves, and not only ourselves, otherwise. Now it is recognised that 'so long as the institutions of modernity endure, we shall never be able to control completely either the path or the pace of the journey' (Giddens 1990, p. 139). Like it, or not, we are increasingly having to learn to live with contingency, to face up to the mixed blessings of modernity, both the new opportunities and the new risks. The implication of this is neither nostalgia, nor panic, but rather the necessity of coming to terms with the consequences of modernity, in particular, of understanding why it is that 'the generalising of "sweet reason" [has] not produced a world subject to our prediction and control' (Giddens 1990, p. 151).

If the idea of progress now seems to be at bay it is probably because its crucial constitutive premises are the subject of doubt, if not disillusionment. The erosion of (i) a sense of a common valued past; (ii) ideas about the superiority of Western civilisation; (iii) the desirability of the goal of economic growth; (iv) faith in scientific reason and knowledge; and (v) belief in the intrinsic value of secular, 'this-worldly', existence seems to invite the conclusion that the idea of progress is in peril, that the 'present is a . . . turmoil of understandable nostalgia, crippling indecision, and bewildering prospect' (Nisbet 1980, p. 329). But nostalgia, indecision, and bewilderment do not exhaust the possibilities. Other more constructive responses are possible, responses which attempt to keep open the prospect of making progress by reconstituting a sense of what is possible, necessary, and desirable.

It is increasingly evident that the accumulation of complex, specialised forms of knowledge about social life has not allowed us to exercise greater control over our destiny. But why? Why have the expectations we inherited from the Enlightenment not been realised? Principally because expectations about progressive developments in rationality leading to increases in prediction and control were, from the outset, misguided, unreasonable, and, fortunately, unrealisable. An increase in knowledge 'does not simply render the social world more transparent, but alters its nature, spinning it off in novel directions' (Giddens 1990, p. 153). Of the various factors that might be advanced to account for the unanticipatedly complex interrelationship which has been shown to exist between social analysis, knowledge, and social life, it is the inescapability of 'unintended consequences' and the unavoidable 'reflexivity or circularity of social knowledge' that are of the most significance.[8] As Giddens remarks, 'no amount of accumulated knowledge about social life could encompass all circumstances of its implementation (Giddens 1990, p. 44). But it is not just a question of the complexity of social processes and events. Knowledge of the social world contributes to its transformation in ways that are difficult, if not impossible, to predict or anticipate. It is the circularity of social knowledge and the reflexive character of modern social life which is 'fundamental to the juggernaut-like quality of modernity' (Giddens 1990, p. 153).

However, while it is not possible to exercise complete control over the social world and its development, it is worth remembering that the reflexivity of modernity may have its virtues. In brief, disappointments arising from the belated discovery that the social world is more complex than we might have been led to believe should not occasion despair. It is neither necessary, nor wise, to conclude that the juggernaut of modernity can only be left to career on, undisturbed. Increasingly we have come to understand that,

> 'History' is not on our side, has no teleology, and supplies us with no guarantees. But the heavily counterfactual nature of future-oriented thought, an essential element of the reflexivity of modernity, has positive as well as negative implications. For we can envisage alternative futures whose very propagation might help them be realised.
>
> (Giddens 1990, p. 154)

This constitutes a difficult, yet increasingly urgent task. It is one which, of necessity, must simultaneously embrace an analysis of existing institutional forms and developments, as well as an elaboration of potential alternative social futures immanent in the present.

2

QUESTIONS CONCERNING TECHNOLOGY AND (POST)INDUSTRIAL SOCIETY

The present is increasingly conceived to be a time of transition. But whether it is judged significantly different in that regard from the past depends on how the various signs of transformation are conceptualised and the significance accorded to any forms of change or transition identified. Such matters remain contentious and continue to stimulate discussion. One prominent contemporary focus for debate has been the idea that the restructuring and reorganisation of industry, associated changes in occupational structure, and related innovations in technology evident in an increasing number of Western capitalist societies since the end of World War II signify a radical transformation of 'industrial society' and the possible emergence of 'postindustrial society'.

The idea of 'postindustrial society' came to prominence in the 1960s and early 1970s, primarily through the work of American sociologist Daniel Bell. But the term does not originate there, even if Bell might be credited, or criticised, for placing it firmly on the agenda for debate. A concept of 'postindustrial society' is clearly employed by Riesman (1958) in an analysis of work and leisure and at a much earlier point in the century, Penty (1917: 1922), seeking to draw attention to the 'potentialities for evil' associated with industrialism, introduced a concept of the 'postindustrial state' to describe a process of reversal in the subdivision of labour, and to argue for a return to some form of craft production, and constitution of a form of guild socialism (cf. Bell 1973, p. 37, n. 45).

Subsequently, in the wake of Bell's agenda-setting contribution there have been a number of related yet distinctively different conceptions of, for example, postindustrial socialism (Gorz 1982: 1985); ecological postindustrialism (Roszak 1972; Bahro 1984); and convivial postindustrialism (Illich 1985). To add to the ambiguity

28

associated with the term there is a string of near synonyms employed to describe the transformations identified, for example 'service society', 'information society' and 'knowledge society'. And to compound further the difficulties involved, the concept of post-industrial society is employed at times as an ideal typical 'conceptual schemata' (cf. Bell 1973), a description of a developing social formation, and as a normative possibility and/or desirable social form. Finally there are a number of significant continuities between the conceptions of 'industrial' and 'postindustrial' society which raise questions about the specificity and distinctiveness of the latter concept (cf. Kumar 1978; Badham 1986).

The idea of a fundamental social transformation arising from a change in the productive system of society is hardly novel; for example it is central to the work of Marx. Indeed it is worth briefly recalling that Marx conceived the industrial capitalist mode of production to be continually in transition, and necessarily so. The means of production are described as subject to perpetual transformation, driven through competition to produce more commodities more 'effectively' in order to maintain if not increase levels of profitability. As Marx and Engels state, in familiar terms,

> The bourgeoisie cannot exist without constantly revolutionis-
> ing the instruments of production, and thereby the relations of
> production, and with them the whole relations of society . . .
> Constant revolutionising of production, uninterrupted dis-
> turbance of all social conditions, everlasting uncertainty and
> agitation distinguish the bourgeois epoch from all earlier ones.
>
> (Marx and Engels 1968, p. 83)

But this was not conceived to be a process without end, rather limits were attached to the developmental potential of the capitalist mode of production. The bourgeois epoch and the capitalist mode of production do not then constitute the end of history; on the contrary history is destined to provide their end and although Marx does not offer much comment on the shape of post-capitalist forms of life he quite clearly indicates that their possibility arises from the development of the forces and social relations of production, and in particular from the increasing application of science and technology to production. With the latter 'real wealth' comes to depend less and less on labour time expended than on the powerful agencies of production set in motion through the progressive deployment of appropriate technologies. In this context Marx begins to touch upon developments which later become central to the 'postindustrial society' thesis, by which I mean the displacement and/or de-centring of human beings and the associated increasing significance of scientific knowledge and technology in the process of social production. As Marx saw it, 'the human being comes to relate more as watchman and regulator to the production process' and labour in the direct form ceases to be the source of wealth. But within the context of a capitalist mode of production labour time, of necessity, remains the measure of value, even though 'the powers of science . . . make the creation of wealth independent (relatively) of the labour time employed on it' (Marx 1973a, p. 706). Almost a century later, after further dramatic increases in scientific knowledge and technological innovation and deployment in the process of social production, Gorz (1982) identifies the growing crisis of postindustrial capitalism in broadly comparable terms, albeit whilst remaining at times oblivious of the extent to which the analysis presented might be considered to be a logical extension of elements of Marx's thesis on the fate of capitalism.

In the work of Marx, advances in science and technology are conceived to be necessary for the development of the preconditions required for a transformation of the capitalist mode of production and its associated forms of social life. Others have been more sceptical about the socially and politically progressive qualities attributed to modern science and technology. Anticipating to some extent views later expressed by the likes of Roszak, Illich, and Bahro, Penty (1917: 1922) introduces the concept of postindustrialism as a resource for documentation, comment and criticism of the problems associated with industrialism. From the turn of the twentieth century fears were beginning to be expressed about the scientific liberation of 'stores of sub-atomic energy' and the effects of labour displacement and un-employment arising from an unrestricted use of machinery in indus-trial capitalist societies. Instead of endorsing the idea that 'unrestricted use of machinery' would ultimately provide the necessary pre-conditions for a liberation of humanity from toil, Penty argues that it has proven to be destructive, and that the idea of machinery as a creative force, present in the work of Marx and the 'socialist theory of society', needs to be corrected. Penty's view is that 'the evidence that industrialism is a blind alley from which we must retrace our steps or perish becomes more conclusive every day' (1922, p. 53). The remedy advocated involves a return to some form of 'medievalism', effectively a return to a form of craft production, 'to handicraft as the basis of production, using machinery only in an accessory way' (Penty

1922, p. 63). The objective outlined is to reverse the subdivision of labour associated with scientific management and industrial civilisation, not to abolish machinery, but to transform the terms and limits within which it is developed and employed. To achieve such an end, Penty suggests, requires appropriate institutions to be responsible for regulating and disciplining economic activity, institutions able to ensure 'the maintenance of economic justice and equity' (Penty 1922, p. 84).

At the centre of Penty's thesis is the idea that the industrial system carries within itself the seeds of its own destruction. As he states:

> Our industrial system is in a state of disintegration, the problem that presents itself to us is not how the industrial and capitalist system can be captured or overthrown, but how a new civilisation can be built out of its ruins . . . Accepting the position that our industrial system is doomed. We should set to work to turn them [the unemployed] into agriculturalists and handicraftsmen. . . . Hitherto our efforts to do anything with the unemployed have been the last word in futility, but that is because the only idea behind the various schemes for dealing with them has been to make work, to mark time, as it were, until trade revived . . . But if the fact that our industrial system is doomed was frankly faced, and men were given a craft or agricultural training to enable them to take their place in the new social order, their work would come to have meaning for them . . .
>
> By such means a new society could be built within the existing one, and as our industrial civilisation falls to pieces this new society would gradually take its place.
>
> (Penty 1922, p. 117)

Contrary to Marx, and to the socialist tradition in general, Penty does not consider the industrial system of production to be the foundation upon which, or from which, a new higher civilisation might be built. Rather what is advocated is a 'return to the past', a revival of agriculture, an abolition of the subdivision of labour, and the development of forms of self-sufficiency, where feasible. Present in Penty's argument are several themes which constitute the heart of the debate about the shape of (post)industrial capitalist society in the late twentieth century, namely the impact of innovations in production technologies on work and the associated problem of unemployment; de-skilling and the increasing meaninglessness of many forms of work;

the futility of many schemes organised for those rendered unemployed; and the destruction of the environment through pollution and the production of waste. Of course there are significant differences, not least of all in the scale and intensity of the problems encountered in the present. Industrialism has not withered and disintegrated in the twentieth century; on the contrary it has increased in scope and its existence and impact is now global.

Penty took the view that 'it is simply impossible for civilisation to continue on the road it is travelling' (1922, p. 123), and argued for a return to 'pre-mechanical standards of thought and industry', and pre-industrial forms of production. Whilst there might be support for the judgment that we cannot continue on our current path, the remedies proposed seem now, to say the least, inappropriate and impractical. Having said that, I should add that some of the contemporary critical postindustrial theorists share many of the concerns articulated by Penty, including the central thesis that the industrial capitalist mode of production is not sustainable. Furthermore, it might be argued that the industrial system has, in any event, metamorphosed into, or at least been transformed by the emergence of, a form of postindustrialism unanticipated by Penty, one which appears to be an extension rather than an antithesis of industrial capitalism. It is with a consideration of this issue that I will begin, proceeding from an analysis of Bell's formative thesis.

THE IDEA OF POSTINDUSTRIAL SOCIETY

Bell introduces the concept of postindustrial society as the central element in a 'social forecast about a change in the social framework of Western society' (1973, p. 9). It is presented as an abstraction which allows consideration to be given to the emergence of particular forms of change along the axis of production. Bell comments that the term constitutes 'a fiction, a logical construction of what *could* be, against which the future social reality can be compared in order to see what intervened to change society in the direction it did take' (Bell 1973, p. 14). Subsequent use of the term by Bell and others (cf. Gorz 1982) suggests that the logical construct has come to be regarded as a reality. However the appropriateness of the concept has been widely challenged and it remains a contentious and awkward term. The concept 'postindustrial society' suggests a radical transformation of social life, if not a wholesale change of society and associated key institutions, and several criticisms of Bell's work proceed on that basis.

Yet Bell is not addressing society as a totality, as a whole, but rather offers a distinction between three levels or dimensions, social structure, polity, and culture, and of these it is the first, curiously conceived to encompass the economy, the occupational system, and science and technology, that constitutes the focus of concern in the thesis on postindustrial society. In this way a series of important issues and questions concerning the inter- relationships of economy, technology, politics, and social and cultural forms are effectively effaced from the analytic agenda. This reflects Bell's analytic assumption that the conception of society as a structurally inter-related whole, organised in terms of a single major principle or determinant, no longer holds. In short, he believes that modern society is 'disjunctive' rather than 'integral', in so far as the three distinct levels or realms of social structure, polity, and culture which comprise it display different rhythms of change and are subject to different, if not contrary, axial principles. Acceptance of the latter, of the existence of different rhythms of change in the various levels or realms, does not necessitate an abandonment of commitment to, or interest in, establishing the connections which exist in a particular conjuncture between social, political, economic, and cultural forms, although it does undoubtedly require an acknowledgement of the analytic complexities involved. In Bell's work no serious attempt is made to establish such connections and in consequence exploration of the idea of postindustrial society proceeds without any significant analysis of the socioeconomic, political or cultural context of emergence.

Essentially for Bell the term 'postindustrial society' refers to changes in the sphere of production arising from developments in science and technology. Five main changes are identified, namely a relative shift of emphasis from goods production to service provision in the economic sector, and an increase in health, education, research and development, and government agencies in particular; growth in numbers and influence of a professional and technical class; primacy of theoretical knowledge as a resource for innovation and policy; 'control of technology and technological assessment'; and the 'creation of a new "intellectual technology"' (Bell 1973, p. 14). Bell argues that of these changes the increasing significance of theoretical knowledge is the most important for it constitutes the axial principle of postindustrial society. Whereas industrial society is held to revolve around the coordination of workers and machines for the production of goods, postindustrial society is 'organised around knowledge, for the purpose of social control and the directing of innovation and change' (Bell 1973, p. 20). The major industries of industrial society are described by Bell as largely the inventions of 'tinkerers'; in contrast the new productive enterprises of postindustrial society are held to be the product of planned technological innovation predicated upon the increasing integration of science, technology and economics in research and development. It is from planned initiatives, from research and development programmes, that the new science-based postindustrial fields of computers, electronics, optics and polymers have emerged to 'dominate the manufacturing sector of the society'. The scenario outlined is one in which developments in all fields of knowledge come increasingly to depend upon advances in theoretical work conducted within the 'axial structures of the emergent society', namely universities and research organisations. Advances in forecasting techniques facilitate a planned or controlled development of technology and provide the means for minimising the unwanted consequences of technological innovation (e.g. pollution) and the emergence of the intellectual technology of the computer allows the 'major intellectual and sociological problems of the post-industrial society . . . , those of "organised complexity"' (Bell 1973, p. 29) to be addressed, if not managed effectively. But such elements or dimensions are conceived to be potentials rather than realities by Bell and the implied goal of a rational organisation or ordering of society is not unequivocally endorsed. To the contrary, Bell appears at times to be critical of such a goal, commenting that if the utopian dream has faltered it may be less a consequence of human resistance to rationality than a problem with the 'very idea of rationality which guides the enterprise – the definition of function without a justification of reason' (Bell 1973, p. 33).

There are a number of problems associated with the concept of postindustrial society. It is introduced by Bell to account for the existence in Western societies of a sense that

> we are in the midst of a vast historical change in which old social relations (which were property bound), existing power structures (centred on narrow elites) and bourgeois culture (based on notions of restraint and delayed gratification) are being rapidly eroded. The sources of the upheaval are scientific and technological. But they are also cultural, since culture I believe has achieved autonomy in Western society. What the new social forms will be like is not completely clear. Nor is it

likely that they will achieve the unity of the economic system and character structure which was characteristic of capitalist civilisation from the mid-eighteenth to mid-twentieth century. The use of the hyphenated prefix *post-* indicates, thus, that sense of living in interstitial time.

(Bell 1973, p. 37)

But if the subsequent proliferation of 'posts' (viz. postmodernity, post-Marxism, post-feminism) constitutes an endorsement of the idea that we are, or at least consider ourselves to be, still very much in an age of transition, living in interstitial time, there nevertheless remain a number of matters concerning the idea of postindustrial society that need to be explored and clarified. These include the following:

1   continuities and discontinuities with the idea of industrial society
2   the question of technology – development and determination
3   articulation of the levels of social structure, culture, and polity.

Bell acknowledges the existence of a relationship of continuity between industrial and postindustrial society and cites as an example the significance attached in each conceptual context to the crucial role of engineers and science in the transformation of society. But he goes on to insist that if there is evidence of continuing historical trends linking the two forms they may nevertheless be rigorously differentiated. The implication is clear – if there are continuities, ultimately the differences or discontinuities matter more. In developing his argument Bell is at pains, once more, to emphasise that postindustrial society is a concept, that it does not constitute an organic, integrated social system, and that it refers to changes in social structure alone and does not assume or imply related or parallel changes in culture or politics. However, one of the difficulties with the argument is that a range of ostensibly different conceptions of society and system continually intrude. For example, in elaborating the case for studying the major societal levels or realms on their own, by implication, autonomous terms, in order to identify axial principles and institutions, Bell refers to *capitalist society* and its axial institution private property; *postindustrial society* and its axial principle the centrality of theoretical knowledge; *Western culture* of which the 'axial thread has been "modernism"'; and *Western political* systems and their axial problem of reconciling bureaucratic forms of organisation and administration with the value of and 'desire for popular participation' (Bell 1973, p. 115). And although no explicit consideration is given to the question of the form(s) of articulation existing at particular moments between the various 'unities' identified, articulation is implied in a number of clear references to the problems and contradictions besetting American society. Indeed the central distinction invoked by Bell, and at issue here, namely between industrial and postindustrial society, is constantly illustrated through references to the American context and experience.

A distinction is drawn between industrial and postindustrial society on a number of counts. Industrial societies are goods-producing; employ machine technology; and their axial principle is economic growth. Their transforming and strategic resources are 'created energy' and 'financial capital' respectively. The former, coupled with the introduction of machine technology and an increasing division of labour, transforms work. Out goes the artisan in comes the engineer and the semi-skilled worker. In such a society 'life is a game against fabricated nature' (Bell 1973, p. 126). Postindustrial societies in contrast are based on services; employ intellectual technology; and their axial principle is the codification of theoretical knowledge. The transformation and strategic resources are information (computer and data transmission systems) and knowledge respectively. In consequence the emphasis in the occupational system shifts to scientific, technical, and professional forms of employment. Once again work is transformed but this time the combination of effects is different. There is an increase in the de-skilling and displacement of many forms of work and employment as a consequence of the introduction of technologies of automation in the production process, as well as an apparent growing requirement for professional workers with 'education and training, to provide the kinds of skill which are increasingly demanded in the post-industrial society' (Bell 1973, p. 127). Out goes the industrial blue-collar worker, in comes the robot, the service and professional worker. Such a society 'is a game between persons', concerned with the quality of life and the provision of health, education, recreation, and the arts as services and amenities 'deemed desirable and possible for everyone', rather than with quantitative questions concerning standards of living. Implied here is the emergence of a new consciousness of the good life which makes post-industrial society a 'communal' society, one emphasising the community rather than individuals and their interests. But just as industrial society has its structural problems which Bell argues 'have been muted if not "solved"' (Bell 1973, p. 116), so postindustrial society faces a number of difficulties. The most significant are the organisation of science, in particular questions of funding, institutional support, and the politicisation of scientific work; a potential for increases in direct conflict arising from the openness and visibility of 'non-market' political decision making; and associated increases in interest groups making political claims or demanding social rights. Within a postindustrial society the distinction between social classes, in terms of ownership and control of the means of production, is deemed by Bell to be less significant than that between a technocracy possessing powers of decision making in organisations and those subject to their authority. As he states:

> If the struggle between capitalist and worker, in the locus of the factory, was the hallmark of industrial society, the clash between the professional and the populace, in the organisation and in the community, is the hallmark of conflict in the post-industrial society.
>
> (Bell 1973, p. 129)

Within a postindustrial society it is not the market or the demands of individuals but the community, public mechanisms, and public choice which shape and influence the provision of services. A communal society is more ready to recognise the rights of marginalised or minority groups, and is more sensitive to the need for government to be exercised over the actions of private corporations and individuals to protect the community and its environment. Demands for more education, better health, rights, and amenities have been associated with an expansion in the 'role of government as funder and setter of standards'. However the ability to deliver has been limited by a lack of appropriate and/or adequate social technologies and funding. The latter has, in turn, been aggravated by rising expectations and what Bell (1976) has termed the 'revolution of rising entitlements'. It seems that in the final instance for postindustrial society the problems encountered are

> not technical, but political, for even though in the nature of the new complexities a large kind of new social engineering is involved, the essential questions are those of values . . . The central question of the post-industrial society therefore is the relation of the technocratic decision to politics.
>
> (Bell 1973, p. 337)

It might be argued that the articulation of technocratic decisions and politics is not only a central question *within* postindustrial society, but in so far as its emergence and development is so closely associated with, if not determined by developments in science and technology, it is *formative* of it. Such concerns, what might be termed the politics of technological innovation and deployment, are not seriously addressed by Bell. In his discussion of the idea of postindustrial society, technological innovation and development appears to be self-propelling, to have a logic of its own. If technology is agreed to be a 'soaring exercise of the human imagination' which instrumentally orders 'human experience within a logic of efficient means, and . . . [directs] nature to use its powers for material gain' (Bell 1980, p. 20), it nevertheless remains necessary to examine the processes of selective stimulation, support and funding, the criteria of efficiency, and the objectives or aims embodied in the decision to develop and deploy a specific technology in a particular form.

A common criticism made of Bell's thesis on postindustrial society is that the changes identified do not signify the development of a new order or form of life. Many of the changes alluded to are accepted, indeed considered important, but are regarded, in turn, as features or trends already strongly evident within industrial society. For example, increasing employment in the service sector of the economy is considered a feature of 'both the United States and England from the beginning of their industrialisations' (Kumar 1978, p. 201), and therefore as an element of continuity between industrial and postindustrial configurations (Heilbroner 1976, p. 72). The shift to a service economy is frequently associated with an increase in white-collar work, but here too there are a number of problems. To begin with the increases claimed for this category might be contested for the term '"services" is amorphous, and covers a wide-ranging and disparate set of activities: for example nursing, teaching, warehousing, selling insurance policies and sweeping streets' (Gershuny and Miles 1983, pp. 10–11). The bulk of white-collar work remains routine and unskilled, 'remote indeed from the humanised, personalised, and self-fulfilling pattern envisaged in the post-industrial scenario' (Kumar 1978, p. 209). Indeed it might be argued that, with what is euphemistically termed the increasing 'rationalisation' of the workplace, computerisation and automation are dramatically reducing differences between office and factory work, in brief virtually proletarianising the office work experience (Lyon 1988, p. 75). Although the emphasis in Bell's work has tended to be on the expansion of human and professional services, on 'teaching, health, and the large array of social services . . . systems analysis and design and the programming and processing of information' (1979, p. 164), this too is a contentious matter. The increases evident in professional, technical and scientific occupational groups are much reduced in significance if consideration is given to the growing signs of an associated deterioration in working conditions, for example longer working hours, greater job insecurity and risk of unemployment, and increases in fragmentation, specialisation, and bureaucratisation in the workplace (Gorz 1976; Heilbroner 1976; Kumar 1978: 1988). One implication is that the status of the professional is changing, and that the process of professionalisation to which many occupations seem to have become subject has been paralleled by a devaluation of the professional coin. Indeed rather than refer to an increasing professionalisation of society it might be more appropriate to note the signs of a growing 'proletarianisation' of the professions.

However the key issue for Bell is the increasing significance of theoretical knowledge and the changing relationship between science and technology. It is here in the new 'axial principle' of knowledge that the distinctiveness of the postindustrial society is located and once again this has proven to be vigorously contested. Examination of the evidence reveals a number of anomalies, for example the inclusion of 'accessories' (e.g. stationery and office equipment) and 'peripheral' activities (e.g. routine testing and marketing procedures) in the indices employed to calculate the contribution of knowledge to GNP in the United States, as well as doubts about the role of institutionalised forms of research and development in the generation of technological and economic development (Kumar 1978, pp. 225–6). Analysis of the contribution of the knowledge industry or knowledge production to GNP in the United States in the period 1958–80 confirms an increase from 28.6 to 34.3 per cent, but it is an 'extremely modest rate of growth relative to the average rate of growth of other components of total GNP' (Rubin and Huber 1986, p 3). However, above and beyond the various anomalies and the less than dramatic rate of growth of the knowledge industry there are two more significant problems associated with Bell's thesis concerning the increasing significance of knowledge, science and technology in postindustrial society. The first concerns the existence of a comparable claim in relation to industrial society, the second the absence of any effective explanation for the alleged 'information explosion'.

On the first point it might be argued that science, wedded to the formation of technologies appropriate for the regulation and/or transformation of various aspects of the environment, the economy, and social and personal life, has been a constitutive feature of the idea of industrial society. As Gellner has commented:

> Industrial society is not merely one containing 'industry' . . . it is also a society in which knowledge plays a part wholly different from that which it played in earlier social forms, and which indeed possesses a quite different type of knowledge. Modern science is inconceivable outside an industrial society: but modern industrial society is equally inconceivable without modern science.
>
> (Gellner 1964, p. 179)

Similar views on the inter-relationship between industrial society and scientific knowledge have been elaborated by Galbraith (1969) and Aron (1972) amongst others. In an analysis of transformations of the industrial system Galbraith examines the impact of the systematic application of science and technological innovation, and the consequent necessity for planning. In a manner which parallels many of the features of Bell's thesis Galbraith argues that high technology and heavy capital use require planning and cannot be left to the vagaries of market demand (Galbraith 1969, p. 321); a relative shift of power has occurred away from capital to a new factor of production, the 'technostructure', that is individuals of 'diverse technical knowledge, experience or other talent which modern industrial technology and planning require' (Galbraith 1969, p. 67); and associated with the latter is the growth of a large educational and scientific estate (Galbraith 1969, p. 286). He suggests that a structural similarity exists between the relationship of banking and finance to the formative stages of industrialisation and that of educationists, scientists and researchers to the emerging new industrial system. Where in the former capital was decisive, in the latter it is an adequate supply of qualified talent emerging from highly specialised educational institutions. As such Galbraith's scenario of the new industrial state anticipates several of the elements at the heart of the thesis on the postindustrial society. However, if there is a considerable degree of complementarity between the two theses there is also an important difference evident in the form of Galbraith's readiness to give consideration to the context within which the new industrial system has developed. Specifically, he shows a readiness to address the question of the relationship between the new industrial system, scientific research and development, and the military, that is, what

Eisenhower referred to as the 'conjunction of an immense military establishment and a large arms industry' (Galbraith 1969, p. 334) or, as it is better known, the military–industrial complex. I will return to this in the next section.

Additional confirmation of the centrality of scientific knowledge and technology to industrial society is provided by Aron who argues that the application of science to production is synonymous with the modern or industrial age (1972, p. 164), and that 'the type of society . . . called industrial, could also be called scientific. Science and technology . . .[having] made it possible for three billion human beings to live on this earth' (1967, p. 99). However, whilst acknowledging the impact of new electronic communications technologies on the development of a number of service industries (e.g. banking, finance, administration, etc.), the existence of a process of redistribution of labour occurring across the respective sectors of the economy, effectively from primary and secondary to tertiary, quarternary, and quinary sectors, and associated changes in occupational categories and statuses, Aron rejects the present relevance of the concept of postindustrial society. Notwithstanding the emergence and deployment of powerful new technologies, it is argued that

> Industry remains the foundation of modern societies, even if increased productivity makes it possible to reduce the percentage of labour used in the primary and secondary sectors. Indeed, such a reduction seems to me to correspond to the nature of industrial society and consequently represents a normal development and not a break with the past or a change of direction.
>
> (Aron 1967, p. 104)

Adopting a broad conception of the term 'industry' as collective effort or activity guided, informed and ultimately transformed by scientific knowledge and technology, Aron implies that the concept of industrial society should remain at the centre of analysis.

Working methods are undoubtedly changing dramatically as a consequence of the employment of new technologies developed through programmes of scientific research. Processes of production are being automated to an increasing extent, the age of the robot is no longer in the future, and 'services' have become an increasingly significant, if not the principal, source of employment. However Aron is cautious about the consequences of such developments and comments that any 'tertiary sector' society will, of necessity, have at its basis the production of material goods, in short 'high productivity (of labour) in factories producing . . . primary and secondary goods will remain one of its indispensable preconditions' (Aron 1967, p. 104). In other words an expansion of services and a concomitant decline of employment in primary and secondary sectors of the economy, automation and the introduction of new micro-electronic technologies of production, do not constitute the end of industrial society, but rather further, more complex, developments of the forces of production, or another stage in the process of industrialisation. Aron argues that industrial societies are to an increasing extent preoccupied with change, with scientific advance, technological innovation, and increasing productivity. The faster the actually experienced and anticipated future rate(s) of change, the greater is the premium on forecasts, estimates, and designs for the future, hence the proliferation of forms of knowledge about the present state of industrial capitalist society and associated extrapolations. It may be that the continuing preoccupation with 'forward-looking' reflects, as Aron suggests,

> the unresolved antithesis between technology and history, between Promethean ambition and the uncertainties of the future . . . [S]cientists are questioned about impending discoveries and an attempt is made to picture what industry will be like in the twenty-first century . . . One speculates about the future of political and economic institutions in the era of the computer. These speculations are legitimate, occasionally instructive and always exciting, but they also entail some intellectual and moral hazards.
>
> (Aron 1972, p. 311)

Intellectual and moral hazards are bound to increase if a consideration of the key institutions and structures which make policy, planning, development and deployment decisions on the basis of selective scenarios concerning the future are omitted from analysis. In the case of Bell's postindustrial society thesis the hazards arise from the omission of any consideration of the sociohistorical and economic context from which the battery of new technologies at the foundation of the 'information revolution' have emerged.

TECHNOLOGY AND THE MILITARY

Central to the idea of postindustrial society is a series of developments and innovations in the fields of science and technology which seem to have spontaneously materialised. Reference is made to the increasing importance of theoretical knowledge, to technological innovation, planning and forecasting but there is little sign in Bell's work of any attempt to examine or explain the processes through which particular potential technological innovations are cultivated, developed and deployed.[1] Where there is an acknowledgement that technologies have histories it takes the form of brief references to selective examples concerning changes in the technology of warfare and the management of the economy by governments. For example in relation to the former Bell comments that:

> Since the end of World War II the extraordinary development of scientific technology has led to hydrogen bombs, distant early warning networks coordinated in real time through computer systems . . . War too has now come under the 'terrible' dominion of science, and the shape of war, like all other human activities has been drastically changed.
>
> (Bell 1973, p. 22)

And he goes on to say that America has taken on the features of a mobilised polity within which scientific research and development has become linked to military and 'defence' requirements (Bell 1973, p. 356). But such observations are not developed. More importantly no consideration is given to the substantial body of evidence concerning either the dramatic transformation of science as it has come under the terrible dominion of military and defence related interests, or the central role of the latter in the generation of a series of new technologies. In contrast Galbraith (1969) has drawn attention to the increasingly close identification between the technostructure and the military, and the significance since the end of World War II of Cold War imagery for realising and legitimating certain fundamental conditions of the industrial system, notably longterm planning and the regulation, stabilisation, and/or stimulation of aggregate demand through large programmes of public expenditure devoted to military procurement of one kind or another (e.g. 'defence'; space exploration and research; 'Star Wars', etc.). In short, the Cold War with its conflictual and competitive image of international relations effectively served the needs of the industrial system by normalising or naturalising an arms race between East and West. On this profitable and privileged site there has emerged a military–industrial complex, a conjunction of industrial corporations with interests in weaponry and a military establishment imbued with values of technological progress, corporate advancement and national security. As Galbraith remarks:

> The industrial system has not become identified with the weapons competition by preference or because it is inherently bloody. Rather, this has been the area where the largest amount of money to support planning was available with the fewest questions asked. And since armies and cannon have always been in the public sector, government underwriting in this area had the fewest overtones of socialism.
>
> (Galbraith 1969, p. 344)

The thaw in East–West relations, *glasnost* and *perestroika* in the USSR, and the transformations under way in the former 'societies of actually existing socialism' in Eastern Europe, notably the introduction of liberal–democratic forms of government and elements of capitalistic economic practice, constitute a challenge to the post-World War II settlement and the established rationales or legitimations for prevailing budgetary allocations. In such circumstances the high priority conventionally accorded to military and defence expenditure may be difficult to sustain. The possibility of a redirection of public expenditure, corporative effort, and scientific research and development away from military ends is raised by Galbraith, but the focus proposed serves, with the benefit of hindsight, to remind us of the problems and hazards of speculation and forecasting. Galbraith suggests that space exploration would provide a safer forum for general scientific, engineering and technological competition in so far as 'competition in space exploration . . . is largely devoid of military implication' (Galbraith 1969, p. 343). Subsequent events, for example the deployment of military satellites and SDI, contradict Galbraith's view of the relative neutrality of space and suggest a contrary tendency, namely a 'militarisation' of space research and development (Webster and Robins 1986, p. 339).

The emergence of a particular technology is not a product of chance, an accident, but a consequence of specific processes of research and development guided by focused questions, articulated concerns and carefully considered priorities, financed in turn by agencies with interests in and expectations of a return in the form of application or deployment (Williams 1974; Noble 1984; Webster 1986; Robins and Webster 1989). The existing form and deployment of any new technology depends, in the first instance at least, on the trajectory of its development. As Weizenbaum has cautioned on the subject of the technology deemed to play a central role in postindustrial society:

> The computer in its modern form was born from the womb of the military. As with so much other modern technology of the same parentage, almost every technological advance in the computer field, including those motivated by the demands of the military, has had its residual payoff–fallout – in the civilian sector.
>
> (Weizenbaum 1979, p. 455)

A more detailed social and historical analysis of the conception and delivery of technological innovations central to the postindustrial society thesis is provided in Noble's account of the relations of power and knowledge which continue to shape both technology and social life.

The development of technology, both its design and its use, is conceived by Noble to be a product of social and political processes in which a technicist ideology of progress promising a technological fix for every problem is the key constituent. Noble argues that the general shape and character of modern science, including patterns of research and development, as well as the frequent equation of additions or increases in scientific knowledge, and the available stock of technologies, with progress, derives its principal impetus from World War II and the influence increasingly exercised since that time by the 'military–industrial' complex. A symbiotic relationship exists between science, capital, and the various agencies and institutions of government, based upon a belief in technological progress and an associated interest in the reduction of chance and disorder, and a concomitant extension of predictability and control (Webster and Robins 1986; Lyon 1988). By virtue of the strong presence of a conception of instrumental reason guiding scientific inquiry and investigation, and the concomitant constitution of knowledge promising, if not actually affording, control, science has become increasingly closely integrated with capital and institutions and agencies of government, that is, with interests and apparatuses seeking to extend and enhance their influence over the course of events.[2] Through such affinities and close relationships science has achieved 'access to the social resources that make . . . achievements possible: capital, time, materials and people' (Noble 1984, p. 43). However, as a consequence of the close connections between practitioners of science and technology, owners of capital and agencies of government, scientists

> tend to internalise and even consciously adopt the outlook of their patrons, an outlook translated into professional habit through such mechanisms as education, funding, reward structures and peer pressure. In various ways this professional habit comes to inform technical and scientific work itself, affecting not only the lives of technical people but their imaginations as well, their notion of what is possible.
>
> (Noble 1984, pp. 43–4)

The central issue is not the choices made by scientists, but rather the relations of power and knowledge which are constitutive of scientific practices. Specifically it is a matter of science, orientated towards increasing certainty or control, becoming in institutional, organisational and cultural terms more and more closely articulated with the 'military–industrial' complex.

Noble contends that the deployment of armed forces around the world and the increasing internationalisation of corporate operations from the end of World War II confronted the American military and industrial apparatuses with a number of logistical communication and control problems. But the basic elements necessary for further theorisation and technical development in the fields of communication and control of information, namely electronics, servomechanisms and computers, were already in existence, having been developed during the course of the war under the sponsorship of the military. The longstanding preoccupation in science with the manipulation of processes and events in order to control the course or pattern of their development coincided with the practical concerns and interests of both the military command and industrial corporations. In short there existed an 'unusual degree of complementarity between the seeming requirements of a new global power and the technical possibilities engendered by a powerful intellectual synthesis within science and engineering, based upon new theories of information, communications, and most appropriately, control' (Noble 1984, p. 45). The technological developments concerned in electronics, servomechanisms and computers, orientated in the first instance towards the war effort and specifically military ends, 'converged in the postwar period to create a powerful new technology and theory of control . . . and . . . gave birth to a host of automatic devices and, most important, to a new way of thinking' (Noble 1984, p. 52). From military origins operations research, combined with developments in the fields of systems engineering and scientific management, gave rise to systems analysis. A computer based systems analysis approach has steadily extended its influence from military and industrial settings and has been employed by social and governmental agencies throughout the social order. It has come to be regarded as an approach relevant to both the natural or physical world and the domain of social life with all its complexities and difficulties, a way of resolving a series of potentially 'catastrophic crises' confronting military, industrial and governmental agencies. Given its ability to handle the scale and complexity of the data and variables involved in a systems approach, the 'intellectual technology' of the computer has increasingly been considered indispensable to the emerging postindustrial or information society (Bell 1979).

Although there now exists an increasingly common and widespread belief in the indispensability of the computer it is clear that before the advent of computer technology and systems analysis complex scientific, technological, and managerial problems were tackled effectively (e.g. the Manhattan Project which led to the atomic bomb). This observation leads Weizenbaum to argue that

> The computer was not a prerequisite to the survival of modern society in the post-war period and beyond; its enthusiastic, uncritical embrace by the most 'progressive' elements of American government, business and industry quickly made it a resource essential to society's survival *in the form* that the computer itself had been instrumental in shaping.
>
> (Weizenbaum 1984, pp. 28–9)

Given a series of 'technical' problems or difficulties within an organisation two quite different categories of response are conceivable. On the one hand the existence of a problem arising from or associated with the limits of organisational practices and conceivable human responses may suggest the necessity of a replacement of human organisations and functions by faster, more efficient computer based technologies. It may also, on the other hand, suggest that modifications need to be made to the structure of human organisations considered to be 'limited', in effect, that tasks need to be revised, changed, or even abandoned. Instead of resorting to the introduction of sophisticated computer based technologies to cope with increasing organisational complexity and associated problems, consideration could have been given to social and political innovation. If the computer did arrive 'just in time' it was not to ensure the continued progressive development of humanity, or to enhance further the quality of life by reducing the toil, degradation, and dehumanisation associated with many forms of labour, but to preserve

> very nearly intact . . . social and political structures that otherwise might have been either radically renovated or allowed to totter under the demands that were sure to be made on them. The computer, then, was used to conserve America's social and political institutions. It buttressed them and immunized them, at least temporarily, against enormous pressures for change. Its influence has been substantially the same in other societies that have allowed the computer to make substantial inroads upon their institutions.
>
> (Weizenbaum 1984, p. 31)

The 'information explosion', centrality of theoretical knowledge, significance of research and development, and increasing deployment of computer technology in business, government, and education are not, as they appear in Bell's work, neutral events. Knowledge and information have not simply emerged to become significant as strategic resources and transforming agents in postindustrial society, they have been developed to that end by particular agencies with specific interests. Proceeding in terms of technology as a given instrument leads Bell to neglect the specific social uses and appropriate forms of organisation inscribed within technological innovations, by virtue of the influences at work during the course of their development. In turn this leads to a rather sanguine view of the associated effects.

A number of recent studies demonstrate that a military–industrial axis continues to orchestrate contemporary developments in the field of information technology (Noble 1983; Roszak 1986; Lyon 1988; Robins and Webster 1989). The information society is not a matter of destiny, but a product of interests shared and decisions taken in a number of key institutional sites to develop a new generation of technologies, and to unleash an 'information revolution'. In both America and Britain the military or defence connection to research and development programmes and information technology industries is a strong one. High technology industries and major computer development investments in America are heavily dependent upon the Pentagon budget for their research and development capital. For example the Integrated Computer-Integrated Manufacturing Programme (ICAM) which is fundamental to computer associated design and manufacturing initiatives in American industry was launched by the Air Force in 1979. The programme 'involves the participation of some seventy industrial and academic contractors, provides risk capital to foster developments that are too broad in scope and too long-term for industry to do on its own – and entails "joint effort between industry and universities, with government funding"' (Noble 1984, p. 330). In Britain there is a comparable connection between information technology corporations and the Ministry of Defence with around two-thirds of the electronics sector's research and development commitment being defence or military related (Robins and Webster 1989, pp. 238–9). The explanation advanced for this 'second Industrial Revolution' involves a number of factors: an intensification of economic competition; increases in the costs of production; technological fetishisation on the part of scientists, managers, and the military; and the latter's shared 'quest for a perfectly ordered universe'. The pursuit of total automation and managerially controlled computerised production systems may continue to be 'promoted in the name of patriotism, competitiveness, productivity and progress. Its twin aims however remain control and domination' (Noble 1984, p. 328).

In exploring the contribution of the American military to the development of the forces of production Noble finds that the Air Force sought to advance development of automation and computer regulated production technologies in order to improve management control, resolve labour force problems, and reduce the level of personnel employed in production. In effect, the aim was to create a future factory in which the manufacturing process would be regulated largely by computers and require minimal human intervention. Through a number of related programmes running under the generic titles TECHMOD (Technology Modernisation) and MANTECH (Manufacturing Technology) the American military and the Air Force in particular has been attempting to promote industry wide adoption of the automated factory and robotics, and through a related initiative has sought to increase the involvement of academia in manufacturing, thereby ensuring that 'the dream of the military, mirrored in industry, is reflected as well in the third arena of the military–industrial–academic triad, the universities' (Noble 1984, p. 332). The principal impetus behind such initiatives appears to be enhanced control and the displacement or replacement of human participants or operators by robots, rather than a carefully calculated conception of economic viability or the problem of skill shortages. If a reduction in manufacturing costs has been the aim of technological innovation the results are ambiguous. Indeed it might be argued that innovations in the forces of production owe as much to the cult or enchantment of technology and management ideology as they do to a concern with increasing productivity and/or reducing production costs (Wilkinson 1983). Equally, the idea of skill shortages as the motive for the introduction of labour displacing technologies is debatable. Whether the introduction of information technology has produced a further de-skilling of labour is not an issue to be pursued here. It is clear that there are arguments for and against on that score, although the weight of opinion would appear to be with the former (Noble 1984; Lyon 1988). But in relation to the introduction of various technologies of automation it is difficult to regard skill shortages as anything more than a rather convenient, if lame justification, effectively a smokescreen for other unexplicated motivations. Undoubtedly there are economic impulses behind the development of the family of numerical control technologies (ICAM; CAD/CAM, etc.), but the prime mover has been the military and its overriding concern with performance and command rather than economic viability or cost.

Identification of the prominent role played by the military in the development of a panoply of new technologies since the end of World War II raises serious questions about the effects of deployment. Technological innovations are not necessarily beneficial or progressive; rather their uses and effects derive in substantial part from the institutional context and cultural form in which they have been developed. In the case of the new technologies considered intrinsic to the emergence of postindustrial society, an examination of the military–industrial context of their development and deployment is vital if an understanding of their potential effects is to be achieved. In so far as Bell treats new technologies as given and avoids an analysis of their development, technological innovations are conceived simply as instruments open to a range of potential uses, which in turn are generally presented as benign, if not progressive. In consequence the dangers or hazards, both potential and real, for example the social and economic problems of unemployment arising from the introduction of 'labour-saving' technologies of production (Gorz 1982: 1985; Webster and Robins 1986; Lyon 1988; Kumar 1988) and the political problems of increasing surveillance associated with the deployment of information and communications technologies (Roszak 1986; Robins and Webster 1989), are largely minimised if not neglected altogether. Whilst Bell (1980) recognises the existence of unemployment arising from the use of labour-saving production technologies the introduction of the latter is not questioned, rationales and motives are not explored. Rather, automation of the bulk of industrial production is simply considered to be 'surely coming', ostensibly driven by its own irresistible progressivist logic. Likewise there is a brief acknowledgement of the political questions and problems posed by the potential for centralised control over communication services and data banks. As Bell remarks, 'control over communication services is a source of power, and access to communication is a condition of freedom . . . these are major questions for the future of the free society' (Bell 1980, p. 43). But while such problems are identified they are left unexplored. Bell is right to emphasise that there is no technological imperative, no immanent logic. It is indisputable that the same technology may be compatible with a range of social organisations, but that does not mean that 'we choose the one we want to use' (Bell 1980, p. 28). If in various ways we do contribute to the making of history, it is not under conditions of our own choosing. In respect of the various information and communications technologies at the heart of the postindustrial society thesis it is quite clear that, for most of us, the choices concerning deployment and anticipated use(s) have already been made. The implication of such remarks is not fatalism or cultural pessimism, but rather that there is a need to understand 'technology in the present tense, not in order to abandon the future but to make it possible' (Noble 1983, p. 11).

NEO-FORDISM AND SURVEILLANCE:FLEXIBLE ACCUMULATION, COMMAND AND CONTROL

Behind the technological manifestations and social developments considered by Bell to be symptomatic of the emergence of a postindustrial society lies a shifting configuration of military, industrial, and political institutions. In consequence it is necessary not only to recognise the contribution of the military to the process of 'postindustrial' technological development, but in turn the significance of economic and political interests (Webster and Robins 1986; Lyon 1988; Robins and Webster 1989; Harvey 1989). If 'postindustrial society' does offer the possibility of a decentralisation of work and industrial structures, as well as an increase in the quantity of information and/or knowledge, it is important to remember that these changes have emerged in particular circumstances, namely of countervailing tendencies towards (re)centralisation; an increasing privatisation and commercialisation of social life; a commodification of information and knowledge; and an extension of surveillance and control. Such major transformations in social relations and forces of production have been occasioned, in turn, by the multinational extension of corporate capitalism, operating in an increasingly global labour market, and military and political preoccupations with command and control, national security, and law and order. Hence 'neo-Fordism', or flexible accumulation, and increasing surveillance or control have been identified as articulated responses to the crisis of corporate capitalism and associated social and political problems arising from the dissolution of the post-war 'Fordist–Keynesian' configuration (Webster and Robins 1986; Harvey 1989).

The transition to 'neo-Fordism' or a more flexible form of capital accumulation has involved significant transformations in the spatial and temporal dimensions of social life. To a degree production has become more decentralised as large unwieldy structures have given way to smaller more flexible forms. To an extent the mass media have been 'demassified' as new potentially more interactive technologies have been developed and marketed. But such forms of decentralisation are occurring within a quite specific context, facilitated by information technology, innovations in communications, automation, and the digital computer, but 'designed by increasingly centralised corporate capital and state agencies' (Webster and Robins 1986, p. 321). The implication is that the restructuring and reorganisation of (post)industrial capitalism may be allowing new forms of diversity, plurality and creativity to emerge but that such developments are in turn vulnerable to commercialisation and increasing commodification. An increase in communication and information resources may allow more choice and flexibility but given the 'delivery system' is designed and marketed within an existing commercially driven system of commodity production the parameters within which choice and flexibility might be exercised are largely predetermined. To that extent decentralisation may be regarded as an effective strategy through which to draw new elements of social life into the commercial marketplace. Certainly at present there is little sign of decentralisation and demassification leading to the process of 'demarketisation' identified as a possibility by Toffler (1983; pp. 295–9). To the contrary, the privatisation of social life implied in Toffler's idea of the growth of home centredness and embodied in the concept of the 'electronic cottage' suggests an increased scope for individualised consumption of commodities. Electronic cottage or neo-medieval mini-fortress? The way in which the electronic home is being reconstituted as the 'locus not only of information and entertainment services, but also of educational, purchasing, banking, and work activities' (Webster and Robins 1986, p. 323) encourages a retreat from public life and public space and serves thereby to increase the sense of insecurity which has become an increasing feature of the 'postmodern' urban environment (Eco 1987). Such decentralised or privatised forms of existence not only increase the market for individualised consumer goods but in turn depend upon highly centralised systems and organisations for essential integrated communications, information and delivery networks. In consequence 'the tendency towards decentralization expresses itself, not in the autonomy of individuals, but in the increasing arrangement of social life by centralized systems' (Webster and Robins 1986, p. 323). And, in turn, this involves the development of new forms of surveillance, security, and control.

Evidence of increases in the service sector of the economy and concomitant reductions in primary and secondary sectors, changes in the occupational structure and work skills, and the growing significance of information technology in the circuits of production and consumption have been regarded as clear signs of a radical restructuring of the industrial capitalist mode of production, of a radical departure from the centralised forms of mass production associated with Fordism and towards a form of 'flexible accumulation' or 'neo-Fordism'. It has been suggested that the current phase of socioeconomic modernisation, and associated cultural and political transformations, parallels radical forms of restructuring which began towards the end of the nineteenth century and subsequently gave rise to Fordism. In brief, that 'both *fin de siècle* periods resonate with similarly transformative . . . socio-spatial processes' (Soja 1989, p. 26). Along with the emergence of a new political economy of capitalism there is in each case 'an altered culture of time and space, a restructured historical geography . . . new visions and designs for the future as the very nature and experience of modernity [postmodernity]

– what it . . . [means] to be modern [postmodern] – [is] significantly reconstituted' (Soja 1989, p. 26). In some explanations the transition from Fordism to flexible forms of specialisation and accumulation has been regarded as symptomatic of the 'end of organised capitalism' (Lash and Urry 1987) or as leading to a 'disorganised capitalism' (Offe 1985). However, such concepts only acknowledge part of the story for, paralleling the deconstruction of established organisational forms, structures, relations, and practices, a process of reconstitution and reorganisation is occurring 'in which capitalism is becoming ever more tightly organised *through* dispersal, geographical mobility, and flexible responses in labour markets, labour processes, and consumer markets' (Harvey 1989, p. 159). It is in this context that the contribution of information technology and developments in telecommunications become critical, for they provide the technical means through which 'productive decentralisation' can be realised, 'tighter organisation and imploding centralisation' effectively and economically articulated (Webster and Robins 1986; Harvey 1989). Information and knowledge have become crucial variables in so far as they permit large corporations to decentralise or 'demassify', and yet continue to exercise effective administrative or organisational control over an extended production network. Decentralised and flexible production systems require continuing streams of information on patterns of consumption in order to meet existing requirements, and anticipate if not stimulate changes in tastes. The corollary of this is that both product and production developments and the achievement of an edge or advantage over competitors come to depend increasingly upon, what Bell terms the transforming and strategic resources of information and knowledge in general, and scientific and technological know-how in particular.

In addition to precipitating a marked spatial reorganisation of social life the processes of restructuring implied in the transition from Fordism to flexible accumulation have had a significant impact on time. Within the production process there has been a tendency for the level of socially necessary labour time required to be reduced as the 'micro-electronic revolution' has increased the scale and extent to which automation has been deployed (Gorz 1985). But if an accelerated development of the forces of production has opened up the possibility of a reduction in the general level of socially necessary labour required in production, the persistence of capitalist social relations has ensured that this is realised in the form of increasing levels of unemployment, and an associated growth of part-time and insecure forms of waged labour. The potential 'paradise' of a reduction in the general level of socially necessary labour has been turned into the subjection of particular communities to the burdens and exclusionary effects of unemployment, a condition which has been deliberately exacerbated by the introduction of 'workfare' schemes, related reductions in the level of social benefit made available, and other policy measures ostensibly designed to reconstitute an allegedly declining commitment to work through a regeneration of the work ethic (Golding and Middleton 1982; Smart 1988). However, the latter objective, in turn, has been made increasingly difficult by the growing meaninglessness of work arising from the de-skilling of many forms of labour, and the associated '*decentring*' of work relative to other spheres of life' (Offe 1985, p. 141), developments intrinsic to the very same process of economic restructuring which has produced the problem of unemployment. The transition from Fordism to flexible accumulation has involved a radical restructuring of the labour market, increases in structural unemployment, and an erosion of the level of membership and influence of trades unions. The introduction of new production technologies and associated 'decentralised' organisational forms has had as the objective not simply a reduction in the level of socially necessary labour time but an overcoming of rigidities and an acceleration of turnover time. For example, new micro-electronic technologies, small-batch production, subcontracting, outsourcing, and 'just-in-time' systems have all been associated with increases in the speed of production. In turn the acceleration of 'turnover time in production entails parallel accelerations in exchange and consumption' (Harvey 1989, p. 285). A range of improvements in communications, information, and distribution systems coupled with changes in banking and financial services made possible by micro-electronic technology have contributed to an acceleration of processes of exchange. Such developments have been matched in the realm of consumption by an acceleration in the rate of 'obsolescence' achieved through the permeation of virtually all areas of social life by the signifying system of fashion and marked shifts in consumption patterns from goods to services. As Harvey observes, given 'there are limits to the accumulation and turnover of physical goods . . . it makes sense for capitalists to turn to the provision of very ephemeral services in consumption' (Harvey 1989, p. 285). It also makes sense for capitalists to welcome the privatisation of formerly publicly pro-vided services. In other words transformations in the service sector considered to be symptomatic of the emergence of 'post-industrial society' constitute part of a broader process of restructuring under way in the capitalist mode of production (Gershuny and Miles 1983).

However, the effects of the transition to flexible accumulation extend beyond the realm of commodity production. Volatility and ephemerality are not confined to the circuits of production and consumption alone but extend to personal values, relationships, life-styles, attachments, and other 'received ways of doing and being'. The turbulence and transitoriness that seem to be an increasingly prominent feature of so many aspects of personal and social life represent, in Harvey's view, a condition which constitutes the cultural correlate of capitalism's current phase of flexible accumulation, a condition tentatively termed 'postmodern'. Furthermore, to operate effectively in a volatile marketplace corporations need to achieve some leverage over consumption patterns, need, to a degree at least, to manage consumption, to ride volatility by anticipating, shaping or manipulating tastes and opinions and this, in turn, necessitates an extension of control over information and knowledge 'beyond the factory to the society as a whole' (Webster and Robins 1986). It is in this context that what is called the 'information technology revolution' has had a significant impact. The introduction of new micro-electronic and telecommunication technologies has undoubtedly facilitated the management of tastes, desires and consumption. Furthermore, insofar as the introduction of information technology has been associated with the commodification of information and knowledge, and with the accumulation of centralised data banks containing information on the personal characteristics, activities, tastes, and desires of individuals, it has contributed to the development of an electronic surveillance network.

If the promise of information technology has generally been presented in terms of a scenario of increasing knowledge and information leading to greater degrees of freedom, independence, and autonomy, the reality of its development and deployment within prevailing social relations of production has been to produce new markets for goods and services, to create new commodities, and to extend the sphere of consumption. Indeed, rather than providing the technical preconditions for achieving a better informed community, it might be argued that deregulation and privatisation of the information sector and the associated commodification of information and knowledge is having the opposite effect. The possibility of information technology facilitating the development of an informed public is being undermined as 'one-time "public" information is put on the market as a commodity [and] . . . private sources of information enjoy growing monopolies' (Lyon 1988, pp. 91–2). Such shifts in the basis upon which information is provided, increasingly from public service to privately purchased commodity, effectively diminish 'the social availability of information' (Webster and Robins 1986, p. 331). The commercialisation of information and communications media is apparent in an increasing number of developments, for example the erosion of forms of public service broadcasting, the privatisation of telecommunications industries and governmental information services and computer operations, the growing market for home computers and recorders of various kinds, video cassettes and discs, and the expansion of cable television and direct satellite broadcasting. Such developments in the field of information and communications technology are contributing to a transformation, if not an erosion, of the public sphere and its institutions, and simultaneously are reducing the public accessibility of knowledge and information. In such a context it is difficult to accept the idea that the emergence of postindustrial society has established knowledge and information as 'collective goods' as Bell (1979) suggests. There has been much emphasis placed on the benefits and virtues of

> the free flow of information for promoting greater communication, understanding, and social harmony. But cursory examination of the new communications media will reveal that, under present conditions, their primary function is not to communicate but to sell. The information revolution is largely about promoting the image of capitalist enterprises and stimulating the consumption of its products.
> (Webster and Robins 1986, p. 334)

It is also responsible for the establishment of a powerful surveillance network (Roszak 1986; Lyon 1988; Robins and Webster 1989).

INFORMATION AND SURVEILLANCE

The increasing deployment of information technology, and the growing use of interactive communications systems in particular, has raised fears about the prospect of an increased potential for intensive and extensive forms of surveillance and, as a consequence, a possible erosion of personal privacy. It has also raised hopes about increases in the form and level of participation of citizens in democratic processes, but these can only be considered unrealistic in a context where development and deployment has been, and continues to be, militarily and industrially, or commercially, driven. Where the principal objective is to increase institutional, administrative, and managerial command and control, and knowledge and information are being increasingly commodified, it is difficult to identify realistic prospects for an enhancement of democratic forms of participation in decision making.

The requirement for information or data on the part of military, political, or industrial institutions and organisations is well documented (Weber 1970; Foucault 1979). The significance of information technology is that it has permitted an intensification and an extension of the 'political anatomy of detail' through which individuals' movements and (trans)actions across time and space may be traced, recorded, and governed. The information technology revolution has transformed the techniques and practices 'of notation, of registration, of constituting files, . . . [and] arranging facts' through which a meticulous observation of individuals can be conducted (Foucault 1979, pp. 190–1). A wide range of commercial and state agencies now collect detailed information on specific aspects of the lives, conduct and interests of individuals. For example, credit agencies, mail-order companies, marketing and public opinion organisations, telephone companies, rental firms of various kinds, banks and government departments concerned with taxation, health, education, social security and welfare, law and order, and the licensing of vehicles and receivers of various kinds, have numerous files on individuals, and through information technology there is now a capacity for speedily integrating the different databases to achieve composite profiles of particular subjects (Roszak 1986; Webster and Robins 1986; Lyon 1988; Robins and Webster 1989).

The increasing documentation of the characteristics and conduct of individuals by industrial, commercial and governmental agencies in electronic data banks has led critics to argue that 'what we confront in the burgeoning surveillance machinery of our society is not a value-neutral technological process; it is, rather, the social vision of the Utilitarian philosophers at last fully realised in the computer' (Roszak 1986, pp. 186–7). It seems our fate is not so much to be trapped in the 'iron-cage' of rationality feared by Weber as monitored, supervised, and ultimately governed by a vast electronic grid or network which has colonised space and time and constituted us as the willing subjects of information, and therefore to an increasing degree complicit in the formation of 'our society . . . [as] one not of spectacle, but of surveillance . . . [in which] the circuits of communication are the supports of an accumulation and a centralisation of knowledge . . . [and] the anchorages of power' (Foucault 1979, p. 217). The contribution of the military to the development of information and telecommunications technologies, and the centralising command and control potential their deployment provides has fuelled concern that Bentham's technical programme, embodied in the architectural figure of the Panopticon, 'to procure for a small number, or even for a single individual, the instantaneous view of a great multitude' (quoted in Foucault 1979, p. 216), has been realised in an electronic form through the development of computer systems.

Integrated information and telecommunications computer systems allow more systematic, intensive, extensive, and covert forms of surveillance to be conducted. This has led references to be made to the existence of a 'surveillance machine' and a 'machine à gouverner' (Roszak 1986), a 'carceral computer' (Lyon 1988) and an 'electronic Panopticon' (Robins and Webster 1989). Common to such analyses is the view that the privacy of individuals is threatened by government agencies, corporations, and military and security organisations which routinely engage in information gathering and storage. Indeed it has been suggested that the 'vast ability of the established authorities to gather information about individuals or groups places in question or even eliminates the distinction between the public and the private' (Poster 1984, p. 114). Certainly a corollary of the convenience associated with computer-driven home-based services, for example in respect of banking, shopping, communication and leisure activities, is that information both enters and exits the private domain, rendering the home subject to surveillance and to that extent problematises the public–private distinction. As Lyon states 'wherever interactive communications systems exist the potential for surveillance is present' (1988, p. 97). And given the lack of adequate legislation to cover problems of privacy, accountability and access associated with information technology, data banks, and the agencies and organisations implicated, that potential remains undiminished.

If the potential for surveillance is undiminished the reality is that it is far from total. The developments outlined by Bell as symptomatic of the emergence of postindustrial society and more broadly accounted for in terms of a shift from Fordism to flexible accumulation or neo-Fordism have not created a nightmare scenario of total social control. Undoubtedly there is a fetishisation of technological progress and technological deliverance abroad which has stimulated the development and use of information and telecommunications technology. These new technologies may have permitted the programme of control outlined by Bentham to be reconstituted and extended beyond 'the architectural and geographical constraints of . . . [the] stone and brick prototype' (Webster and Robins 1986, p. 346). But to date their effects have stopped short of the dystopian scenario of electronic totalitarianism, although the dangers and hazards remain (Roszak 1986; Lyotard 1986; Lyon 1988). The problem is not information or telecommunications technology *per se*, it is political, moral, and cultural. In so far as 'technology is political, it must be recognised that, under current political auspices and for the foreseeable future, the new technologies will invariably constitute extensions of power and control' (Noble 1984, p. 351). In such a context it becomes necessary to examine critically both the institutions and rationales behind technological innovation and development, as well as the design, pattern or form of deployment and (potential) impact. By challenging the cultural fetish of technological development as autonomous, inevitable, and synonymous with progress it becomes possible to reclaim the present. But there remains an added associated responsibility, namely to (re)generate alternative social and political visions moored in the present (Noble 1983).

The question of alternative forms of social, economic and political life is fraught with difficulty. To mount an effective challenge to prevailing forms of life it is necessary to imagine feasible alternatives which go beyond the mere attainment of a more efficient, technocratic management of the present order of things. But it is simultaneously necessary to refrain from an idealised designation of an alternative form of life (Habermas 1986, pp. 171:212). The constitution of an alternative order depends upon the existence of democratic social and political forces willing and able to pursue radical forms of change, and the articulation and implementation of a strategy which acknowledges the existence of determinate structural limits to the range of future possibilities. However, this does not mean that only those changes which might be implemented in the present should be articulated and pursued. To the contrary, as Laclau and Mouffe contend, 'without the possibility of negating an order beyond the point that we are able to threaten it, there is no possibility at all of the constitution of a radical imaginary – whether democratic or of any other type' (1985, p. 190). It is in this context that reference has been made to the need to retrieve and reconstitute utopian forms of thought, in order to obtain a critical purchase on present conditions (Heller and Feher 1988; Giddens 1990).

3

ALTERNATIVE FUTURES

Visions, fictions and forecasts about the future are not peculiar to the modern age. Ideas about future forms of life, social changes and improvements in the human condition are present in the discourses of both classical antiquity and early Christianity (Nisbet 1980; Kumar 1987). What seems to distinguish the modern age is the strong conviction that a progressive growth of scientific knowledge will uncover the natural order of things, making possible the construction of technologies through which control might be exercised over the course of the development of events. In effect scientific knowledge and associated technological forms are considered to provide the capacity through which the world might be progressively transformed (Roszak 1972; Bell 1980).

A conception of inexorable progress, from the past through the present and on into the future, has been a persistent and distinctive feature of modern Western civilisation. And if the prevailing grand narrative has been that of increasing progress towards an emancipation or liberation of the human condition from want, disease, conflict and toil, the necessary means has been scientific knowledge and the forms of technological innovation it facilitates. Such has been the 'project of modernity' from the time of the Enlightenment (Habermas 1981). The idea of an information technology revolution and much of the discussion over the possible emergence of postindustrial forms of life belong in this context, in so far as they represent contemporary manifestations of a view which constitutes one prominent element of the Enlightenment legacy, namely that the development of technical rationality promotes an increasing understanding and control of natural and social phenomena, and in consequence makes possible the cultivation of improved conditions of existence.

If there continues to be a firm commitment to and resilient confidence in the idea of technological progress, there also exists a substantial and quite diverse range of criticisms of prevailing forms of technology and their effects, as well as a series of associated alternative visions or scenarios for the development and deployment of technological innovations (Bahro 1984; Gorz 1982: 1985; Illich 1985; Roszak 1972). There is no suggestion here that technology *per se* is the problem; rather it is the constitution and promotion of technological innovations as the source of solutions to social, economic and political difficulties that is problematic. 'Technophilia', or an infatuation with technological innovation, in part lies behind the pursuit of a 'technical fix' for problems which ultimately are political, economic, cultural, and moral in kind (Roszak 1986; Robins and Webster 1989). But it is not simply enchantment or infatuation that accounts for the persistence of this state of affairs. More importantly it is the preservation or enhancement of an existing system of domination that is both served and masked by 'infantile dreams of technological salvation' (Noble 1983, p. 92). Furthermore, if there are postindustrial scenarios which might be criticised, as Robins and Webster (1989) imply, for endorsing an ideology of technological progress, it is evident that there are a number of alternative versions or visions of postindustrial futures which are more critical of prevailing hegemonic forms. It is with a consideration of key aspects of some of these alternative futures that this chapter is primarily concerned.

ON THE RECONSTITUTION OF UTOPIAN THOUGHT

Growing evidence of the problems associated with existing forms of science and technology, and parallel criticisms of the idea of progress as an inexorable process of economic growth, best exemplified by the development of Western civilisation, have provided the context in which a reconsideration of utopian forms of thought has begun to occur (Kumar 1987; Frankel 1987). If More's *Utopia* describing an imaginary island with a perfect system of government is an unrealisable fiction, it does not follow that all contributions to utopian thought are equally incapacitated, because they are equally unrealistic and hence unrealisable. As employed in the generation of alternative versions of postindustrial futures, utopian thought is not necessarily concerned with the constitution of perfect systems or ideal forms of life, but rather with challenging the one-dimensionality of prevailing forms of technical rationality, and the seemingly preordained or 'natural' character of existing or established patterns and trends of development. The alternative postindustrial scenarios which are constituted through this process are only utopian in the sense that they require a departure from prevailing forms and patterns of development and, as a corollary, fundamental changes in key institutions and social practices. It is because the analyses provided and the alternative visions or scenarios outlined effectively challenge existing practices and policies, informed by a technical rationality and legitimated through an ideology of scientific and technological progress, that they have come to be regarded as utopian. It is in the context of accumulating doubts about the modern scientific and technological project, doubts prompted by the growing evidence of the hazards and dangers associated with the various forms in which the project has been realised, that the idea of a return to some form of utopian thought needs to be situated.

Utopian thought has had a bad press, particularly within the critical tradition of inquiry developed by Marx. In Marx's work utopian thought is compared unfavourably with what is constituted as a scientific analysis of history. Given the adequacy of a materialist conception of history, the irresistible accumulation of class antagonisms, and the associated emergence and development of an enlightened and revolutionary proletariat which will usher in a post-bourgeois post-capitalist social formation – 'socialism' – there is no need for abstract, ahistorial, utopian formulations. If socialism, or a higher more progressive social formation, is considered to be the product of a determinate process of historical development, to be gestating within an inexorably crisis-ridden capitalist mode of production, simply awaiting the 'decisive hour' to emerge, then there is really no need for 'an imaginative reminder of the nature of historical change: that major social orders do rise and fall, and that new social orders do succeed them' (Williams 1985, p. 13). There is, in brief, no need in such circumstances for utopian thought. For Marx and Engels utopian forms of socialist thought were, at best, symptomatic of an early stage in the development of the capitalist mode of production, 'fantastic pictures of future society, painted at a time when the proletariat is still in a very undeveloped state and has but a fantastic conception of its own position' (1968, p. 116). At its worst utopian socialism was deemed to be a product of the neglect of class antagonism and struggle, to involve a rejection of political and revolutionary action, and to favour the pursuit of a new order through peaceful means that were ultimately 'doomed to failure'. The criticisms of utopian forms of socialist thought outlined by Marx and Engels simultaneously served to advance their own counter-conception of 'scientific socialism'. But in addition such criticisms and the associated strong emphasis placed upon scientificity serve to occlude the utopian traces which remain present in their work. As Kumar comments:

> when we look at Marx's account of the social changes that are bringing the new society into being, still more when we consider the glimpses that we are given of the future communist society, we may be inclined to think Marx's own vision more dazzling in its utopianism than that of even the most utopian of utopian socialists.

(Kumar 1987, p. 53)

On the question of the process of transition from capitalism to socialism and the various comments that are made on the subject of the 'free development of individualities' in a future post-capitalist society, elements of utopian thinking are consistently present in Marx's work (1973a: 1973b: 1976). But given Marx considers his project to be not merely interpreting or analysing the world, but changing and improving upon it, it is hardly surprising that a vision of the potential yet to be realised persists throughout the work, even if its quasi-utopian character is concealed under the cover of science. A century later the idea of laws of history or development has few advocates; the primacy of class antagonism and conflict is questionable, as is the very existence of the proletariat; the capitalist mode of production continues to demonstrate a remarkable capacity to mutate and displace its crisis tendencies; and the first fruits of scientific socialism, the societies of 'actually existing socialism', appear to be withering on the vine, if not decomposing on the ground. Such 'local' difficulties, confined largely to Marxist discourse, are further compounded by the expression of increasing doubts concerning the more general 'project of modernity'. This is the broad context in which it has been argued that there is a need to develop alternative social and political visions and to cultivate utopian forms of thought.

In the course of the nineteenth century an ideology of technological progress served to legitimate the constant upheavals and turmoil associated with the development of the industrial capitalist mode of production. Furthermore, in so far as development of the forces of production, through the application of science and technology, promised to provide the preconditions necessary for deliverance from capitalist exploitation, an ideology of technological progress constituted the cornerstone of socialist critiques of capitalism. The difference was that where 'the capitalists apologised for and rallied behind technological progress, the socialists revered it. For them technological progress was not simply a means to economic ends and a convenient justification of domination, it was a historical vehicle of emancipation' (Noble 1983, p. 20). If subsequently there has been some loss of faith in the idea that technological innovation leads to social advance and an improvement in the human condition, the ideology of technological progress continues, rekindled by the information technology revolution, to be prominent within contemporary capitalist societies. But it no longer provides a basis or a resource for critique. Technological innovation within the capitalist mode of production does not constitute progress towards a post-capitalist or socialist order; to the contrary it is now apparent that, 'development of the productive forces is functional exclusively to the logic and needs of capital. Their development will not only fail to establish the material preconditions of socialism, but are an obstacle to its realisation' (Gorz 1982, pp. 14–15). Leaving aside the complex question of the desirability, feasibility and form of a future 'socialism', it is clear that scientific and technological innovations are not neutral but the products of determinate political and cultural processes. There is no autonomous, unilinear, progressive process of technological development bearing us into the future, but there is in the present an increasing deployment of technological innovations which are precipitating major changes in social relations, and thereby influencing the possibilities for future forms of life. To counter the agendas which are being constituted and the parameters which are being set in accordance with a revived ideology of scientific and technological progress, it is necessary to 'envision other technological possibilities and alternative futures' (Noble 1984, p. 351). It is in this context, as a challenge to existing social circumstances and the future forms of life they promise, or threaten, to deliver that utopian forms of thought have been reconstituted. As Williams remarks,

> the utopian impulse . . . runs not only against the dis-
> appointments of current politics or a more generalised despair,
> but also against the incorporated and marketed versions of a

libertarian capitalist cornucopia . . . Its strongest centre is still
the conviction that people can live very differently.

(Williams 1985, p. 14)

It is to a consideration of critical analyses of the present and
conceptions of possible alternative future forms of life, or 'realistic
utopias', contained in the respective works of Toffler and Gorz, and
to a lesser extent those of Illich, Bahro and Roszak that I will devote
my attention. None of the theorists to be considered here offers a
vision of an ideal form of life or a perfectly harmonious society. All of
them, however, share an interest in identifying the scope and
potential for a considerable improvement in the condition of
humanity. Whether that makes them utopian is debatable. Frankel
suggests that in the final analysis they are utopian because their
respective ideas for postindustrial futures are 'not linked to concrete
plans of action and organisation' (1987, p. 18). But on that criterion
it would be necessary to include most social theorists who have
sought critically to analyse the present and comment on the future –
a long list. Certainly the theorists concerned are conscious that their
views may be regarded as utopian, and in the case of two of them,
Gorz and Bahro, the term is positively embraced. Gorz outlines a
'Utopia for a possible dual society' which tells the story of a future
France in which emphasis is placed upon the quality of life rather than
the pursuit of ever increasing standards of living or levels of GNP; on
the production and consumption of goods which meet the criteria of
'durability, ease of repair, pleasantness of manufacture, and absence of
polluting effects' (1982, p. 147). In a parallel manner Bahro argues
that 'today utopian thought has a new necessity', namely to overcome
the idea of historical spontaneity, of objective economic laws (1978,
p. 253). Subsequently, after moving to the West, Bahro described his
intellectual trajectory as involving a movement from scientific
socialism to 'utopian socialism' (1984, p. 220).

A radically different response to the topic of utopian thought is
articulated by Illich who ultimately differentiates his analysis from the
idea of utopia. For Illich the declared aim is to contribute to the
development of a 'post-industrial era of conviviality'. The difficulty
lies in the poverty of our imagination, the fact that 'our vision of the
possible and the feasible is so restricted by industrial expectations that
any alternative to more mass production sounds like a return to past
oppression or like a Utopian design for noble savages' (1985, p. xi). A
less radical but more ambiguous response to the topic is provided by

Toffler, whose work reveals a significant change of mind, a volte-face, on the question of utopian forms of thought. Outlining a 'strategy of social futurism' in *Future Shock* Toffler categorically asserts the need for 'powerful new utopian and anti-utopian concepts', a 'revolution in the production of utopias', and 'utopia factories' (1971, p. 421). But in a subsequent work Toffler declares that he is 'not a utopian' (1984, p. 36) and, more importantly, that the alternative scenario outlined does not warrant the description, for it is 'agitated by deep problems'. Indeed the potential 'Third Wave' civilisation projected by Toffler is described as neither a utopia nor an anti-utopia. Instead it is portrayed as a 'practopia',

> neither the best nor the worst of all possible worlds, but one that is both practical and preferable to the one we had. Unlike a utopia, a practopia is not free of disease, political nastiness, and bad manners . . . Conversely, a practopia does not embody the crystallised evil of a utopia turned inside out . . . In short a practopia offers a positive, even a revolutionary alternative, yet lies within the range of the realistically attainable.
>
> (Toffler 1983, p. 368)

The question of whether, or not, the respective analyses provided by Bahro, Gorz, Illich, Roszak and Toffler are, in some essential sense, utopian is not a matter to be pursued here. The focus of my concern will be on their different analyses of the problems and possibilities immanent, or emerging, in the present.

SHOCKWAVES OF CHANGE – THE TOFFLER THESIS

The emergence of a postindustrial society is depicted by Bell as synonymous with a change in merely one element or dimension of modern society, namely the social structure. For Toffler the stakes are somewhat higher and the range of changes identified are extensive, and regarded as signifying nothing less than the emergence of a new civilisation. The new forms of change constitute 'not a straight-line extension of industrial society but a radical shift of direction, often a negation, of what went before. It adds up to nothing less than a complete transformation at least as revolutionary in our day as industrial civilisation was 300 years ago' (1983, p. 359). In Toffler's view the range of terms introduced to describe the changes taking place, for example information age, technetronic age, postindustrial society, and his own initial suggestion of a 'super-industrial society'

(Toffler 1971, p. 23), are far from adequate because they fail to capture the scale, scope, and complexity of the transformations we are facing. To that extent Toffler is not a 'post-industrial' theorist, although the transitions and transformations he explores are, for the most part, comparable to the concerns articulated in the various contributions to the debate over the idea of postindustrial society.

Toffler's work is located very much within the futures study field in so far as it attempts to provide an imaginative exploration of future possibilities. The principal concern is not to prophesy or predict on the basis of extrapolations drawn from the present, but to produce an 'imaginative picture of future states of the world'. As such the analysis presented constitutes less of an ideal type against which reality might be measured or compared than a model of social change and social structure, a model derived from a variety of source materials including 'technical journals, . . . newspapers . . . statistical summaries . . . reports . . . novels, films, or poetry' (1984, p. 190), plus interviews with authorities drawn from a variety of relevant fields of inquiry. Just as Bell's agenda-setting notion seems to have been widely circulated in governmental and policymaking circles in the USA, so Toffler's thesis has received world-wide promotion on television, has been recommended for study in China, and in addition has gained the attention of the White House.[1] What precise effect, if any, Toffler's work has had on policy formation is a matter of speculation, although it might be argued that through its generation of an image of the future it 'not only indicates alternative choices and possibilities, but actively promotes certain choices and in effect puts them to work in determining the future' (Polak 1973, p. 300). Certainly Toffler provides a readily accessible, if controversial, account of key aspects of contemporary forms of social change and the prospects and possibilities for future forms of life.

Toffler employs a three-stage model of social change. An early version is outlined in *Future Shock* where a distinction is developed between 'agricultural', 'industrial' and 'super-industrial' stages of development. It is with the latter that Toffler is principally concerned, with the accelerating pace of change in everyday life which is producing an increasing experience of transience in people's relationships with one another, with material things, places, institutions, ideas and information; a breakdown of bureaucratic administrative structures; and a related emergence of new task specific, less hierarchical organisational forms ('ad-hocracy'). Toffler is quite categorical at this stage about the changes identified – they signify the creation of 'a new society. Not a changed society. Not an extended, larger-than-life version of our present society. But a new society' (1971, p. 172). Toffler suggests that with technology as the engine of change and knowledge as its fuel the 'super-industrial revolution . . . threatens to alter not merely the "how" of production but the "why". It will, in short, transform the very purposes of economic activity' (Toffler 1971, p. 202). Transformations anticipated include a shift from 'productivity' or 'efficiency' as the goal of economic activity to 'psychic fulfilment', or rather a reconceptualisation of the former in terms of the latter, an associated expansion of the 'psychic component' of services, and a concomitant growth of 'experiential industries'. The latter service industries may also of course be generated in order to conserve or enhance the productivity or efficiency of a particular form of economic activity, but such an extension of the commodification of life is not seriously countenanced. However, if Toffler anticipates an increase in the significance of experiential products and services, simulated environments and experiences, in effect a 'psychologisation of the economy', these possibilities do not receive an unqualified endorsement, they are far from celebrated developments. To the contrary the movement towards a 'psyche' economy is described as morally repellent, given the abject poverty and starvation to which the majority of humanity are subject, and it is suggested that,

> The technosocieties could defer the arrival of experientialism, could maintain a more conventional economy for a time by maximising traditional production, shifting resources to environmental quality control, and then launching absolutely massive anti-poverty and foreign aid programmes.
>
> (Toffler 1971, p. 216)

But the absence of any consideration of the political, economic, and cultural transformations required to implement such programmes means that the statement, well-intended as it might be, has a hollow ring to it. Furthermore, the intentions themselves might be questioned given Toffler's comment that a 'campaign to erase hunger from the world . . . would buy the techno-societies badly needed time for an easier transition to the economy of the future' (Toffler 1971, p. 216).

Toffler clearly has mixed views about the possible emergence of a super-industrial society. Standardised goods and services, standardised mass culture and associated life-styles may no longer be as problematic as they were once conceived to be, because the 'super-industrial revolution' has introduced increasing diversity and individualisation. But now, rather than an erosion of choice, we seem fated to confront the converse, the prospect of a paralysing surfeit of choice. The increasing proliferation of choice in the sphere of economic production and consumption prompts the suggestion that we may be approaching a point of 'overchoice', where the 'advantages of diversity and individualisation are cancelled by the complexity of the buyer's decision-making process' (Toffler 1971, p. 246). A parallel tendency towards diversity is evident in art, education, and mass culture. For example, in literature and painting there is 'evidence of a powerful international shift towards cultural destandardisation' and this trend is paralleled by a diversification of educational programmes. Such forms of diversity and individualisation are considered to be producing a fragmentation of cultures and communities, precipitating a proliferation of subcultures and encouraging a 'crazy-quilt pattern of evanescent life styles' (Toffler 1971, p. 275). These changes introduce a bewildering diversity of styles, values and subcultures, and a 'super-abundance of selves', of identities and forms of subjectivity, creating problems of both social and individual integration. In short, increasing diversity and transience, coupled with an emphasis upon novelty, is producing an historical crisis of adaptation which Toffler terms 'future shock'.

After having diagnosed the present as a time in which uneven, rapidly accelerating and uncontrolled forms of change appear to be occurring in an increasing number of areas of social life, Toffler commences to outline a possible non-technocratic strategy for the management of change which involves a humanisation of planning, an extension of time horizons, and the introduction of democratic forms of goal formulation. The assumption is that 'we are witnessing the beginning of the final breakup of industrialism and, with it, the collapse of technocratic planning' (Toffler 1971, p. 404). Technocratic planning is described as 'econocentric', relatively short range in time horizon, hierarchical and undemocratic, and ill-equipped to cope with the emergence of 'super-industrial' forms. As evidence of the limitations of our ability to regulate and control our social and physical environment has increased, so has disillusionment with modern science. In this 'postmodern' context there has been a 'garish revival of mysticism'; an emphasis on the emotional rather than the rational and/or scientific; a 'reversion to prescientific attitudes . . . accompanied . . . by a tremendous wave of nostalgia in the society', a promotion of spontaneity; and an antipathy shared by a 'strange coalition of rightwingers and New Leftists' towards planning, which manifests itself in 'a "hang loose" approach to the future' (Toffler 1971, p. 407). In contrast to what is described as a 'plunge backwards into irrationality', Toffler outlines a strategy of social futurism, which involves adding to the anticipation of *probable* futures a broadened conception of *possible* futures. Given our present circumstances, it is argued that

> we need a multiplicity of visions, dreams and prophecies – images of potential tomorrows. Before we can rationally decide which alternative pathways to choose, which cultural styles to pursue, we must first ascertain which are possible. Conjecture, speculation and the visionary view thus become as coldly practical a necessity as feet-on-the-floor 'realism' was in an earlier time.
>
> (Toffler 1971, p. 418)

The Third Wave represents Toffler's attempt to provide such a vision of present possibilities.

In *The Third Wave* Toffler conceives of history as a 'succession of rolling waves of change' (1983, p. 27) which collide, overlap, ebb and flow. Following the waves of change unleashed by the agricultural and industrial revolutions respectively it is argued that a 'Third Wave phase [is] now beginning'. The first wave of change, synonymous with the rise of agriculture, the establishment of settled communities, and cultivation of the land, is considered to have 'virtually subsided'. The second wave, which arose with industrialisation, has radically transformed life in many parts of the world and continues to have a considerable impact, although in Toffler's view it is past its peak and is increasingly disturbed by the emergence of a third wave of change. It is the 'collision between the Third Wave and the obsolete, encrusted economies and institutions of the second' that is, as I have indicated, at the centre of Toffler's discussion. The implication is that we are in the midst of a struggle between, on the one hand, 'industrial' or second wave vested interests, 'conservatives' of all political parties and persuasions who are attempting to incorporate and/or subordinate emerging new forms, whether in technology or social practices, beliefs, and life-styles, within the 'old' order of industrialism and, on the other hand, those who conceive the afore-mentioned changes to signify the emergence of a new civilisation, and therefore to require new social, political, economic, and cultural responses. As Toffler remarks:

> most people, irrespective of their politics, see the future as a simple, straight line extension of the present. I think they are in for a big surprise. We've reached the end of an age – and at that point all bets are off.
>
> (Toffler 1984, p. 86)

BEYOND CAPITALISM AND SOCIALISM?

In a series of comments that parallel in some respects the thesis outlined by Kerr *et al.* (1960) on the 'logic of industrialism', Toffler argues that, notwithstanding differences of history, culture, and politics, all second wave societies, by virtue of their industrial form, share a number of fundamental features. The most significant of the features identified is the division of production and consumption and its necessary corollaries, the constitution of particular forms of subjectivity, 'producers' and 'consumers', and an associated 'marketisation' of the economy. Prior to the Industrial Revolution the bulk of food, goods, and services was produced for self and familial consumption rather than for exchange. Subsequently there has been an increasingly marked shift from production for use to production for exchange and as this has occurred the market 'once a minor and peripheral phenomenon [has] moved into the very vortex of life' (Toffler 1983, p. 53). These developments, in turn, are considered to have precipitated, in all second wave societies, whether capitalist or socialist in form, the introduction of a number of distinctive principles of organisation, namely standardisation; specialisation; synchronisation; concentration; maximisation; and centralisation. In other words, beneath the diverse features manifested by second wave industrial societies, and 'regardless of their cultural or climatic differences, regardless of their ethnic and religious heritage, regardless of whether they call themselves capitalist or communist' (1983, p. 50), there exists a latent stratum of similarity. In addition to the common features and organisational principles noted above a further set of similarities is identified in the techno-sphere and the structure of political power. For example, 'Just as the factory came to symbolise the entire industrial techno-sphere, representative government (no matter how denatured) became the status symbol of every "advanced" nation' (Toffler 1983, p. 86). Or more succinctly, 'a Second Wave political unit was needed to match the growth of Second Wave economic units' (Toffler 1983, p. 93).

It may appear at times as though Toffler is propounding a determinist thesis in which economic or technological factors are the catalysts for change. However, such an objection is anticipated, firmly denied, and countered by the argument that no single force is responsible for the changes identified (1983, pp. 128; 369–70: 1984, pp. 208–9; 212). Yet virtually no consideration is given to the social and historical forces which have shaped the information and tele-communications technologies identified with the third wave of change, and in the absence of such an address understandable doubts about Toffler's position have persisted (Roszak 1972; Frankel 1987). Certainly, before the environmentally friendly, appropriate scale, and more humane technologies referred to by Toffler can be realised, it is necessary to examine the existing configuration of forces, and the social relations of innovation and production which have been responsible for the introduction of the present generation of technologies, specifically the military–industrial complex which has constituted the catalyst for the development of the information and telecommunications technologies on the crest of the 'third wave' of change.

However, industrialism is more than a socioeconomic, technological and/or political formation for Toffler; it also constitutes a cultural form and involves a distinctive 'new way of thinking about reality'. This new way of thinking involves a number of ideas and assumptions that have been identified with the 'project of modernity'. Three inter-related ideas are of significance to the world-view of industrial society – 'indust-reality' – outlined by Toffler, namely an instrumental–rational orientation to nature; a conception of humanity as the 'pinnacle of a long process of evolution'; and an understanding of historical development as a process of inexorable progress. In turn these ideas are associated with a deeper set of assumptions about reality concerning time, space, matter, and causality.

Toffler argues that a new 'software of time' emerged with second wave civilisation, that time was made 'linear'. No longer mystified by the pre-industrial first wave idea of time as circular and repetitive, second wave societies are impaled on the arrow of time, for it is linear time that makes their evolution and progress conceivable. Just as time has been transformed so space, too, has been redesigned by industrial civilisation. Industrialisation has been associated with the emergence of a 'spatially extended' culture, with the elaboration of many specialised types of space, which in turn has necessitated the development of forms of spatial organisation and coordination. The necessity to coordinate the proliferating range of specialised spaces 'was the exact spatial analogue of temporal synchronisation. It was in effect synchronisation in space. For *both* time and space had to be more carefully structured if industrial societies were to function' (Toffler 1983, p. 119). Paralleling the precise standardisation of units of time and their linear organisation, space, in its turn, has been subjected to measurement and standardisation, has been defined and mapped in a manner that is comparable to the 'linearisation of time'.

As with time and space so too a distinctive conception of matter emerged with second wave civilisation, namely atomism. Philosophical and physical atomism, the idea that the universe consists of an assembly of discrete parts and elements, is identified as indispensable to the development of industrial society with its emphasis upon 'mass production of assembled machine products composed of discrete components' and constitution of autonomous individuality as the basic element of social and political life. The theme of atomism, the conceptualisation of physical, social, and political phenomena in terms of distinctive autonomous elements or units, is a constitutive feature of second wave civilisation. Likewise a conception of causation, a fixed, predictable law-like patterning of events and relationships, is identified by Toffler as a core assumption of industrial societies. The new way of thinking which emerged has produced positive developments in the fields of science and technology and in social, economic and political life. It articulated 'perfectly with the new energy systems, family systems, technological systems, economic systems, political and value systems that together formed the civilisation of the Second Wave' (Toffler 1983, p. 127). But in Toffler's view this civilisation, its established ways of thinking, key institutions, technologies and cultural forms, is now experiencing an 'irretrievable crisis', one which through a combination of external and internal pressures is rendering a '"normal" continuation of industrial civilisation' inconceivable. Accumulating evidence of ecological damage; problems associated with both the increasing price and declining availability of energy and raw materials; 'internal' crises affecting the provision of welfare, health care, education, and employment; the problems affecting modern city life; the international financial system and the nation-state: all these suggest the imminent collapse of second wave civilisation, but not necessarily the

75

emergence of a third wave civilisation. Industrialism may be ebbing and the changes taking place may signify the emergence of new non-industrial third wave forms but, Toffler cautions, that does not mean a new civilisation will inevitably emerge (1983, pp. 360:370).

The features attributed to second wave industrial civilisation are deemed to be common to both capitalism and socialism and in consequence they too are considered to be in a terminal state. Contemporary capitalism and actually existing socialism constitute industrial forms; both

> are dependent on fossil fuel. Mass production. Mass distribution. Mass education. Mass media. Mass entertainment. Both make the nuclear family the basic model for society. Both are built on big cities and the nation-state. Both impose the same principles of standardisation, synchronisation, centralisation, maximisation, and so forth
>
> (Toffler 1984, p. 91)

And because they share certain core structural features which are being eroded by a third wave of change Toffler anticipates their demise. As phenomena predominantly of the industrial era, modern capitalism and actually existing socialism are unable to survive the effects of increasing diversity and demassification, and an acceleration in the pace of change, associated with the third wave. As flexible rhythms and schedules, diversity and segmentation, and dispersal, appropriate scale and decentralisation replace synchronised assembly line production, standardisation, and concentration, maximisation and centralisation respectively, so modern capitalism and actually existing socialism experience 'crisis'. Changes occurring in respect of energy, production and distribution systems, social institutions and relationships, and culture, communications and politics represent for Toffler the foundations for a possible new civilisation, but its realisation is by no means inevitable, for the collision between the second and third waves 'will be marked by extreme social disruption, as well as wild economic swings, sectional clashes, secession attempts, technological upsets or disasters, political turbulence, violence, wars, and threats of war' (1983, p. 360). Yet if there are great dangers Toffler considers the odds lie with ultimate survival and the construction of a more democratic, economically and ecologically more 'coherent and workable' civilisation.

This admission seems to leave open the possibility of the continuing existence of an 'abnormal' industrial civilisation, one which attempts to adapt and accommodate to some of the elements of change identified with the third wave. It also raises the question of the possibility of third wave forms of capitalism and socialism. Toffler offers relatively little comment on the first point, virtually nothing beyond references to the 'super-struggle' which is occurring between the two forms of civilisation, between interests, regions, and nations completing their industrialisation, or attempting to conserve and protect their existing industrialised forms of life, and the diverse interests and forces associated with the emerging third wave.[2] In Toffler's view this constitutes the single most significant political conflict confronting us. It 'cuts like a jagged line across class and party, across age and ethnic groups, sexual preferences and subcultures. It reorganises and realigns our political life . . . [and] points towards escalating crises and deep social unrest in the near-term future' (Toffler 1983, p. 449). As for the prospect of third wave forms of capitalism and socialism, Toffler insists that in both instances their contradictions will prove fatal and that they will not survive the oncoming tide of change.

The contradictions deemed to be fatal to capitalist and socialist forms of life derive from their respective core organisational principles, namely private property and centralised planning. On the question of advanced capitalist societies Toffler affirms a separation of ownership and control thesis (Burnham 1962; Gailbraith 1969) and argues that 'decisional power and control' has steadily displaced ownership in importance as information has become the essential property. But if 'info-property' is indeed potentially infinite, non-material and non-tangible, it nevertheless has, within the prevailing social relations of production, become a commodity, subject to copyright, patent and ownership. Furthermore, whilst it might be the case that corporations are not *narrowly* driven by the maximisation of profit, the latter needs must be pursued if market shares and financial investment levels are to be maintained. Likewise, if the increasing significance of metasymbolic 'info-property' contradicts the conventional notion of property as scarce and material, there nevertheless remains an important continuity. If, as Toffler contends, what really matters to shareholders is 'the organised information it [the share] controls' (1984, p. 104) it is because of the increasing strategic significance of information in the production and profit-making process. If information has emerged as the essential property it does not constitute a fatal contradiction for contemporary capitalism. To the contrary it might well be argued that it has facilitated 'restructuring' by allowing more flexible forms of production and accumulation to develop. Toffler might be right in believing that the 'information revolution' has made 'ideological goulash out of all old economic theories', but that does not mean capitalism has become an anachronism. The third wave principles of flexibility, diversity, dispersal, appropriate scale and decentralisation, in and of themselves, constitute no particular threat to the capitalist system of production. Similarly, associated shifts away from bureaucratic forms of organisation towards less hierarchical more flexible structures need not be a problem. And the development of smaller work and production units, including the much vaunted 'electronic cottage', might be regarded as virtual functional prerequisites for a more cost-effective, flexible and industrial-conflict free form of capitalism. From its inception capitalism has been a technologically and organisationally dynamic and revolutionary mode of production, and the transformations identified above suggest that 'the tension that has always prevailed within capitalism between monopoly and competition, between centralisation and decentralisation of economic power, is [now] being worked out in fundamentally new ways' (Harvey 1989, p. 159).

If there is a problem for capitalism on the horizon identified by Toffler it is that of the prospect of an 'end of the process of marketisation', a process which is paralleled by the emergence of 'prosumption', that is, a return to production for self-consumption rather than exchange. The fission of production and consumption and the corollary, the increasing significance of the mediating mechanism of the market, is identified as the event which transformed first wave 'agricultural' economies into second wave industrial economies. Likewise the blurring of the distinction between production and consumption evident in the rise of 'prosumption' and the emergence of the 'prosumer' represents for Toffler important evidence of a shift from second to third wave economic forms. Although factories and offices will continue to exist they are 'destined to be revolutionised in the decades ahead'. Changes are anticipated in the international division of labour, in levels of employment, the size of production units, the relationship of production and consumption, and the nature and location of the activity of work. In particular Toffler makes reference to the increasing possibility that work will be transferred to the home, to the 'electronic cottage', to which there is surely a responsibility, if not an obligation, to add the additional, more sober and realistic, if less evocative, imagery of the electronic flat, or tenement, which will surely constitute the fate of most 'home-workers'.

The information revolution, the computer, telecommunications, the changing nature of productive activity and the reduction in the size of work units make possible a transfer of work from factory and office to the home. This possibility is paralleled by the rise of production for use, 'prosuming' in Toffler's terms. Self-help groups and movements concerned with various issues, problems, and difficulties (e.g. health, disease, addiction, etc.), the 'externalisation' of labour costs and forms of DIY, involving not simply home construction and decoration, but education and other services, demonstrate for Toffler the existence of a growing movement from passive consumption to active prosumption. Such a trend is not confined to services, but extends to goods, and the suggestion is that 'the more we de-massify and customise production, the stronger the customer's involvement in the production process' becomes (Toffler 1983, p. 284). In this way, through third wave high technology, prosumption is regenerated and this has consequences for the exchange mechanism of the market predicated on the split between production and consumption.

In my view Toffler does not go so far as to propose a 'withering away of the market' (Frankel 1987, p. 35) or the emergence of a 'demarketised future' (Frankel 1987, p. 152). On the contrary, he states categorically that 'the market is not going to go away' and that there will be no return to a pre-market form of economy (Toffler 1983, p. 287). However, two related yet quite distinctive and relevant developments are anticipated. The first concerns a 'de-marketisation' of activities, involving both goods and services affected by the rise of prosuming, the second the prospect of an end to the process of market expansion. On the first point it is argued that, other things being equal, an increase in prosumption is likely to lead to a less market intensive society, hence a degree of 'de-marketisation'. This contributes to the end of the process of marketisation, but other additional factors are involved. The market expanded by locating new populations of consumers, extending the commodification of life, and increasing the number of intermediaries involved in transactions between producers and consumers. Toffler argues that all these forms of expansion are approaching their limits, and that there are no significantly new populations to be drawn into the market. The prospect of a further commodification of life through the introduction of new goods and services is undermined by the rise of prosumption and increases in the costs associated with the exchange process are leading to simplified forms of distribution. The implication of the approach of these limits is an end to the process of marketisation. Toffler believes that the second wave mission to 'marketise the world' has been virtually completed, and that although there will continue to be a need to maintain, renovate and redesign the market mechanism this will not constitute a central feature of a third wave civilisation. The latter is described as a 'trans-market' civilisation, one which depends upon exchange networks provided by the market mechanism 'but is no longer consumed by the need to build, extend, elaborate, and integrate this structure' (Toffler 1983, p. 298). Given the market is conceived to be not merely an economic structure but in addition a psychosocial structure, Toffler anticipates a potential release and redirection of energy, imagination, and action formerly devoted to market building. This would represent a fatal development for the capitalist mode of production dependent, as it is, upon the pursuit of increasing levels of capital accumulation through the generation of expanding markets for goods and services.

Both of Toffler's general points on the question of the market and its future are, however, open to challenge. To begin with, accepting the reality of a level of prosumption and the rise of the prosumer, consideration needs to be given to the prospect that an increase in forms of production for immediate, direct or own use or consumption may create a need for, if not actually depend upon, the availability of additional new goods and services in the marketplace. Increases in forms of prosumption may, in short, be a corollary of the production of potentially limitless new generations of *consumer* goods and services. In other words the rise of the prosumer may not signify 'de-marketisation' but the development of a new accumulation cycle (Gorz 1985). Furthermore, even if the idea that rising costs of exchange leading to a simplification of market mechanisms is accepted, along with the observation that there are no remaining vast new populations awaiting market seduction, the assumption that further increases in commodification are unlikely is unwarranted and contentious. To begin with, there exist dramatic variations in the pervasiveness and significance of the market mechanism in different societies and, in so far as that is the case, there would seem to be scope for a further expansion of the market although, as Toffler cautions, such a second wave strategy might 'turn the entire planet into a single giant factory and wreak ecological havoc' (1983, p. 341). Of greater significance however is the potentially limitless scope for increases in the commodification of life. An ever increasing range of improved, novel, more up-to-date, and fashionable goods and services are being designed for the market. This form of market expansion is not merely 'theoretically possible', as Toffler contends, it is being realised. Indeed this very possibility is clearly implied in his earlier identification and discussion of the emergence of a 'throw-away society' characterised by transience, the pursuit of novelty, an expansion of the psychic component of services, and associated growth of 'experiential industries' (Toffler 1971). The prospects for continuing marketisation arise not only from the scope for a commodification of (relatively) unexploited areas and aspects of life, but in addition through the generation of an increasing acceleration of the pace of consumption. Developments of this order do not signify the demise of capitalism but its restructuring and reorganisation, specifically its transition to a form of more flexible accumulation, or 'neo-Fordism' (Webster and Robins 1986; Harvey 1989).

Addressing the question of socialism in present circumstances poses a number of difficulties. References abound to a growing 'common marketisation' of international relations, the end of history, and the triumph of liberal democratic Western capitalism (Fukuyama 1989); the end of the Cold War and the prospect of a 'New World Order' (Sommer 1991); the radical transformation of those Eastern European geo-political 'unities' which once claimed to represent 'actually existing socialism' (Bahro 1978); and the possibility of an associated renaissance of Europe. In one way or another each of the above assessments of contemporary developments raises the question of the very survival of socialism. Toffler's answer is that socialism based upon centralised forms of planning will not survive the third wave of change. Even within industrial economies centralised planning has proven cumbersome, inefficient and increasingly inadequate for organising the activities of large complex socioeconomic units.

With the emergence of new, more diverse, non-standardised, demassified, flexible and fast changing social, economic, and technological forms Toffler argues that the '"decision load" of the planners becomes literally unmanageable' (1984, p. 96). Central planning cannot cope with increasing diversification, an accelerating pace of change, and associated shifts towards 'flexible, customised decisions'. In consequence it becomes necessary to decentralise decision making, but doing so necessarily risks a transformation of the prevailing system. As is clear from the complex and difficult processes of adjustment underway in Eastern Europe there is relatively little room for manoeuvre for the former societies of 'actually existing socialism'. To ride the third wave of change they have had to liberalise their social, economic and political systems, and encourage independence, risk-taking and creativity, for the difficulties they confront cannot be resolved simply by importing high technology from the West:

> Technology by itself can't bring the Third Wave. A Third Wave economy requires a Third Wave culture and a Third Wave political frame. This suggests to me that they will have to decentralise and democratise eventually, whether they want to or not . . . In short, if they want the benefits of an advanced economy, they'll have to transform their entire system.
>
> (Toffler 1984, p. 100)

However, such a transformation still leaves open the question of the possibility of third wave non- or post-industrial forms of socialism.

THE PROSPECTS FOR POST-INDUSTRIAL SOCIALISM

The idea that a series of inter-related changes are carrying modern, predominantly Western societies beyond both capitalism and socialism is present in a number of analyses. 'Post-socialist' post-industrial society is described by Bell as merging in its problems, if not in its outcomes, 'with the post-capitalist societies in that the new determining feature of social structure (but not necessarily of politics and culture) is the scientific and technological revolution . . . the centrality of theoretical knowledge as the axial principle of social organisation' (1973, p. 112).[3] A broader and more extensive pattern of changes is described by Toffler as making both capitalism and socialism, 'products of the industrial revolution', obsolescent. In each instance the changes involved are considered to be precipitating disorder, conflict and disorganisation, in short producing a crisis in the existing industrial systems of capitalism and socialism. The problems associated with the emergence of new social, economic and political forces and phenomena evidently require novel solutions and remedies, new institutions and structures, and new forms of organisation, rather than recourse to old formulae and programmes. Ultimately Bell seems to have relatively little to offer on this score, for whilst there is a recognition of the scale of the problems to be confronted, proposals extend no further than a vague 'reaffirmation of liberalism' and a suggestion that the market principle be used for social purposes in order to resolve the contradictions between private interest and public provision besetting contemporary capitalist societies (Bell 1980, p. 227). More imaginative in his conception of the kind of changes and policies which might be required (and possible), Toffler argues that if the transition to a third wave civilisation is to be successfully accomplished, then our obsolescent political institutions need to be replaced by alternatives based upon the key principles of 'minority power, semi-direct democracy and decision division' (1983, pp. 451–2). Predictably both Bell and Toffler conclude that the pressing problems of the present and the future are political. Some things do not change.

A parallel analysis which attempts to present a range of radical measures and policies which might be regarded as necessary, possible, and/or desirable to cope with fundamental changes occurring in the structure and organisation of modern capitalist societies is provided in Gorz's discussion of the prospects and possibilities for a 'post-industrial socialism'. Gorz's contribution belongs within a tradition of critical socialist inquiry and analysis which acknowledges the analytic limits and limitations of Marxist analysis and the increasingly evident inadequacies of both contemporary capitalism and actually existing forms of socialism. But the objective of the work is not to abandon the entire conceptual apparatus of Marxist analysis, or to undermine the prospect of imagining and working towards an alternative social formation capable of transcending the limitations of modern capitalism and the various perversions and devaluations of the 'notions of "socialism" and "communism" by regimes and parties that claim to represent them' (Gorz 1982, p. 12). The aim is to provide an analysis of the changed circumstances synonymous with the 'post-industrial revolution' and to outline the prospects and possibilities for the development of a 'liberated society' (1985, p. 32). There are a number of important points of contact between Gorz's work and the analyses provided by Toffler and Illich and, to a lesser extent, Bahro and Roszak respectively. In each case there is a critical concern with the problems associated with economic growth, environmental damage, and the growing crisis confronting the industrial system in general, although Gorz is more explicit in analysing the industrial *capitalist* mode of production as the locus of the problem, and identifying the question of communism as intrinsic to the constitution of a 'liberated' postindustrial society (1982, pp. 123–4).[4]

Gorz endorses the view that advanced industrial societies have reached a critical stage in their development and are poised to move beyond both capitalism and socialism. The choice confronted now is not the one identified by Marx between 'barbarism' and 'socialism', it is between, on the one hand, the emergence of a 'programmed' or technocratic society and, on the other, a genuinely liberated society within which the benefits of advances in knowledge and technology will be deployed so as to enhance, rather than reduce or eradicate, forms of individual autonomy. A complex multi-dimensional crisis confronting the advanced industrial societies is conceived to be evident in virtually every area of social life, 'in the relation between the individual and the economic sphere . . . in the character of work . . . in our relations with nature, with our bodies, with our sexuality, with society' (1980, p. 12). It represents a crisis of industrialism *per se*, for realising the central goal of perpetual economic growth – increasing capital accumulation and rising material standards of living – through the exercise of control over nature by means of the deployment of technological innovations has become increasingly more difficult; indeed, Gorz suggests that it is now approaching its structural and physical limit.

There are two clear elements in Gorz's work, the first an analysis of the current crisis afflicting Western industrial capitalist societies in particular, the second an outline of a programme or set of measures through which a technocratic totalitarian end to the postindustrial revolution might be avoided. The crisis has both an economic and ecological dimension and, although the focus of Gorz's analysis falls upon Western capitalism, the societies of Eastern Europe are deemed to encounter comparable problems as a direct consequence of their adoption of Western technologies and production systems, and equally relentless pursuit of a policy of economic growth (Bahro 1984). Of these two dimensions to the crisis it is the 'economic' that constitutes the principal concern, for in the final instance ecological accommodations and costs may, like other costs, be incorporated within the capitalist mode of production (Gorz 1980, pp. 4–7). Indeed it is possible that ecological concerns, in so far as they open up new territories for 'marketisation' and 'commodification', may make a contribution to the regeneration of capitalism. The 'greening' of capitalism is more than conceivable, it is under way.

Economic crisis derives from the fact that all the principal conventional sources of economic growth are approaching exhaustion. Market saturation, a falling rate of profit, rising costs in the form of wages, benefits and raw materials, and in addition over-capacity in industries that were formerly amongst the fastest growing, suggest that economic growth is no longer revivable through the conventional remedies of 'reflation through demand' and the alternative, 'reflation through investment'. The former is considered to be increasingly ineffective because, like Toffler, Gorz believes the market for consumer products is virtually saturated. Reflation through investment confronts not only problems of declining levels of profitability, rising costs and over-capacity, but in addition the fact that the new technologies of computerisation and robotisation, introduced to achieve rises in productivity necessary for reflation or growth, 'require the writing off of greater amounts of existing capital than the amounts newly invested, and destroy more jobs than they create' (1985, p. 13). In addition to the problems of investment, profitability and direct and indirect wage costs, there is the accumulating problem of 'social costs' which have been rising consistently faster than overall production.[5] An increase in social costs derives from two principal sources. First, the capitalist model of increasing individualised consumption of goods and services creates a tendency for people to demand and expect 'individual', personal, more novel and sophisticated 'solutions' or remedies to what are often collective or communal problems and difficulties. Through its reinforcement of 'individual commodity demand' the state sector, and welfarism in particular, has played a decisive role in the reproduction of the ethos of individualism. Second, a revolution of rising consumer expectations has been followed by a 'revolution of rising entitlements', an accelerating demand for protections, rights, and services from all groups in society (Bell 1976, pp. 232–6). Together these processes have produced a continual increase in social costs, a state of affairs which Gorz argues has led both 'left' and 'right' to conclude that a way has to be found to reduce public sector demand. The alternative proposals for reducing social costs are fundamentally different, as are their respective social and political consequences.

AUTO-PRODUCTION, AUTO-INTEGRATION AND AUTO-SURVEILLANCE

The introduction of information technology represents the method adopted within the capitalist system to reduce social costs, extend the market for commodities, and launch a new accumulation cycle. The expectation is that information technology will reduce the costs of producing the appropriate consumers. It should furthermore make it possible to industrialise one-to-one services, namely those of physicians, psychologists, educators etc.; to transfer the production of consumers to the consumers themselves – with the help of computer programmes which will be sold to them with a sizable profit.

(Gorz 1985, p. 25)

Self-production or auto-production of consumers to the level required by industry is currently being promoted in two key areas in particular, namely education and health, both of which are costly, staff intensive and characterised by declining productivity. The scenario outlined for education is one in which commercial teaching machines, computers and instruction programmes are introduced on a growing scale, effectively creating a situation in which 'individuals pay industry for the means (terminals, teletext, receivers, access to memory storage and specific programmes) of auto-production, auto-integration and auto-surveillance – the means to ward off anxiety, isolation, fear of demotion, unemployment and marginalisation' (Gorz 1985, p. 25). A comparable process of industrialisation of personal social services, involving the substitution of personnel by technologies promoting self-assessment, is on the agenda in the sphere of health.

What formerly had constituted a drain on profit levels, a 'social cost', is being turned, through the extension of industrial capitalist logic into the sphere of public provision, into a potential source of profit. Formerly publicly provided and funded services become, via the marketplace, services and commodities produced commercially for individual consumers. With the turn towards flexible forms of accumulation domestic, self, and public provision of services essential to the reproduction of the labour force are being steadily transformed in order to provide a new market for capitalist commodity production (Gorz 1980, pp. 86–8: 1982, pp. 84–5; Harvey 1989, pp. 156–9). However, such an attempt at a resolution of the current economic crisis has two inter-related consequences in Gorz's view, namely a deterioration in the prospects for individual autonomy and self-control, and ultimately a negation of the very commodity relations that lie at the foundation of the capitalist mode of production.

Industrialisation of the network of key personal or social services necessary for the reproduction of the labour force is beneficial for the capitalist system in so far as it creates scope for new commodities and markets, and contributes to an increasing individualisation of consumption. Such a development has been promoted as a step which gets government 'off people's backs', gives greater freedom of choice, and, through the generation of increasing competition, improves the standard or quality of provision. However, the reality, as Gorz cautions, appears to be otherwise, for auto-production and auto-services, contrary to Toffler's assumption about the prospects for prosumption, are not necessarily synonymous with increases in autonomous activity, or an extension of self-control. To the contrary, the deployment of information technologies, developed within the prevailing social and political relations of production, facilitates centralised programming by promoting circumstances in which

> individuals can be made to train themselves, maintain themselves and 'produce' themselves to fit a social norm which is preprogrammed by the auto-production technology that they use. The desire for autonomy and free time is exploited and turned against its subject. What should be the material basis for our control over our own lives serves instead to imprison us in solitary autoconsumption.
>
> (Gorz 1985, p. 27)

Furthermore, if micro-electronic technologies promise to reduce social costs they also threaten to transform the structure of commodity relations at the foundation of the capitalist mode of production. Unlike the technologies associated with the industrial era the new micro-electronic technologies allow for higher levels of production at lower cost per unit of output – they effectively allow savings in investment, labour and raw materials. However, a corollary of the reduction in labour required within the production process is a possible reduction in wage-earners and, in turn, consumers for the growing volume of commodities and services produced. Because capital investment in new technologies now destroys more jobs than it creates it presents consumer capitalism with a critical paradox: the very solution to the economic crisis being pursued may be eroding the conditions necessary for a continuation of capitalist economic relations.

The micro-electronic revolution has precipitated a reduction in the levels of labour necessary for production, eliminated established crafts and skills, and accelerated the growing disaffection with waged work. Nevertheless in all industrial capitalist societies a similar pattern of response to the micro-electronic revolution has emerged. Although levels of unemployment have increased considerably, full-time employment has continued to constitute the norm, and employment or waged work has retained its central structuring role both in the organisation of everyday life and the formation of human subjectivity. In consequence a division has emerged between 'an elite of permanent, secure, full-time workers . . . [and] a mass of unemployed and precarious casual workers without qualifications or status, performing menial tasks' (Gorz 1985, p. 35). To maintain this state of affairs a number of strong measures and policies are required, including the disciplining, regimentation and segregation of non-workers; institutionalisation of a dualistic stratification of social activity into the 'highly productive and internationally competitive' and 'low-productivity occupations which have no effect on the first sector's costs and do not need precise profit and productivity norms' (Gorz 1985, pp. 36–7); and, in order to make demand effective, the treatment of consumption as on a par with work, a development which signifies a major transformation of the system of production. This leads to the conclusion that the emerging system bears only

> a *formal* resemblance to capitalism . . . What is being preserved *is not the capitalist system but capitalism's system of domination, whose chief instruments were the wage and the market.* For now the goal of production is not and cannot be capital accumulation and valorisation. Its primary objective is control and domination . . . Production system and control system become one and the same. We are much closer to a totalitarian society run by a technocracy with a quasi-military hierarchy than to bourgeois capitalist society.
>
> (Gorz 1985, p. 39)

But such a programmed 'resolution' by no means constitutes an inevitable or necessary response to the crisis affecting industrial capitalist societies. A 'living-dead capitalism' may be avoided, for there is scope for an alternative deployment of micro-electronic technology, one allowing a redistribution of socially necessary labour which could effectively reduce the time spent in employment, thereby alleviating some of the constraints and alienating effects associated with work, excessive levels of consumption, and increasingly centralised forms of social control.

POST-SOCIALIST POSTINDUSTRIAL SOCIETY

The micro-electronic revolution and associated developments in the capitalist mode of production have rendered many of the tenets of scientific socialism inoperative. As the deployment of new technologies has reduced both the *quantity* of labour required for socially necessary production and the *quality* of work experience, so it has become increasingly difficult to sustain the idea that work constitutes a potential source of meaning, fulfilment and identity for the majority of the population. Instead of the promised growth of a class-conscious, work-centred, potentially revolutionary proletariat, Gorz observes the emergence of a non-class of postindustrial neo-proletarians, a new historical subject, composed of the unemployed and underemployed, those engaged in casual, insecure, temporary, and part-time forms of employment, and those disaffected with their work. Increasingly it is the latter who constitute the majority, rather than those in relatively stable, secure, and protected forms of employment, and as a result the conventional socialist political strategy of workers taking control of production and pursuing personal fulfilment through their work becomes highly problematic. Indeed, if the objective for the non-class of neo-proletarians is, as Gorz contends, to free themselves '*from* work by rejecting its nature, content, necessity and modalities' (Gorz 1985, p. 67) the aims and objectives of conventional forms of socialism become virtually obsolete.

The postindustrial revolution not only transforms the nature of production, work and employment but, in addition, is associated with an increase in forms of social and cultural diversity, and political pluralism. Gorz suggests that actually existing socialism, committed to centralised planning, is unable to accommodate social and cultural diversity, or to embrace pluralism, and that in consequence it 'will remain an unattractive proposition', effectively 'condemned . . . to a minority position' (Gorz 1985, p. 80). However, the transformations which have led to a crisis of socialism may simultaneously provide the basis for a political resolution. The revolutionary development of the productive forces under the capitalist mode of production may have rendered a transitional stage of socialism historically obsolete, and made a conception of 'postindustrial socialism' inappropriate, by producing the preconditions necessary for a reconsideration of the question of communism. The level to which the means of production have been developed makes possible a radically different organisation of the economy in Gorz's view, one in which it is possible both to satisfy needs and reduce the amount of socially necessary labour required. But if a postindustrial communism is to become a reality it will be necessary to regulate and stabilise social production, and to promote non-market, non-commodity goals and values. A positive conception of communism as an alternative to capitalism can only emerge if

> it is practically demonstrated not only that it is possible to live better by working differently and consuming less, but that voluntary, collective limitation of the sphere of necessity is the way, the only way, to guarantee an extension of the sphere of autonomy.
>
> (Gorz 1985, p. 124)

It is to the tentative articulation of this controversial possible alternative that Gorz's work is in part directed.

Gorz's conception of a possible alternative to industrial capitalism and existing socialism utilises a distinction, developed in Illich's work, between two distinctively different types of activity, namely autonomous production of use-values and heteronomous production of goods for their exchange value, for the market of anonymous consumers.[6] The sphere of heteronomy encompasses two elements, the production of 'necessities' and the conditions appropriate to ensure the continued 'functioning of society as a material system'. The sphere of autonomy involves self-structured, self-managed, and self-motivated activity and encompasses the self-production of goods and services. Gorz, following Illich, holds the view that the constitution of an alternative to industrial capitalism necessarily requires a subordination of the sphere of heteronomy to that of autonomy.[7] To achieve such an outcome requires radical social and economic change, in particular an abandonment of the goal of economic growth and reorientation of economic activity away from production for profit and towards production for need, and significant policy innovations in the areas of unemployment, income distribution, and 'free-time'. Of these a policy of time is central, for whereas technological innovations deployed in material and non-material production currently precipitate increasing levels of unemployment, they might equally well facilitate a reduction in the time spent in heteronomous labour and allow an increase in free-time, that is time for autonomous activity.

As heteronomous labour is reduced it becomes necessary to revise, if not transform, the relationship between employment or jobs, work and income. In effect it means a way has to be found to ensure 'that citizens can live and work without an employer to "give" and buy their work' (Gorz 1982, p. 143). But if there is to be some form of income or wage for life, as well as a reduction in hours spent in heteronomous work, and a concomitant distribution of responsibility to ensure that all those deemed able actually participate in appropriate socially necessary or useful activities, a regulatory political body or state mechanism is going to be required. Gorz recognises that a continuing element of depersonalising and unfulfilling work will remain a necessary feature of the postindustrial future, for such heteronomous activity constitutes the source of the convivial tools which may be creatively employed and enjoyed in autonomous activity. In turn, the necessity of some form of executive power or authority, a 'minimal' state, to control or regulate relations between the various self-managing local communities engaged in micro-social activity, and to oversee the production and reproduction of material and non-material goods and services that continue to be the object of macro-social activity, is acknowledged. The implication of Gorz's comments is a continuing significant state presence, staffed by professionals performing essential tasks that either cannot be decentralised, or alternatively would be less effectively or less efficiently provided, if decentralised. But, although there is an acceptance of the need for the continuing existence of specialists and professionals (e.g. surgeons, agronomists, chemists, geologists, mechanics, legal experts) there is also an acknowledgement that a means has to be found to 'stop them forming a class or caste' (1985, p. 76). In contrast to Illich's (1978) advocacy of a 'post-professional ethos', Gorz believes that there will always be professionals and, in order to overcome the problem of hierarchy associated with specialisation, proposes a policy which will reduce the time spent in professional practice, and thereby create a need for more people with specialised competences.

An executive–administrative state mechanism is essential, for it represents the medium within which appropriate laws, prohibitions, and objectives concerning the material and non-material necessities of communal life may be constituted and implemented. It effectively designates the circumference and content of the sphere of autonomy and possesses the appropriate authority to ensure that socially necessary macro-social activity is carried out. The problem is how to retain an executive and administrative apparatus, albeit reduced in scale, whilst preventing effects of domination. In response to the problem identified, Gorz argues that the state is capable of simultaneously reducing both the sphere of heteronomy and the range and scope of its own activities (1982, p. 115). In the present context, where the state in both capitalist and socialist societies constitutes the principal source of military, legal, and not infrequently economic power and domination, such a response appears excessively optimistic. But it is a 'transformed' state that is implied:

> The state can only cease to be an apparatus of domination over society . . . if society is already permeated by social struggles that open up areas of autonomy keeping both the dominant class and the power of the state apparatus in check. The establishment of new types of social relations, new ways of producing, associating, working and consuming is the fundamental precondition of any political transformation. The dynamic of social struggles is the lever by which society can act upon itself and establish a range of freedoms, a new state and a new system of law.
>
> (Gorz 1982, p. 116)

In Gorz's discussion of this transformation there is the implication that social struggles may cohere into a movement. However, the basis on which a plurality of groups and individuals comprising the non-class of postindustrial neo-proletarians might constitute a movement is left unexplicated (1982, p. 116). Clearly this prospective 'unity' serves for Gorz as the potential agency for change and, as such, it constitutes a postindustrial functional equivalent to Marx's conception of the industrial proletariat (Keane and Owens 1986, pp. 171–2).

Accepting the necessarily tentative and at times speculative character of Gorz's work there nevertheless remain a number of problematic features and contentious aspects. To begin with there is the implication in Gorz's work that a radical socioeconomic transformation might be achieved within a national context, a position which is at odds with the growing internationalisation of the capitalist mode of production and associated erosion of the sovereignty of the nation-state. As Keane and Owens comment:

> the new international division of labour, changes in the global monetary and trading systems and super-power strategies would

all loom large as obstructive factors in any single employment society's attempt to make a transition to socialism in Gorz's sense.

(Keane and Owen 1986, p. 169)

Furthermore, even if it were possible to discount the obstructiveness of global or international forces, there would remain the difficult question of the conditions under which an effective social movement, oriented towards the kind of radical changes and measures proposed, would be likely to emerge. As I have noted above, although Gorz gives some consideration to the 'dynamic of social struggles' the analysis is brief and questions of the organisational and programmatic coherence of 'the movement' are left unresolved.

We might accept that the world of waged-work is changing along *some* of the lines identified by Gorz. Unemployment has increased in incidence in Western industrial capitalist societies and there has been a growth of temporary, casual, and part-time forms of employment. But what do these changes signify? Proponents of the 'service society' thesis have argued that although there can be no guarantee of a return to full employment the new 'information technologies' do not necessarily lead to higher levels of unemployment. Much depends on how IT is utilised (Gershuny and Miles 1983). It has been suggested over and over again that new markets for innovative goods may be developed, and that, in addition, the time and resources freed by new technology may be used in the 'increased consumption of more traditional types of services' (Gershuny 1987, p. 13). Both of these possibilities constitute potential sources of additional employment. To an extent Gorz anticipates such an objection by commenting that most forms of employment are vulnerable to technological innovation. But this leaves considerable scope for further argument concerning both the feasibility and the desirability of developing new markets for new commodities and services, and the potential effects of such developments on the prospects for employment.

The question of a significant deterioration in the intrinsic value or meaning of waged-work is perhaps less contentious. Indeed it might be argued that the process has been exacerbated by the deployment of new technologies which have 'driven workers from the assembly line . . . [and] turned many areas of highly technical work into relatively simple routine operations' (Morris-Suzuki 1984, p. 18). But it has not diminished the demand for waged-work or employment, or for that matter the desire to consume commodities and services. The scenario for a radical transformation outlined by Gorz requires both a policy of time and a form of income redistribution. If a reduction in hours of work might be appealing, the corollary – a reduction in income and associated capacity to purchase goods and services – is less likely to be so. Gorz argues that 'consumption or the buying of goods and services is ceasing to be the primary aspiration' (1982, pp. 140-1). This is a crucial point, for if Gorz is correct it would signify a major cultural transformation with enormous socioeconomic and political implications, not least of all for the constitution of a radically different postindustrial society. However, the evidence presented refers almost entirely to small surveys of people's opinions, and only in a minority of cases to the experiences of individuals participating in schemes involving a reduction of hours spent in employment, and as such it is, at best, indeterminate and unconvincing.

The beginnings of a cultural transformation of the magnitude required to realise a conception of postindustrial communism cannot be identified in the studies cited by Gorz of wage-workers expressing various degrees of disenchantment with their work. 'Work less, live more' is a very appealing slogan, but its attractiveness is diminished by the corollary 'consume less'! Notwithstanding the perceptiveness of Gorz's critical comments on the increasing deterioration of the general quality of life experienced by the majority, the desire to consume has remained undiminished, if it has not increased in intensity. But perhaps this is to be expected given that, in Western industrial capitalist societies, the reality is one in which

> bourgeois appetites . . . resist curbs on acquisitiveness, either morally or by taxation . . . and an individualist ethos . . . at best defends the idea of personal liberty, and at worst evades the necessary social responsibilities and social sacrifices which a communal society demands.
>
> (Bell 1976, pp. 248–9)

The fact that a majority of the population in Western industrial capitalist societies seems to be imbued with an increasing desire to consume, that their very identities may be synonymous with their status as consumer subjects, raises serious questions about the prospects and possibilities for a radical transformation of the social system in the direction advocated by Gorz.

ECOLOGICAL POSTINDUSTRIALISM

Although there is generally some form of acknowledgement in postindustrial scenarios of the extent to which the future fates of industrial and non-industrial societies, First, Second and Third World nations, and Northern and Southern Hemispheres are inextricably connected, the focus of analysis and discussion tends to fall predominantly on the forms of life peculiar to Northern Hemisphere, First World, Western industrial capitalist societies. Given that it is these societies that are in the vanguard of the transformations associated with the postindustrial revolution such a focus is understandable. However, since part of the argument is that the changes and effects involved extend beyond the boundaries of the 'developed' nations, albeit unevenly, to the globe as a whole, the relative neglect of the impact upon, and consequences for, Third World, Southern Hemisphere, non-industrial societies and communities is problematic.

While both Toffler and Gorz make reference to the predicament in which non-industrial societies find themselves, their analyses are in the final instance inconsistent and unconvincing. The growing crisis of industrial civilisation leads Toffler to argue that industrialisation is no longer an appropriate model of development for non-industrial societies. But equally, an alternative 'first wave strategy', involving labour intensive, low capital and low energy using forms of production, employing 'appropriate', 'intermediate', or 'soft' technologies, is regarded as unacceptable because it 'condemns hundreds of millions of desperate, hungry, toiling peasants to perpetual degradation' (1983, p. 346). Toffler does not attempt to offer a coherent alternative development strategy; rather he argues for the possibility of a fusion of elements associated with the first and third waves, for indigenous strategies 'matched to actual local needs'. However, the assumption that elements of the first and third waves might prove compatible is open to question. The idea of some kind of balance being achieved between, on the one hand, scientific knowledge and associated forms of technology and, on the other, a Gandhian conception of village republics – 'Gandhi with satellites' – is vulnerable on a number of counts. These include the incidence of exploitation and poverty amongst home-workers; the existence of foreign control and domination of advanced technology; the effects of the international debt crisis; and the presence of highly centralised authoritarian military and political regimes (Frankel 1987, pp. 136–7).

Similarly, although Gorz makes reference to the connection between the levels of affluence and excessive consumption characteristic of the industrialised capitalist countries and the poverty and famine of the non-industrialised countries of the Southern Hemisphere, it is hard to understand how the transformation proposed for the former will effect any significant improvement in the latter. As Frankel has commented, 'it is difficult to accept that Gorz's concern with ecological goals and the abolition of imperialism in the Third World goes any deeper than a generalised moral critique of Western affluence and wasteful consumption' (Frankel 1987, p. 138). Gorz's scenario seems, at best, to propose a self-sufficient labour intensive, low-tech, subsistence future for the Third World, whilst the First World and to a lesser extent the Second World enjoy the benefits of a reduced level of socially necessary labour, a high level of material well-being, and significant increases in personal autonomy. However, if Gorz's work shares aspects of Toffler's overriding ethnocentric Western bias, or preoccupation with the present reality and future prospects of Northern Hemisphere industrial capitalist societies, it also displays traces of a radically different position. In so far as Gorz is concerned with the growing problem of the global impact of ecologically wasteful and destructive forms of production associated with industrial capitalism, his work draws upon a more austere or ascetic variant of 'postindustrial' analysis, exemplified by the works of Illich, Bahro, and Roszak. As will become clear below, 'ecological postindustrialism' does not necessarily involve or require a policy of 'reversionism' in which an idealised past is reconstituted as the model for the future. *Contra* Toffler the 'Greens, the environmental movement, and other groups critical of industrial mass society' are not peddling despair or mindlessly criticising all technology, rather they are critically addressing the central problem, namely 'the oppression, misery, . . . ecological degradation and inequities of the industrial world . . . from the point of view of the future' (1984, pp. 90–1).[8] In the analyses developed by Illich, Bahro and Roszak this takes the form of a critique of the industrial mode of production and associated technocratic or instrumental forms of Western rationality intrinsic to the project of modernity. It constitutes a critique of prevailing processes of economic development and influence, and technological innovation, as well as the associated assumption that 'the rest of the world [constitutes] . . . an effectively vacant lot from which . . . [to] extract raw materials' (Williams 1985, p. 216). As such, it provides a basis from which to begin to reflect on the prospects for a genuinely new form of social and economic life.

A continuation of the present pattern of development, in which the earth and its various life forms are regarded as available for appropriation and transformation in increasing circuits of production and consumption, threatens to precipitate the collapse of the biosphere and with it our whole system (Bahro); to create a wasteland in which human beings are subjected to a programmed society (Roszak); and to bequeath to the next generation the 'gruesome apocalypse predicted by many ecologists' (Illich). As evidence of an escalating global crisis has accumulated so the limits and limitations of the industrial (capitalist) mode of production and associated instrumental forms of rationality, promising growth, efficiency, and progress through an extension of mechanisms of domination and control, have become increasingly apparent. In consequence Bahro, Roszak, and Illich argue that it is now necessary to consider possible alternatives to the industrial capitalist mode of production. Although their respective alternative conceptions differ considerably, both in form and content, they share an antipathy to the perpetual pursuit of economic growth, or the goal of ever increasing levels of material prosperity, synonymous with the industrial capitalist mode of production, and a conception of an emerging ecological catastrophe.

Bahro, emulating elements of the analysis of Western reason developed by Adorno and Horkheimer, argues that 'European culture of the past two or three thousand years . . . has been exterminist in its most inner dispositions, modelling itself on individual competition and the Olympia principle of "more, higher, faster, better". These dispositions have in the recent period led to capitalism' (1984, p. 213). Evidence of a disposition towards exterminism is present in the arms race and associated threat of nuclear war; the existence of mass starvation in the Third World; the destruction of nature; and a preoccupation with power and control characteristic of *homo occidentalis* in general, and *homo occidentalis oeconomicus* in particular (Bahro 1984, pp. 214–5; Galtung 1984, pp. 17–18). But above all, for Bahro, exterminism is synonymous with industrialism, hence the conclusion that it will become necessary 'to undertake a complete transformation of our civilisation, right down to its material foundations' (1984, p. 172).

The transformations required to change the existing system constitute a 'cultural revolution' and involve the generation of new patterns of consumption 'geared to the *qualitative* development of the individual', a revision of needs, interests and exigencies independently of the forms established in any particular historical situation, and a stabilisation of economic activity at a significantly lower level than that currently common in the industrial capitalist system. Because industrialism and militarism are deemed to be inextricably connected, militarism being regarded as a 'natural consequence of the dependence on raw materials of our over-worked production system' (Bahro 1984, p. 138), Bahro outlines an eco-pacifist strategy of industrial disarmament. The strategy involves an end to competitive, aggressive industrialism and the constantly increasing accumulation of goods and services, and a subordination of technology to the goals and values of new stable self-sufficient communal forms of socioeconomic life (Bahro 1986). But the 'commune perspective' outlined by Bahro leaves open a series of questions concerning the organisation and coordination of communes, the extent of their self-sufficiency, the kinds of hierarchical and centralised structures that might prove necessary for social planning and be compatible with 'basic communes', and the feasibility of 'industrial disarmament' (Frankel 1987). However, given that the principal concern for Bahro is to develop a critique of prevailing industrial capitalist forms of production and consumption responsible for the growing global ecological crisis, the absence of detailed consideration of the social, economic and political mechanisms appropriate for a potential ecologically friendly postindustrial alternative form of life is understandable, if nevertheless problematic.[9]

A comparable analysis of the impact of industrial capitalism on the environment is present in the work of Roszak (1972). But where Bahro tends to place emphasis upon the problems of industrialism Roszak focuses more upon scientific rationality and technology as the 'prime expression of the West's cultural uniqueness, the secret of our extraordinary dynamism, the keystone of technocratic politics, the curse and the gift we bring to history' (Roszak 1972, p. xxiv). The difference is ultimately one of emphasis for, just as Bahro makes reference to the exterminist disposition of European culture and, by implication, Western rationality, so Roszak critically analyses the impact of industrial capitalism on the environment. Roszak argues that within industrial capitalist society the measure of progress has increasingly become the degree of artificiality of the environment, a condition achieved through an elimination or predictive anticipation and control of natural phenomena and forces. If science and technology have constituted the means of control, the resources in power–knowledge relations through which an artificial environment has been fabricated, the design, the technocratic agenda, has to a substantial extent been set by the 'interests of dominant commissars or capitalists or bureaucrats'.

The industrial capitalist system is not a pure technocratic system, but in Roszak's view contemporary politics is technocratic in so far as there continues to be an assumption that industrial expansion and development is progressive, and further that increases in both the reliability and quantity of knowledge available will enhance mastery over the environment, and thereby improve the effectiveness and efficiency of the '*machine à gouverner*'. Roszak argues that citizens have been reduced to a condition of helpless awe and dependence before the 'arsenal of wonders' provided by science and technology, and that increasingly the 'world is being bound together by the affluent societies in ingenious networks of investment, military alliance, and commerce which, in themselves, can only end by propagating an oppressive urban–industrial uniformity over the earth' (Roszak 1972, p. 22). Evidence of a general inability to imagine alternatives to the prevailing artificiality of industrial capitalism, deference to scientific–technical–professional expertise, and the associated capacity of modern technology to 'grow strong by virtue of chronic failure', to claim 'progress' in resolving earlier technologically induced dislocations, leads Roszak to identify an emerging urban–industrial cataclysm and to argue for the necessity of a new vision. The implication is that the existing pattern of development will lead to

'an air-conditioned nightmare' of endemic malfunction and slapdash improvisation. Glowing advertisements of undiminished progress will continue to rain down on us from official quarters; there will always be well-researched predictions of light at the end of every tunnel. There will be dazzling forecasts of limitless affluence; there will even be much *real* affluence. But nothing will ever quite work the way the salesman promised; the abundance will be mired in organisational confusion and bureaucratic malaise, constant environmental emergency . . . breakdowns in communication, overburdened social services . . . The scene will be indefinably sad and shoddy despite the veneer of orthodox optimism . . . Everything will take on that vile tackiness which only plastic can assume, the look of things decaying that were never supposed to grow old . . .

When public education collapses under the weight of its own coercions and futility, the systems teams will step forward to propose that schools invest in electronicised-individualised-computerised-audio-visual-multi-instructional consoles. When industrial pollutants finally make the air unbreathable, we will be advised to cover the cities over with plastic domes and air-condition them. Technological optimism is the snake oil of urban industrialism.

(Roszak 1972, pp. 64–5)

Roszak argues that the damaging impact of industrial capitalism on both the environment and social life stems from the predominance of a depersonalised, instrumental, 'progressive' conception of science and technology, the key elements of which are present in Francis Bacon's (1855) articulation of a new philosophy. It is in Bacon's work that the paradigm of scientific work, of science providing 'knowledge, power, dominion without limit', is to be found, and it is the development of this dehumanising 'single vision' as the reality principle of industrial capitalism and 'legitimising mystique of the technocracy' that Roszak attempts to challenge and counter. Science, once considered synonymous with Reason and all things good, now appears not to be working so well. Detached, impersonal, 'objective' scientific knowledge has proven, in its application, to be ecologically disastrous. In short the accumulating environmental crisis is the inescapable price of 'Baconian power–knowledge'. Science and technology have no necessary relationship to social health and freedom; on the contrary 'an infatuation with the stern exactitudes of mathematics and physics, a distaste for the unruliness of human ways, a mania for system, centralisation [and] control' are leading us towards a programmed society (Roszak 1972, p. 246). If the realisation that the scientific world-view does not work becomes widespread it will simultaneously undermine the associated grand narrative of endless progress at the centre of Western culture, as well as the citadel of professional expertise which has disqualified the understanding and knowledge of 'ordinary' people.[10] Roszak comments that the 'free-floating worldview of the Enlightenment', the idea that science and technology can guarantee 'good liberal values', is now disintegrating all around us, and that the associated emergence of alternative forms of life raises the prospect of a 'transition to a truly postindustrial society'.

Roszak proposes that a potential repeal of urban industrialism should not be considered a 'grim sacrifice' but rather a positive move necessary to terminate the infatuation with power, growth, efficiency and progress which has consigned us to the wasteland of an increasingly artificial environment. The objective is defined as moving 'freely and in delight toward the true postindustrialism', by which Roszak does not mean an anti-technological future, one entirely bereft of urban or industrial production forms, but one in which selective and appropriate forms of technology are subordinated to a preferred alternative pattern of life. The alternative involves a selective reduction of industrialism, a reconsideration of the necessity of certain forms of work, and the cultivation of a zero growth, 'economics of permanence' as a potential source of fulfilment. As Roszak acknowledges, good intentions will be ineffective and politically futile, if they are expressed in terms of puritanical forms of self-denial. To have any chance of success it is important to emphasise that an alternative, ecologically sound, healthy and humane form of life to industrial capitalism can also be fulfilling. Signs of an emerging postindustrial alternative are considered to be evident in a 'thousand fragile experiments throughout America and Western Europe', but it is argued that it is not possible to provide a blueprint of how exactly 'this bizarre postindustrial alternative . . . would hang together and function' (Roszak 1972, pp. 422: 432). Two important reasons are offered for refraining from a detailed discussion of a possible post-industrial alternative. First, to generate motivation for change it is necessary to counter the technocratic constitution of bureaucratic programmes for alternative futures, and to challenge people to articulate their own visions and set their own priorities. Second, if the aim is to generate an active participatory democratic system, the provision of a detailed programme, or set of abstract social prescriptions, is going to be counter-productive. It would constitute a contribution to the reproduction of professional–client, expert–layman relationships, and thereby extend rather than counter the technocratic game.[11] In consequence Roszak offers merely a list of the problems to be thought through, namely the appropriate mix of heavy industry, intermediate technology and handicraft; the balance of decentralised and centralised forms of organisation and administration; the need for new economic, legal, welfare, and educational institutions and services; and matters concerning personal and community life (Roszak 1972, p. 432). The blunt response to those who bemoan the absence of detail is that:

those who demand the complete blueprints of a postindustrial alternative are only looking for as many academic bones of contention as possible – and finally for an excuse to turn off and rest content with the conventional wisdom. They are not ready to change their lives and the most studied Utopian prospectus will not bring them around. They will always find loopholes.

(Roszak 1972, p. 434)

A complimentary address of the crisis confronting industrial capitalism and the prospects for an alternative form of life is provided in the work of Illich. Whilst Illich shares Roszak's critical concern about experts, professionals, and technocrats, the discussion provided of a possible alternative postindustrial form of life is more detailed but still well short of a blueprint for change.

TOWARDS A 'CONVIVIAL' POSTINDUSTRIAL SOCIETY

Illich shares with Gorz, Bahro, and Roszak the view that modern industrial societies have created forms of life which are unjust, poverty producing, and disabling in a variety of fundamental respects. However, whereas Gorz considers the required cultural transformation is, in some respects, under way, but ultimately leaves the question of the costs arising from radical forms of change unaddressed, and Roszak believes the signs of a potentially more fulfilling alternative form of life are already gradually emerging, Illich outlines a more austere view that seems, in some respects at least, to be closer to Bahro's position. Illich argues that a trade-off between heteronomous management and autonomous action requires a 'Copernican revolution in our perception of values' (1978, p. 36), one which will necessitate sacrifices and the development of a life-style of 'modern subsistence'. The changes required, for example a reduction in dependence on the market, the use of 'convivial' tools to create use-values, and the promotion and protection of equity and personal liberties, are regarded as difficult to achieve in so far as:

The richer we get in a consumer society, the more acutely we become aware of how many grades of value – of both leisure and labour – we have climbed. The higher we are on the pyramid, the less likely we are to give up time to simple idleness and to apparently non-productive pursuits.

(Illich 1985, p. 80)

Such a diagnosis leads to the conclusion that, only when the problems confronting industrial society become critical, only when there is a movement from breakdown to chaos will 'enlightened self-interest' persuade people that business as usual cannot continue, or that the 'organisation of the entire economy toward the "better" life has become the major enemy of the *good* life' (Illich 1985, p. 102).

The industrial mode of production is conceived to have reached a point where its negative effects or consequences far outweigh its benefits. Increasing scientific rationalisation, specialisation, and professionalisation places individuals in a situation of dependency upon institutionally produced commodities and services. Individuals, as increasingly passive appendages to manipulative 'tools', which prevent the self-production of use-values, have of necessity become consumers of exchange values, of industrially produced commodities and services. Industrial 'tools' (viz. hardware; machines; commodity producing institutions; and systems producing intangible commodities such as health, education, knowledge, decisions, etc.) have produced a progressive homogenisation of persons and relationships, and an erosion of individual autonomy and creativity. Such 'tools' may offer 'growth', escalating levels of production, development, material 'affluence', and 'progress', but professionally engineered delivery models, judgments, and evaluations have undermined independence and belief in self-competence, and thereby have eroded the conditions necessary for autonomy. As the other theorists considered above affirm, the problematic developments which arise with the industrial mode of production are not confined to the capitalist West, but extend to the formerly socialist societies of Eastern Europe, societies which have been equally imbued with the virtues of industrially organised production and the pursuit of economic growth. If an autonomy-enhancing decentralised form of society is to emerge, existing institutions and the industrial tools with which they are associated need to be fundamentally transformed, if not displaced by 'convivial tools . . . which give each person who uses them the greatest opportunity to enrich the environment with the fruits of his or her own vision' (1985, p. 21). But what are the prospects of such a radical transformation?

The existing industrial mode of production is 'dynamically unstable' in that it is constantly engaged in the pursuit of economic growth and its corollary, the constitution of new forms of human 'need'. But even if the benefits of the existing system are questionable, inequitably distributed and at times degrading and disabling, Illich suggests that it is extremely difficult for people to envisage the possibility of a viable, appealing, alternative postindustrial or convivial society, in which control and mastery might be exercised over tools, thereby facilitating autonomy, choice, and diversity in the expression of creative energies. It is not enough

> to show that a convivial life style is possible, or even to demonstrate that it is more attractive than life in a society ruled by industrial productivity. We cannot rest with the claim that this inversion would bring society closer to meeting the goals now stated as those of our major institutions. It is not even enough to show that a just or socially equal order can become a reality only through a convivial reconstruction of tools and the consequent redefinition of ownership and power. We need a way to recognise that the inversion of present political purpose is necessary for the survival of all people.
>
> (Illich 1985, pp. 43–4)

What needs to be demonstrated is that the industrial mode of production is threatening our very survival, and this Illich attempts to do through a discussion of the various manifestations of imbalance which have become apparent.

Illich identifies five examples of the way in which growth orientated industrial tools appear to disturb the balance of life. These concern damage inflicted on the environment through faulty technology; the way in which forms of radical monopoly displace autonomous, self or personal provision of use-values and satisfactions, by standardised industrial forms of production; a process of overprogramming which transforms the potentially autonomous act of 'learning' into the controlled business of 'education', through which 'people are constantly taught, socialised, normalised, tested, and reformed' (Illich 1985, p. 76); a growing polarisation of power and inequality, and an associated 'modernisation of poverty'; and finally a pervasive tendency towards engineered obsolescence, which constantly devalues past and prevailing forms. To combat the forms of imbalance which arise from the above Illich argues that it is necessary to 'develop constitutive boundaries within which tools must be kept . . . Without constitutive limits translated into constitutional provisions survival in dignity and freedom is squelched' (Illich 1985, p. 77).

The achievement of a postindustrial mixed mode of production which makes possible an enhancement of autonomy and creativity does not require an abandonment of all forms of industrial production, nor a halt to innovation, change, and scientific exploration. 'Convivial reconstruction' does not require 'industrial disarmament', but the constitution of limits to the rate of change of tools, and a withdrawal from the addiction to growth. The major question which remains to be considered is how the various transformations central to the possibility of a convivial postindustrial society are to be realised. 'Counterfoil research' may indeed succeed in outlining both the negative consequences of existing industrial mega-tools, and the ways in which science and technology might be redirected away from the provision of innovations geared to industrial development and the displacement of human creativity and autonomy, and towards the creation of decentralised forms of 'high' technology. However, whether these and other fundamental changes take place depends in the final instance on a restructuring of political procedures and processes, in effect an inversion of existing political structures and purposes and the generation of a 'post-professional ethos'. An escape from the vicarious pleasures, illusions, and frustrations associated with modern industrial capitalist forms of life requires an end to the domination of heteronomous forms of production, a reversal of the process of increasing market dependency, and opposition to professionally induced forms of dependence, disability, and disqualification. It is also simultaneously necessary to foster the development of an ethic of 'austerity', the implication of which is not that we should don Bahro's hairshirt, but rather that we might share Roszak's joyful vision of the possibilities before us of 'a new ecology, a new democracy, and a new vitality of spirit' (1972, p. 444). The sense of austerity invoked by Illich does not imply grim self-denial and the exclusion of all enjoyments, 'only those which are distracting from or destructive of personal relatedness' (1985, p. xiii).

POST-PROFESSIONAL, POSTINDUSTRIAL AND POSTMODERN?

Before a convivial postindustrial society can be established it is necessary to overcome a number of obstacles and illusions associated with forms of 'radical monopoly' and 'disabling professionalism'. In particular there is the key issue of the cult of the expert or authority associated with the pervasive institutionalisation of forms of scientific knowledge, and the corollary, the marginalisation, delegitimation, and disqualification of other forms of knowledge. Where Gorz remarks that he has 'nothing against professionals' and suggests that 'they will always be there', Illich emphasises the disabling effects of professional dominance and develops an analysis which bears comparison with the critical position taken by both Roszak (1972) and Foucault (1981) on the question of experts and professionals.

Illich argues that people have become too accustomed to relying on 'experts' and professionals for their knowledge. In effect individuals have become knowledge-consumers, dependent upon the provision of 'objective' knowledge commodities by institutions accorded authority and responsibility for the discovery and dissemination of more and 'better' forms of knowledge and information. As a result the confidence of people in their own ability to make judgments, take decisions, and find out about events and processes occurring in the world, has been eroded, if not entirely undermined. The associated 'paralysis of the moral and political imagination' leads Illich to argue that there is a need for diagnosis and decision making to be retrieved from its professional locus and returned to the political community, so that people may participate in the making and taking of decisions which affect them. This does not necessitate a retreat from formal procedures and processes, to the contrary. Notwithstanding the current ends towards which the existing structures of law and politics are directed, formal and legal procedures provide an essential mechanism for 'hampering, stopping, and inverting our major institutions'. Indeed Illich suggests that 'any revolution which neglects the use of formal and legal procedures will fail' (1985, p. 99).

As things stand people have become increasingly immobilised through a series of socioeconomic and cultural structures and institutions within which they are constituted as clients or consumers of professionally organised and produced services and commodities. Use-values are denigrated, and autonomous, self-produced services and values rendered obsolescent or deficient by the endless circuit of innovation, production, marketing, and consumption. In part this condition is rationalised as a sign of technological progress, but in practice the emergence of ever more complex and specialised tools 'in the service of market orientated institutions' undermines creative activity and effectively 'licences more professional domination' (Illich 1978, pp. 74–5). The form in which particular technologies have been developed owes nothing to any 'imperative'; rather it is a matter of development being directed towards the fulfilment of particular socioeconomic, political and cultural ends, by professionals concerned to extend forms of radical monopoly. Given the military and industrial interests which have influenced the funding of scientific research and technological developments, it is not surprising that Illich should find that 'needs for autonomous action are precluded, while those for the acquisition of commodities are multiplied' (Illich 1978, p. 76).

Furthermore, even if the more 'enlightened' multinational corporations, governments, and international organisations have belatedly begun to recognise the need for limits to the process through which the provision of commodities and services is continually extended to meet increasing, socially engineered needs and desires, it is evident that problems remain. Illich argues that the emergence of a new category of professionals, articulating the need for limits to growth and an end to environmental pollution, itself constitutes a problem, in so far as the essential relationship of expert to client or consumer remains unchanged. All that is really at stake in such circumstances is the prospect of a trimming of levels of consumption, as 'entire populations socialised to need on command are assumed ready to be told what they do not need' (Illich 1978, p. 78). Professionally defined and managed 'austerity' is no more convivial than professionally induced accelerating levels of excessive consumption. Well intended as such forms of modern 'enlightened' professional intervention might be, the risk is that the balance of liberties and rights in society is disturbed. As Illich cautions:

> liberties protect use-values as rights protect the access to commodities. And just as commodities can extinguish the possibility of producing use-values and turn into impoverishing wealth, so the professional definition of rights can extinguish liberties and establish a tyranny that smothers people underneath their rights.
>
> (Illich 1978, p. 79)

Granting professionals the licence to define for us what we need and do not need can lead to a confusion of liberties and rights, if not an erosion of the former through professional specification of the latter. In brief the public promotion of rights not only fails to protect or guarantee liberty, it may actually serve to reduce freedom and autonomy, and thereby render more difficult the cultivation of a convivial postindustrial society.

107

The transformations identified and proposed by the postindustrial theorists discussed above may suggest the presence of a strong antipathy towards the 'project of modernity', if not a revolt against it (Frankel 1987, p. 177). Certainly the idea of a perpetual process of progressive, orderly growth or development, achieved through scientific and technological mastery or control over events, is questioned and challenged. However, the analyses presented ultimately reveal substantially different conceptions of potential alternative postindustrial forms of life. Whilst Bahro advocates 'industrial disarmament' and 'basic communes' and comes close to an anti-modern 'reversionist' position (Toffler 1984, pp. 89–90), Toffler proposes a more 'comprehensive' notion of progress, new forms of science and technology, and generally implies a regeneration of the 'project of modernity'. And although Gorz alludes to the need for a different rationality, and endorses the idea of more convivial tools, ultimately he appears also to subscribe to an essentially orderly totality, and to that extent his work might be said to constitute an endorsement of the modern project. In contrast Illich, and perhaps to an even greater extent Roszak, directly challenge the singular vision of Western rationality, and critically question prevailing modern forms of scientific knowledge and technology, associated modern institutions and their effects, and to that extent suggest the possibility, and desirability, of a different, possibly more radical alternative.

Although the respective conceptions advanced of an alternative postindustrial form of life vary significantly, the theorists considered are unanimous in regarding the present as a time of transition. By demonstrating that industrial capitalism has precipitated increasing levels of inequality and exploitation, an accelerating deterioration in the quality of life, and a growing ecological crisis, the desirability of an alternative form of life is established. But in so far as prevailing forms of social, economic, and political life cannot, in any event, be sustained, the cultivation of an appropriate and acceptable alternative to the modern obsession with material wealth, economic growth, control technologies, and relentless 'progress', embodied in the idea of Western industrial civilisation as the model of development, becomes a necessity.

4

ART, WORK AND ANALYSIS IN AN AGE OF ELECTRONIC SIMULATION

Reflections on a series of transformations in, on the one hand, the structure, organisation and experience of work and production and, on the other, art and culture, have been at the centre of debates which have developed around the respective ideas of postindustrial society and postmodern forms of life. Amongst other things what appears to be at issue in the various analyses is the possibility that the world of work has changed in significant ways, that the activities and practices, the skills and techniques, the associated structures and forms of organisation, and in turn the experience, meaning, and place of work in the lives of people, have all been radically transformed. Likewise it has been argued that in relation to art, communications, and culture no less significant transformations have occurred.

The introduction of micro-electronic 'information technologies' (IT) into the workplace, for example computer numerical control systems (CNC), computer-aided design and manufacturing systems (CAD/CAM), robotics and various advanced forms of automation, has undoubtedly transformed the structure, organisation, experience, and meaning of work, its availability but not yet its necessity. And change remains a continuing feature of the workplace. Indeed the goal of innovation in computer-integrated manufacturing systems (e.g. ICAM) seems to be nothing less than the abolition of work and workers, save for a managerial stratum which would be free to exercise uncontested control over the sphere of production. The motivation behind the continuing development and deployment of labour-saving automated and computer controlled production technologies when there is no shortage of labour remains a matter of concern. Certainly it is questionable whether the principal impulse behind such developments is economic rather than, for example, the 'combined and compounded compulsions, interests, beliefs, and

109

aspirations of the military, management, and technical enthusiasts' (Noble 1984, p. 339). To a considerable degree we seem to be in the presence of a self-generating fixation, automation or IT for automation's sake. But above and beyond any infatuation with technology there lies the interest shared within military and industrial organisations in reducing uncertainty and enhancing control. The accelerated introduction, in the absence of parallel socioeconomic and cultural changes, of additional labour-displacing forms of production affecting both goods and services may in practice be socially and politically undesirable, even if technologically and economically practicable, but this possibility does not seem to have been accorded much significance in the quest for enhanced levels of certainty and control.

While it is important to examine, criticize and attempt to 'dismantle the dominant social imaginary, the technocratic ideology' (Robins and Webster 1989, p. 270), it is at least equally necessary to consider the various ways in which the deployment of particular forms of technological innovation may have transformed social, economic, political, personal, and intellectual life. As technology is not independent of its complex context of formation and deployment, so social, cultural, economic, and political practices and institutions, as well as forms of personal life, do not remain unaffected by technological innovations.

Changes in the relationship between science, technology, and production have been identified as an increasingly significant feature of transitions in the (post)industrial capitalist mode of production. The impact of the introduction of machinery on the labour process and the associated subordination of workers to the status of living accessories to machines is a prominent theme in Marx's analysis of the development of the capitalist mode of production. Marx anticipated the development of further levels of mechanisation in the labour process leading ultimately to a metamorphosis of the means of labour in an 'automatic system of machinery . . . set in motion by an automaton, a moving power that moves itself; this automaton consisting of numerous mechanical and intellectual organs' (1973a, p. 692). With such a development the creation of wealth depends less and less on the quantity of labour, or labour time, employed in production and more on 'the general state of science and on the progress of technology, or the application of this science to production' (Marx 1973a, p. 705). Technological and organisational innovation, based upon scientific research and development, is crucial to the displacement or temporary resolution of the crisis tendencies to which capitalism is perpetually prone (Harvey 1989). The introduction of micro-electronic 'information technologies' in systems of production undoubtedly constitutes a key feature of the latest phase in the development of capitalism (Gorz 1982; Noble 1984; Webster and Robins 1986; Harvey 1989). But if such technologies have been introduced in part to resolve the accumulation problems of contemporary capitalism it is evident that their effects extend beyond the intended realm and impinge directly on social, cultural, and political life, on forms of human sensibility, and often in unintended and unanticipated ways on economic institutions and practices themselves. It is to a consideration of these concerns as they are broached in the respective works of Benjamin, McLuhan, and Baudrillard that this chapter is directed.

FROM MECHANICAL REPRODUCTION TO ELECTRONIC SIMULATION

With the systematic application of scientific knowledge and technological innovation to production the features noted by Marx have become more pronounced. Invention has not simply 'become a business', it is now virtually synonymous with business. Furthermore, the process by which the 'living worker's activity becomes the activity of the machine' (Marx 1973a, p. 704) now affects a growing number of workers. With developments in information and communications technology even the residual or accessory position to which living labour has been relegated within the production process ('as watchman and regulator') is threatened, and the prospect of a new generation of computer technologies promises to do much the same for the professionals, service workers, and programmers who have been in the vanguard of the so-called 'information revolution'. But the effects of technological innovation extend well beyond the immediate sphere of production and the world of work, as Benjamin (1973) acknowledges in an essay on the impact of changes in the methods and techniques of production and reproduction of works of art upon aesthetic and cultural forms, human sense perception, and judgment.

Benjamin is concerned with the effect(s) of reproduction on works of art and their reception. The possibility of imitation and replication of works of art has always been present, but the development of mechanical forms of reproduction, for example the Gutenberg

111

technology of printing which allows writing to be mechanically repro-duced (McLuhan 1967), lithography, photography and film, represent 'something new' (Benjamin 1973, pp. 220–1). If the technology of printing represents a significant reference point in the development of forms of reproduction of works of art, it is in Benjamin's view the development of photography which first transformed the relationship between human senses and artistic endeavour by freeing 'the hand of the most important artistic functions which henceforth devolved only upon the eye looking into a lens' (Benjamin 1973, p. 221). Associated with the displacement of hand by eye is not only an acceleration of the process of pictorial production but a foreshadowing of an even more significant event, namely the development of the art of the sound film. By the turn of the twentieth century the technical standards achieved allowed repro-duction of 'all transmitted works of art' and thereby transformed both the impact of art works upon the public and, in addition, art itself in its traditional forms. In particular what changed with the development of technical means of (re)production was the unique existence or presence in time and space of an art work, what Benjamin refers to as its 'authenticity'. Subsequent innovations in technologies of reproduction have contributed to the 'development of cultural production and marketing on a global scale' (Harvey 1989, p. 348), and thereby to a transformation of experiences of space and time.

Contrasting manual with process forms of production Benjamin argues that whereas in the former the authority of the original is largely preserved and reproductions are consequently regarded as forgeries or as counterfeit, in the latter the original loses its authority. Indeed it might be argued that the very notion of an original begins to become problematic as techniques of (re)production develop. With the advent of process forms of reproduction, techniques of enlargement and slow motion begin to reveal aspects and images of the original which escape unaided or 'natural' vision. In addition such processes of reproduction transform the contexts of appreciation, reception and 'use' of the original through the provision of 'copies' which can enter spaces and situations beyond the reach of the original (i.e. a reproduction of an orchestral concert, a football match, or other 'live' event in the home). Benjamin argues that such developments have interfered with the 'authenticity' of the object and that 'in the age of mechanical reproduction . . . the aura of the work of art' withers (Benjamin 1973, p. 223).

Through the substitution of a plurality of copies for a 'unique existence' and the associated reactivation of the reproduced object, in situations and contexts chosen by viewers, listeners, or consumers, the technique of reproduction detaches the reproduced object from its traditional domain. Such processes are deemed to be 'intimately connected with . . . contemporary mass movements'. To be precise, the decay of the authenticity and authority of the object is related to the desire of 'the masses' in contemporary social life both to 'bring things "closer" spatially and humanly' and to 'overcome the uniqueness of every reality by accepting its reproduction' (Benjamin 1973, p. 225). There is here the implication of a movement from 'uniqueness and permanence' to 'transitoriness and reproducibility' which Benjamin conceives to be part of a process of unlimited scope, namely the 'adjustment of reality to the masses and the masses to reality' (Benjamin 1973, p. 225). For Benjamin the new forces of artistic production and reproduction hold out the prospect, if not the necessity, of the creation of new social relations between artists and audiences, writers and readers, producers and consumers of texts. Technical means of reproduction raise the prospect of art ceasing to be the privilege of a few. The new media of film, photography, radio, and recorded music are considered to lend themselves to a radically different, 'popular' and 'progressive' development, and simultaneously to offer the means through which the more traditional modes of artistic production might themselves be transformed. The development of the new forms identified by Benjamin, and in particular the impact of a later form of televisual reproduction, is at the heart of McLuhan's analysis of the 'modern' media and their effects, and Baudrillard's later speculations concerning electronic simulation and the ecstasy of 'postmodern' communication. Although Benjamin addresses the question of the potential effect(s) of changes in media technologies on forms of artistic practice or production and appreciation, reception, and use, he does little more than note the impact such transformations might have on sense ratios and perception. But references to the way in which innovative technologies of artistic and cultural reproduction create a 'deepening of apperception', increase mass participation, and transform modes of participation foreshadow concerns which are developed in more detail in McLuhan's and Baudrillard's respective analyses of the media in an age of electronic simulation.

The question of the impact of media technologies on sense ratios, human experience, and social life is at the centre of McLuhan's analysis of the present as a time of transition from an earlier 'mechanical age' to a 'new electronic and organic age'. McLuhan

113

identifies the 'Gutenberg configuration', by which he means the impact of the technology of printing on forms of experience, outlook, and expression, as a principal factor in social and sensory change. With the development of a 'typographic and mechanical era' it is argued that a shift occurred from an auditory to a visual emphasis in habits of perception in Western culture, and that a 'high degree of visual shaping of spatio-temporal relations' began to occur. The introduction of new technology is then associated with the establishment of new sense ratios, in so far as there is an extension of some form(s) of human sensory capacity or function and a concomitant suppression of others. As McLuhan cryptically comments, civilisation having given 'the barbarian or tribal man an eye for an ear . . . is now at odds with the electronic world' (1967, p. 26). The implication is that just as the 'typographical and mechanical age' precipitated a displacement of oral culture, so the development of an electronic age in its turn challenges the literary and visual bias installed at the centre of Western culture. Because of our literary and visual bias we are, in other words, ill-prepared and in consequence inept in the way we handle the new electronic technology. In short there is a need to understand that the new electronic technologies, new media of communication, new patterns of information and associated novelties of automation not only transform the spheres of work and production, and social or community life, but in addition have far reaching consequences for perception and action.

In a manner which parallels some of the key elements of Benjamin's discussion of features of an 'age of mechanical reproduction' McLuhan sets out to reveal the ways in which prominent technological innovations have been associated with significant forms of social and personal transformation. Although the deployment of new technologies is conceived to be a 'principal factor in social change' the thesis outlined is not explicitly deterministic. Indeed the stated aim of the work is to contribute to an understanding of the effects of media technologies on human sensibilities and social life, and thereby to help bring about a 'genuine increase of human autonomy'. As McLuhan comments, 'the influence of unexamined assumptions derived from technology leads quite unnecessarily to maximal determinism in human life. Emancipation from that trap is the goal of all education' (1967, p. 247).

ANTICIPATING BAUDRILLARD

> After three thousand years of explosion, by means of fragmentary and mechanical technologies, the Western world is imploding.
>
> (McLuhan 1973, p. 11)

There are traces of several of the themes which are at the centre of the various debates over the possible emergence of postindustrial and/or postmodern forms in McLuhan's analysis of the social and psychic effects associated with the development of communications technology. For example, the anxieties of our age are considered to be bound up with the effects and problems of adjustment arising from the development of electronic technology. Electric technologies of communication are conceived to have 'extended our central nervous system . . . in a global embrace' which abolishes 'both space and time as far as our planet is concerned' (McLuhan 1973, p. 11). Our former fragmented space and time patterns become inappropriate, if not redundant, in a context where 'electrically contracted, the globe is no more than a village' (McLuhan 1973, pp. 12–13).

For McLuhan the key feature of any technology or medium, its 'message', is the change of pace or scale, pattern or organisation, it introduces into prevailing forms of social life and human experience.[1] The central thesis is that many of the long established features of Western culture and civilisation are at odds with, if not rendered obsolete by, the emergence of an 'electric age'. Fragmentation and centralism, separation of function and lineal specialism, analysis of components, isolation of the moment and the cultivation of detachment are deemed to be synonymous with a mechanical age. In contrast the new electronic technologies of communication are integral and decentralist in depth, and as they create 'conditions of extreme interdependence on a global scale, we move swiftly again into an auditory world of simultaneous events and over-all awareness' (1967; pp. 28–9). Many of the anxieties of our age are held to derive from the fact that the literary and visual bias associated with print culture has left us 'unready to face the language of . . . electro-magnetic technology' (1967, p. 30). At issue then are a series of fundamental transformations in social and psychic life as the 'mechanical' age is overshadowed by the gathering momentum of a micro-electronic age.

It is not only the work of art or the art of work which is transformed by the advent of new technologies of (re)production, but the artist, producer, worker, spectator, viewer, and consumer, not to mention the practices and experiences of creativity, production, work, consumption and so on. The new electronic technologies transform the scale, structure, and pattern of human activities and relationships, through an extension and amplification of sense and capacity, which brings 'all social and political functions together in a sudden implosion' (McLuhan 1973, p. 13). Furthermore, just as the impact of literacy and the typographic principles of 'uniformity, continuity and lineality' proved problematic for many non-Western cultures, so McLuhan suggests that with the development of electronic media a comparable experience of difficulty is encountered *within* Western cultures – 'we are as numb in our new electric world as the native involved in our literate and mechanical culture' (McLuhan 1973, p. 25). Because we have tended to equate 'rational' with uniform, continuous and sequential forms, that is 'reason with literacy, and rationalism with a single technology', the electric age appears virtually synonymous with the 'irrational'. And as we continue to associate a uniform, connected, and visual order with the 'rational' we find ourselves in an 'electric age of instant and non-visual forms of interrelation . . . at a loss to define the "rational"' (McLuhan 1973, p. 129). Implied here is a series of changes and problems which have subsequently been diagnosed as symptoms of a 'postmodern condition' associated with the emergence and development of postindustrial social and economic formations.[2] If McLuhan does not employ the latter terms to describe the transitions and extensions with which he is concerned it is nevertheless evident that the 'inventory of effects' identified anticipates many of the themes addressed in the several debates which have revolved around the respective notions of postindustrial society and postmodern forms and conditions. Above all McLuhan places emphasis upon the growing significance of information systems, their reversal of established patterns and processes of fragmentation and differentiation, and the transformation of prevailing sense ratios.

The distinctive feature of the 'electric age' is then the increasing significance of information. Information has become the crucial commodity as, in turn, commodities have increasingly assumed the character of information. With the advent of automation, programmed production, and associated technological extensions of our senses, a dynamic is set up 'by which all previous technologies . . . will be translated into information systems' (McLuhan 1973, p. 68). Where mechanical technologies are based upon partiality and fragmentation, visual separation and analysis of functions, explosion and expansion, electronic technologies are 'total and inclusive', synonymous with 'implosion and contraction'. With the transition from mechanical to electronic technology we come to regard 'all technology, including language, as a means of processing experience, a means of storing and speeding information' (1973, p. 367). In sum McLuhan suggests that learning and knowing become increasingly central, that with electronic technology 'all forms of employment become "paid learning" and all forms of wealth result from the movement of information' (1973, p. 69). Formerly, in the mechanical age, for which we might read the era of 'industrial society', work had involved hierarchical forms of organisation and authority, processing of materials, and fragmented assembly line operations or methods of production – in short, division of labour and specialisation of functions. With the electronic age, computers and information systems, the job, or work, is transformed. Increasingly it is the movement or processing of information that constitutes the task of work. The most appropriate and obvious example of the way in which the effort and experience of work, including its availability, is being transformed occurs in relation to the impact of automation. It is in his discussion of automation and its effects that McLuhan most clearly reveals his enchantment with electronic technology and a forgetfulness concerning the social relations responsible for the development and deployment of the same.

Automation is conceived not only to eradicate jobs but, in turn, to transform the experience of work, and to end the 'old dichotomies' (viz. between culture and technology, art and commerce, work and leisure). McLuhan comments that automation 'is a way of thinking, as much as it is a way of doing' and that its effects extend beyond production to marketing and consumption. With automation

> energy and production . . . fuse with information and learning. Marketing and consumption tend to become one with learning, enlightenment and the intake of information. This is all part of the electric *implosion* that now follows or succeeds the centuries of *explosion* and increasing specialism.
>
> (McLuhan 1973, p. 373)

Although within the prevailing social relations of production automation is synonymous with a reduction in the demand for labour, McLuhan remarks that there is no need for alarm about unemployment, for paid learning is becoming the principal kind of production and consumption – 'both the dominant employment and . . . source of new wealth'. This is a familiarly optimistic and clearly misguided scenario, one which fails to consider the possibility that the very electronic computer technologies referred to may, in turn, be extended or developed to displace knowledge and information workers. It is a scenario which fails to take into account an earlier underdeveloped caution that the electronic media may have the potential to 'move the world' but that they have been leased to private corporations.[3] One implication of this is that private corporations have a degree of leverage over the world and aspects of its transformation. This is not to suggest that the effects of technology should once again be considered simply and solely in terms of the realisation of specific vested interests or the development of a late, disorganised, cybernetic or postindustrial capitalist formation. But on the other hand the technologies identified have both a history and a specific context of deployment, and a consideration of effects and subsequent consequences needs to take such factors into account. Doing so would have allowed McLuhan to recognise that 'alarm about unemployment' hardly constitutes folly.[4]

McLuhan attempts to draw attention to the subliminal impact of technological transformations on organisational forms, ways of living, human conduct and experience. In a sense the focus is upon unintended and unprogrammed effects which follow from the development and deployment of electronic technologies, on the technological medium itself as the message, rather than upon the medium as the bearer, conveyor, or communicator of a content. As McLuhan argues, the 'conventional response to all media, namely that it is how they are used that counts, is the numb stance of the technological idiot . . . The effects of technology do not occur at the level of opinions or concepts, but alter sense ratios or patterns of perception steadily and without any resistance' (McLuhan 1973, pp. 26–7). In consequence the emphasis in the analysis falls upon changes in participation, sense ratios, and socioeconomic and political forms. Because we have tended to neglect the question of the impact of new technologies on our 'sense-lives', on the ratios and relationships between our faculties, we have tended to assume that distinctions, capacities, and social and political forms synonymous with the development of mechanical technologies will persist. However, where mechanisation is synonymous with differentiation, fragmentation and specialisation, electrification is precipitating de-differentiation, creating if not requiring a high degree of inter-dependence. Where 'the typographic extension of man brought in rationalism, industrialism, mass markets, and universal literacy and education' (McLuhan 1973, p. 184), the implosion of the electronic age is eroding national boundaries and precipitating an 'organic structuring of the global economy'; and in turn is rendering the 'uniformly trained and homogenised citizenry . . . a burden and problem to an automated society' (1973, p. 377). Implicit here is the idea of a transformation in education, away from conceptions of uniformity, excessive specialisation and training, and towards a conception of a form of liberal education as mandatory. It is suggested that there is now no need to continue with social organisations, practices and institutions designed for an age of servile toil and mechanical production, for what 'we had previously achieved mechanically by great exertion and coordination can now be done electrically without effort' (McLuhan 1973, pp. 380–1). This too is a familiar theme reiterated in somewhat different ways in the respective works of Bell, Toffler, and Stonier on the implications of the emergence of a postindustrial society.

Ironically the way in which education appears to be changing, in the short term at least, as governments attempt to come to terms with the impact of the micro-electronic revolution and associated restructuring of the international capitalist economy, is away from the liberal conception recommended by McLuhan and towards a more vocational training-orientated model. This development, in its turn, is clearly articulated with governmental responses to the problem of funding the public sphere which involve introducing quasi-free market economic policies and practices into the domain of education. As I have noted already the health, education and welfare sectors identified as potential growth points in a postindustrial society have been designated appropriate targets for privatisation and industrialisation. What has been termed 'the computer revolution' is facilitating a process of industrialisation of person to person services, allowing health, education, and welfare to be commodified, to become much more explicitly industries, their 'products' a potential source of profit. But McLuhan is not concerned with the question of the impact of private corporate interests on the 'extensions' and developments identified. The persistence of capitalist social relations of production, their articulation with and impact upon electronic technologies and their complex associated effects are matters that receive little, if any, consideration.

Whilst it might be agreed that 'official culture is striving to force the new media to do the work of the old' (McLuhan 1967, p. 94), or that we 'look at the present through a rear-view mirror . . . [and] march backwards into the future' (1967, p. 75), there are other factors involved which need to be addressed. If we are indeed currently 'threatened with a liberation that taxes our inner resources of self-employment and imaginative participation in society' (1973, p. 381), it is a condition which arises in a context where labour-saving technological innovations (IT, CNC, CAD/CAM, etc.) are being deployed to resolve, albeit very temporarily, the increasing control and accumulation problems besetting the capitalist mode of production. McLuhan is correct when he observes that people are increasingly control and coming to realise 'how much they had come to depend on the fragmentalised and repetitive routines of the mechanical era' (1973, p. 381). Their dependency has been considerable, as identity, income necessary for the provision of goods and services, and participation in the public domain, have all been bound up with 'job', 'waged-work', or 'employment' of some form or another. With the 'spectre of joblessness' people have indeed become nomads, but not quite in the sense McLuhan intends to convey. We have not suddenly become 'nomadic gatherers of knowledge . . . free from fragmentary specialism as never before – but also involved in the total social process as never before' (1973, pp. 381–2). On the contrary, if the 'nomads' are indeed gathering, it is because of the increasing frequency with which the unemployed are having to move from one region of a country to another in search of work, leaving families and friends behind them whilst they become part-time, temporary, and/or insecure 'guest workers' in another city or country. Such a condition might be described as one of *freedom* from fragmentary specialism, one of *involvement* in the total social process as never before, but only in the cynical sense that specialised skills have been rendered obsolescent by technological innovation and those subject to such displacement marginalised, if not actually prevented from participating in the commodity game which is central to (post)modern consumer societies.

RECALLING McLUHAN

In exploring the configuration of 'postmodernism' and its complex articulation with emerging socioeconomic formations (e.g. postindustrial or cybernetic capitalism; 'information society')

Baudrillard has drawn upon appropriate elements of the respective works of both Benjamin and McLuhan (cf. Kellner 1987; Poster 1988). Baudrillard approaches the questions of reproduction, implosion, and simulation posed by Benjamin and McLuhan through a critical address of Marx's theory of historical materialism and critique of political economy.[5] At issue in the engagement with Marx's work is a shift from an analysis of the commodity form to that of the sign form. Baudrillard's argument is that the centre of gravity within the capitalist mode of production has moved from

> the form-commodity to the form-sign, from the abstraction of the exchange of material products under the law of general equivalence to the operationalisation of all exchanges under the law of the code.
>
> (Baudrillard 1975, p. 121)

This constitutes a passage to the political economy of the sign.

For Baudrillard the process of material production is no longer the epicentre of the contemporary capitalist has system. The waning of the competitive phase of capitalism has led to a process of 'complete restructuring' from which, of necessity, a different logic has emerged. With the advent of monopoly capitalism consumer demand becomes the strategic element, people are 'mobilised as consumers; their needs become as essential as their labour power' (Baudrillard 1975, p. 144). In turn, the emergence of a cybernetic or postindustrial capitalism promises to make the mobilisation of consumers or consumer power *more* essential than labour power.[6] Baudrillard's view is that by 'expanding the field of social abstraction to the level of consumption, signification, information and knowledge, by expanding its jurisdiction and control to the whole field of culture and daily life, even to the unconscious' (1975, p. 142) capitalism has radicalised its own logic. In a manner which at times parallels elements of the thesis outlined by Habermas on the contemporary 'legitimation crisis', Baudrillard argues that the partial contradictions arising from economic relations of production have been resolved, to an extent, through a process of displacement. However, capitalism continues to be vulnerable at the level of the production of social relations, in so far as it is incapable of reproducing itself symbolically.[7] To explore the ways in which social relations and political forms have been radically transformed by the increasing centrality of the sign as the object of both production and consumption, Baudrillard examines the media, communications technologies and their effects, in short develops a number of themes already addressed by McLuhan.

An adequate understanding of the new communications and media technologies and their effects cannot be derived simply from an expansion of 'analysis in terms of productive forces to the whole murky field of signification and communication' (Baudrillard 1981, p. 164). An analysis which proceeds in terms of the metaphors of 'infrastructure' and 'superstructures' and associated conceptions (e.g. forces and social relations of production; use and exchange value, etc.) ends up conceiving of the media simply as conveyors of ideology, 'as marketing and merchandising . . . the dominant ideology'. Following McLuhan, Baudrillard argues that it is through their form and operation, rather than the content they carry, that the electronic media of communication have transformed social relations. The existing mass media are considered to undermine communication as an exchange, to 'fabricate non-communication', and prevent response other than in the form of a simulation, which itself is already inscribed in the process of transmission–reception. In so far as Baudrillard is a critic of the system of social control and power implied in the existing configuration of the media, there are clear differences with McLuhan's position, which tends to celebrate the emergence of an 'electric age' and view the prospects and possibilities of associated developments with optimism. However, if the 'medium is the message' is not a critical proposition, it nevertheless does have analytic value. The proposition emphasises that it is the form of the media that matters most, and this leads Baudrillard on to argue that attempts to democratise content and/or control the information process are bound to have little effect, for they leave the form unchanged, and it is the form of the media which 'inexorably connects them with the system of power' (1981, p. 173).

As I have implied, Baudrillard's analysis of the impact of electronic technologies of communication extends and develops key elements of the work of both Benjamin and McLuhan. Benjamin is credited with having recognised the implications of technical reproducibility, in particular that technique needs to be understood as 'medium, form, and principle of a whole new generation of sense'. Furthermore, if the analysis of the impact of technological innovation on the process of production, product, producer, and consumer is confined almost entirely in Benjamin's work to the terrain of art, we know that today all material production enters into this sphere. We know now that it is on the level of reproduction (fashion, media, publicity, information and communication networks) . . . that is to say in the sphere of simulacra and of the code, that the global process of capital is founded.

(Baudrillard 1983a, p. 99)

The developments identified by Benjamin, and later McLuhan, have reached a critical stage. In contrast to Benjamin who is principally concerned with the emergence and development of the industrial simulacrum, with the serial and technical era of reproduction, McLuhan is preoccupied with the emergence of a subsequent order of simulacrum in which 'generation by means of models' replaces serial production. It is the development of this new order of simulacrum that is central to Baudrillard's analysis of the present. In brief '"The Medium is the Message" is the very slogan of the political economy of the sign, when it enters into the third-order simulation' (1983a, p. 154, n. 4).

Baudrillard posits the existence of three orders of simulacrum since the Renaissance. The first based on the natural law of value is the order of counterfeit. The second is that of serial production based on the commercial law of value. The third, and present order, is that of operational simulation based on the structural law of value. The key transition is from the second to third orders, from the industrial simulacrum to the metaphysic of the code. With the industrial revolution objects are produced in a serial form. Uniqueness is no longer a critical issue, for the relationship between objects is no longer, as in the first order, that of 'original' to 'counterfeit'. As Baudrillard adds, in serial production 'objects become undefined simulacra one of the other' (1983a, p. 97), as do their producers. But just as counterfeit was abolished by serial production, so in turn the latter has had to yield to 'generation by means of models'. In effect, a transition has occurred from a 'capitalist–productivist society to a neo-capitalist cybernetic order' (1983a, p. 111). The transformation conceptualised by Baudrillard is effectively from

a universe of natural laws to one of forces and tensions, and finally, today, to a universe of structures and binary oppositions. After the metaphysics of being and appearance, after that of energy and determination, we have the metaphysics of indeterminacy and the code. Cybernetic control, generation by

123

models, differential modulation, feed-back, questionnaires (question/response?): such is the new *operational* configuration . . . Digitality is its metaphysical principal . . . and DNA its prophet.

(Poster 1988, p. 139)

Regulation in terms of the model of the genetic code has permeated beyond the walls of the laboratories and the postulates of the theoreticians to everyday life. In brief, digitality is said to haunt 'all the messages, all the signs of our societies'.

The entire communication system is now taking the form of a binary sign system of question and answer, and within the process of perpetual testing, which is a corollary, answers are effectively 'designated in advance' by the unilateral nature of the question. Such a situation does not allow for contemplation, rather it requires, if it does not actually demand, 'instantaneous response, yes or no'. In effect media communications and images no longer inform as much as test and control. As Baudrillard comments, 'objects and information result already from a selection, a montage, from a point of view. They have already tested "reality", and have asked only questions that "answered back" to them' (1983a, p. 120). The medium has quite literally become the message. Through the style of montage, *découpage*, and interpellation, and solicitation and summation, the medium controls the process of meaning. Before considering the impact of associated developments in the realm of politics and its contemporary double, 'public opinion', I want briefly to reconsider the changes in work and production identified by Baudrillard.

The analysis developed by Baudrillard can be located within the various debates which have arisen over the question of a possible transition to a late, hyper, disorganised, postindustrial or information capitalism. The argument is that capitalism has changed in a number of significant ways, and that it 'no longer corresponds to the order of political economy'. The dialectical articulation of use and exchange value, which defines the rational configuration of production regulated by political economy, no longer holds in Baudrillard's view. With the emergence of a third order of simulation 'the two aspects of value . . . are disarticulated'. The appeal to referential value is nullified, and in the absence of referentials (of production, signification, history etc.), signs exchange without reference to a 'real'. The operation is repeated in respect of labour power and production – an 'elimination of all finalities of content allows production to function as a code, and permits the monetary sign . . . to escape in indefinite speculation, beyond any reference to the real or even to a gold standard' (Poster 1988, p. 126). The implication of such comments is not the demise of capitalism; on the contrary, it is capital that has put an end to 'social determination through the mode of production' and substituted the structural form of value for the commodity form. The historical and social mutations identified are synonymous with the emergence of a system based upon indeterminacy, a system whose strategy derives from capital. Indeterminacy may rule, but this is far from an acceptable state of affairs, as is evident from the following statement:

> All the great humanist criteria of value, all the values of a civilisation of moral, aesthetic, and practical judgment, vanish in our system of images and signs. Everything becomes undecidable. This is the characteristic effect of the domination of the code, which is based everywhere on the principle of neutralisation and indifference. This is the generalised brothel (chaos) of capital . . . of substitution and interchangeability.
>
> (Baudrillard 1983a, p. 128)

Within the economic sphere the process of indeterminacy identified leads to a transformation of both production and labour. It is no longer appropriate to proceed from the conventional terms associated with a critique of political economy, for 'everything has changed'. With the shift from the commodity law to the structural law of value the social form of production has been undermined and the status of labour transformed, such that now 'labour and production . . . only function as signs, as interchangeable terms with nonlabour, consumption, communication etc' (Baudrillard 1983a, p. 131). As a result, production and its ends are increasingly in question as labour becomes marginalised as a productive force. Yet if labour is less and less a productive force it has increasingly become reproductive of 'the assignment to labour'. There is, then, no implication here of the disappearance of labour, to the contrary it increasingly

> invades all of life as a fundamental repression, as control, and as a permanent job in specified times and places, according to an omnipresent code. People must be *positioned* at all times: in school, in the plant, at the beach or in front of the TV, or in job retraining – a permanent, general mobilisation. But this form of

labour is no longer productive in the original sense . . . This is the tendency of every current strategy that concerns labour . . . You are no longer brutally removed from daily life to be delivered up to machines. But rather you are integrated: your childhood, your habits, your human relations, your unconscious instincts, even your rejection of work. You will certainly find a place for yourself in all this, a personalised job, and if not, there is social welfare provision that is calculated based on your individualised statistics. In any case, you will never be left on your own . . . the die is cast, . . . the system of socialisation is complete. Labour power is no longer violently bought and sold; it is designed, it is marketed, it is merchandised. Production thus joins the consumerist system of signs.

(Baudrillard 1983a, p. 134)

In effect the sign of labour has been dispersed throughout everyday life. The important thing is occupation, being busy, or occupied. Labour has the function of localising each individual in a social nexus, and to that extent 'all that is asked . . . is not that you produce . . . but that you be socialised' (Baudrillard 1983a, p. 131).

In these observations Baudrillard is outlining, albeit somewhat pessimistically, the implications associated with the development of new technologies. Whilst there are differences of emphasis and, as we will see, development, there remain clear parallels with some of the more critical postindustrial scenarios, for example with Gorz's observations on the impact of micro-electronic technologies on work and production, in particular the drift from production to consumption as the gravitational centre of the system. But for Baudrillard questions of economy, production, and labour become increasingly secondary to those of communication.

COMMUNICATIONS, SIMULATION AND POLITICS

In respect of the analysis of communications and the media Baudrillard contends that McLuhan's dictum is far from exhausted. Not only has there been an implosion of the message and its meaning in the medium, but in addition it is argued that there has been an 'implosion of the medium itself in the real'. For McLuhan the medium is the event, the contents or messages carried become secondary in so far as they are constituted and thus compromised, if not neutralised, by the particular form of the medium itself. Within this formulation Baudrillard believes there remains the possibility of manipulating the medium in its form, and thereby perhaps transforming the real. In short, a potentially subversive use of the medium remains a possibility. But what if the distinction between medium and reality can no longer be sustained? It is exactly this state of affairs that Baudrillard considers has arisen with the development of electronic media of communication. With the implosion of 'the medium' and 'the real' a nebulous hyperreality emerges which effaces their difference(s) and distinctiveness. In Baudrillard's view 'the medium and the real are now in a single nebulous state whose truth is undecipherable' (1983b, p. 103).

This comment needs to be placed in the context of the broader argument concerning the emergence of a third order of simulacra in which differences between 'true' and 'false' and 'real' and 'imaginary' are rendered increasingly problematic. With simulation there is a 'generation by models of a real without origin or reality: a hyperreal' (1983a, p. 2). Signs of the real are substituted for the real itself and in consequence 'truth, reference and objective causes' cease to exist. For Baudrillard it is television that most clearly embodies the transformations described, the merging of medium and message and implosion of the former in and with the real – 'the dissolution of TV into life, the dissolution of life into TV' (1983a, p. 55). The media are conceived to be akin to a genetic code which regulates the 'mutation of the real into the hyperreal', and which in turn erodes the traditional poles of analysis as one enters into simulation. In so far as the conventional conceptions of causality and determination, and distinctions between cause/effect, active/passive, subject/object and means/ends are called into question, critical analysis is made difficult, if not of necessity fundamentally transformed.

In drawing attention to the complex effects associated with developments in communications media Baudrillard does not endorse the idea of the increasing significance of information. To the contrary, an appropriately sceptical response is provided to all the hype about an 'information revolution' arising from the introduction of micro-electronic technological innovations, and to that extent the work may, in this respect at least, be considered to add weight to the criticisms advanced by others concerned about the 'technical fix' on which we have become ever more dependent.[8] In Baudrillard's view we encounter a paradox: 'there is more and more information, and less and less meaning' (1983b, p. 95). Following a line of analysis that may be traced back, albeit tenuously, to the theorists at the Institute for Social Research in Frankfurt, Baudrillard analyses the inter-relationship between the media, communications and information, and those subjects constituted as the silent terminals of the process – the silent majority or the masses. The latter are not portrayed as cultural dopes, but rather as the bearers of a positive counter-strategy, as positively expressing an indifference to the exhortations to be better informed, as silent in the face of the noise and interference of 'information', and as opposing 'their refusal of meaning and their will to spectacle to the ultimatum of meaning' (1983b, p. 10). In opposition to the familiar argument that the masses are manipulated by the media, a different view is proposed, namely that the mass and the media constitute one single process, that,

> Instead of transforming the mass into energy information produces even more mass. Instead of informing as it claims, instead of giving form and structure, information neutralises even further the 'social field'; more and more it creates an inert mass impermeable to the classical institutions of the social, and to the very contents of information.
>
> (Baudrillard 1983b, p. 25)

The mass refuses socialisation and derives its strength from its very 'destructuration and inertia'. Hence Baudrillard's simulation of McLuhan's dictum becomes, 'Mass(age) is the message' (1983b, p. 44), the corollary of which is the simultaneous decline of the social and the political.

The social has a history; it is neither timeless nor universal. There have been societies before, and without, the social and Baudrillard implies that perhaps we are now witnessing the 'end of the social'. Much of course depends on what is meant by the concept of 'the social'. Four possibilities need to be considered, namely that the social has never existed, that it has only ever been a simulation; it has existed as a 'rational control of residues and a rational *production* of residues', but that as the residues become equivalent to the whole of society the social itself becomes residual, a remainder; it has taken the form of reality principle 'from the perspective space of a rational distri-bution . . . which is also that of production – in short in the narrow gap of second order simulacra, and absorbed into third order simulacra, it is dying' (Baudrillard 1983b, p. 83); and finally with simulation there is 'an implosion of the social into the masses' (1983b, p. 91, n. 12). It is the third and closely related fourth possibilities that Baudrillard elaborates upon, arguing that all the institutions which have been associated with the extension of the social (urbanisation, production and work, medicine, education, etc.), of which *capital* is described as the 'most effective socialisation medium of all', have simultaneously been contributing to its erosion. As Baudrillard comments:

> the social is formed out of abstract instances which are laid down one after the other on the ruins of the symbolic and ceremonial edifice of former societies . . . But at the same time they consecrate that ravenous, all-consuming abstraction which perhaps devours precisely the 'essential marrow' of the social . . .
> The process accelerates and reaches its maximal extent with mass media and information. Media, *all* media, information, *all* information, act in two directions: outwardly they produce more of the social, inwardly they neutralise social relations and the social itself.
>
> (Baudrillard 1983b, p. 66)

By implication our society is considered to be in the process of burying the social under a simulation of the same.

The absence of a 'real social substance' is associated with the fall of the 'political', its loss of specificity. For the political there is no longer anything to represent, no clearly delineated social referent (a people, class, proletariat, etc.). The only referent that remains is that constituted through the media, the silent majority of public opinion, the existence of which is not social 'but statistical, and whose only mode of appearance is that of the survey' (Baudrillard 1983b, p. 20). Politics works with an imaginary referent, the masses, and because the (imaginary) existence of the masses is constituted through the survey, rather than expression, representation is no longer an element of the political game. Baudrillard thus posits the simultaneous decline of both the social and the political. Both succumb to the mass(age) and associated proliferation of electronic media. The political sphere loses its specificity 'when it enters into the game of the media and public opinion polls' (1983a, p. 124), when the formation of public opinion is displaced by polls which constitute a simulacrum of public opinion. It is not the manipulation or deception of the public through media constructed opinion polls that constitutes the issue for Baudrillard, for only members of the political class 'believe in them'. The problem of the polls is 'the operational simulation that they institute over the entire spectrum of social practices: that of the progressive *leucemiazation* of all social substance, that is the substitution for blood of the white lymph of media' (1983a, p. 129).

Although Baudrillard argues that we are subject to a binary sign system of communication – 'of question/answer – of perpetual *test*' – which effectively undermines contemplation and stimulates instantaneous response, the political outcome is clearly not mass manipulation. To the contrary the political sphere is no longer capable of representing anything at all, it has become empty. Politics has become a regulated game in which media simulated polls of public opinion effectively short-circuit representation. From this standpoint the 'advanced democratic' systems appear increasingly to be based on a bipartite alternation between fractions of a homogeneous monopolising political class. This state of affairs is synonymous with a simulation of opposition between contesting parties, and a neutralisation of *social* antagonisms under the sign of public opinion, 'mediated and homogenised by anticipation (the polls) that will make alteration possible "at the top"' (1983a, p. 133). Such developments are associated with an increasing scepticism towards both the political system in general and the democratic credo of 'free choice', a scepticism which manifests itself in a withdrawal from participation, and an absence of response, that might be regarded as a 'counter-strategy of the masses' (1983b, p. 105).

Like McLuhan Baudrillard makes much of the impact of the electronic mass media, and television in particular. Television is described as the 'most beautiful prototypical object of this new era' of simulation (1988a, p. 12). In turn it is considered to prefigure a series of transformations in the private sphere, work and production, consumption, leisure and play, as well as in social relations. Some of Baudrillard's more flippant and ambiguous remarks appear to suggest not simply an identification or analysis of new techno-cultural configurations and their effects, but a celebration of them.[9] However, such an interpretation is hard to sustain and difficult to reconcile with the general tenor of other comments made on the problematic effects associated with the development of new cultural and economic forms. For example, a number of developments in electronic technologies of communication (i.e. miniaturisation, transistorisation, telematics, etc.) are judged to have condemned central aspects of our everyday lives to 'futility, obsolescence and almost to obscenity'. The mere presence of television is said to have transformed the home into a 'closed-off cell, into a vestige of human relations whose survival is highly questionable' (Baudrillard 1988a, p. 18). Overstated perhaps, but celebratory? Hardly.

Miniaturisation, remote control and microprocessing have had dramatic impacts upon virtually every aspect of human existence. Bodies and pleasure, work and leisure, public and private spheres or spaces, the social and the political have all been progressively transformed. Time has been reduced to a series of instants, the body to superfluousness as 'everything is concentrated in the brain and the genetic code' (1988a, p. 18). Everything in short has become subject to the obscenity of the universe of communication, has become transparent, visible and exposed. Developments in information and communication are synonymous with an obscenity of the 'all-too-visible', with superficiality, saturation, harassment, and a dissolution of interstitial space. With increasing media saturation of space, our culture moves from 'forms of expression and competition' towards an 'extension of forms of chance (*alea*) and giddiness' (1988a, p. 25). But if Baudrillard is not necessarily celebrating such transformations, it is also clear that he does not wish to be interpreted as offering a reflex negative judgment, for pleasures, perceptions and forms of human sensibility have also changed. And here we encounter a problem, namely that:

> In applying our old criteria and the reflexes of a 'scenic' sensibility, we run the risk of misconstruing the irruption of this new ecstatic and obscene form in our sensorial sphere.
> (Baudrillard 1988a, pp. 25–6)

Interestingly, where Stuart Hall finds Baudrillard in celebratory mode in discussions of 'new trends or tendencies', Doug Kellner uncovers a nihilism 'without joy, without energy, without hope for a better future' (1988, p. 247). In both cases analysis proceeds from the terrain of a Marxist problematic, and in consequence the respective addresses of Baudrillard's work produce friction, difference, and criticism. For Hall, postmodernist theories might currently draw attention to problems and contradictions associated with modern culture, but they are simultaneously considered to be guilty of invoking a conception of a categorical break or rupture with the modern era, which suggests another 'new' epoch or historical moment, a criticism endorsed by Kellner (1988, p. 267). In opposition to this tendency Hall questions whether there is 'any such absolutely novel and unified thing as *the* postmodern condition' (1986, p. 47), and reminds us that the old certainties have been in question for some time now, from at least the turn of the century. There really is no need for argument here, as most of the more measured contributions to the various debates over postmodernism and postmodernity make clear. There is no singular or unified postmodern condition, as Kellner acknowledges in comments on 'the diversities between theories often lumped together as "postmodern"' (1988, p. 241). Even in Lyotard's much maligned *and* over-celebrated address of 'the condition of knowledge in the most highly developed societies' (1986, p. xxiii) the concept of the 'postmodern' is utilised to refer to mutations, problems, developments, and difficulties associated with, arising out of, and prompted by, features of the modern. As for the question posed by Hall of the geo-political relevance of postmodernism – is it 'irrevocably Euro- or Western-centric', 'a global or a "western" phenomenon?' (1986, p. 46). An obvious response, virtually solicited by the question, is that the term seems to have been coined to describe a number of developments in Western Europe and America. But in so far as these include a questioning of grand narratives and a recognition of the limits and limitations of Western forms of rationality and associated linear conceptions of history and development (viz. economic, cultural, social, and political) it might be argued that it has a broader global significance.

The key issue through which both Hall and Kellner engage with Baudrillard's work is that of a set of problems concerning questions of meaning – signification – representation. Hall suggests that Baudrillard's work displays an infatuation with the 'facticity of life', with what seems to be immediately present, and that in consequence it rejects not only the idea of a final, absolute meaning or ultimate signified, a justifiable move, but in addition asserts that 'meaning does not exist'. Whether Baudrillard makes such a facile comment is a moot point. Certainly reference is made to the way in which 'information dissolves meaning'; to the implosion, neutralisation, and absorption of meaning; to a 'catastrophe of meaning' which awaits us; and to the way in which the masses, through their silence, and the media, through its fascination, engage in a defiance of meaning. Such statements derive from a consideration of the impact of the electronic media on information, communications and meaning, and a related observation that

The cycle of meaning is infinitesimally abridged into minute quantities of energy/information . . . This is the equivalent of

the code's neutralisation of signifieds, the instantaneous verdicts
of fashion, advertising, media messages.

(Poster 1988, p. 142)

Where Hall accepts that meaning may have broken into fragments,
the aura of the unique and singular may indeed have been destroyed,
but considers that this has given rise to an 'infinite multiplicity of
codings' (1986, p. 50), Baudrillard emphasises the presence of
regulation on the model of the genetic code throughout everyday life,
a genetic social code which 'irradiates the social body with its
operational circuits' (Poster 1988, p. 141).

Although Hall notes Baudrillard's indebtedness to McLuhan he
does not seem to appreciate the consequence, namely that the
emphasis in the subsequent discussion of the electronic mass media
falls on the impact of medium on message, communication, or
meaning. Baudrillard argues that the growth of electronic mass media
of communication, and associated effects of simulation, produce a
'short-circuit between poles of every differential system of meaning,
the effacement of terms and of distinct oppositions' (1983b,
pp. 102–3). In effect, meaning, the message, is absorbed within the
medium and, in turn, the end of the message is paralleled by the end
of the medium, in so far as the electronic media cease to exist in the
literal sense of the term as 'a power mediating between one reality and
another, between one state of the real and another' (Baudrillard
1983b, p. 102). This does not constitute a celebration of the demise
of meaning but, to the contrary, represents an attempt to explore the
impact of the development of electronic mass media on information,
communication and meaning. To that extent the work constitutes a
potentially critical counter-balance to analyses of the communications
and information 'revolutions' that do indeed celebrate the emergence
of a 'post-industrial' social formation. The analysis effectively
challenges the idea that electronic mass media are neutral conveyors
of more and, by implication, better forms of information. But it also
cautions that

It is useless to dream of revolution through content or through
form, since the medium and the real are now in a single
nebulous state whose truth is undecipherable.

(Baudrillard 1983b, p. 103)

A parallel set of objections has been raised in relation to Baudrillard's
conception of the masses. It has been argued that the masses are

133

depicted as indifferent and apathetic, as an 'apathetic silent majority' (Kellner), and as 'nothing but a passive reflection of the historical, economic and political forces which have gone into the construction of modern industrial mass society' (Hall 1986, p. 52). Ironically the oppositional position articulated by Hall bears a striking resemblance to the criticised thesis. Hall argues that if the masses are silent it may be because they have been deprived of the 'means of enunciation'. Yet whilst so deprived 'their continuing presence, as a kind of passive historical–cultural force, has constantly interrupted, limited and disrupted everything else' (Hall 1986, p. 52). The comparable thesis in Baudrillard's work is the inverse of McLuhan's optimistic global village scenario, in which intensification of the media increases liberty. Baudrillard's position is that 'the media and especially television accord no right of reply', that the media 'produce the masses in their silence', but silence itself is conceived to be a strategy, a 'massive reply'. Silence is taken to be more than simply a symptom or sign of passivity, it is a refusal, a neutralisation of social, cultural and political impositions from above – 'all of that comes . . . through the media, and the masses reply to it all with silence; they block the process' (1984a, p. 22). The comment that the masses refuse or block meaning that comes from above, rather than pursue a negative or subversive reply, might be regarded as at least compatible with Hall's observations that 'the masses have kept a secret to themselves while the intellectuals keep running around in circles trying to make out what it is' (Hall 1986, p. 52). My point is not that Baudrillard and Hall share a common view, but that their respective positions may be closer than the criticisms advanced suggest.

Hall clearly wishes to take issue with postmodernism, including the 'post-Marxist' strain engineered by Laclau and Mouffe, but to do so effectively it is necessary to abstain from parody.[10] There may indeed be analyses and discussions of postmodernism which celebrate 'the American age', and deep disillusionment amongst some left-bank Parisian intellectuals may have rendered them 'vulnerable' to ideas about a postmodern condition. But by no means all versions of postmodernism celebrate American culture, and Paris does not have a monopoly on intellectual disillusionment. More to the point, within Hall's own analysis there are the traces of another way of thinking about 'the postmodern' that does not feed on disillusionment, or require an abandonment of modernism and modernity *in toto*. Consider for example the following statement:

if postmodernism wants to say that such processes of diversity
and fragmentation which modernism first tried to name, have
gone much further, are technologically underpinned in new
ways, and have penetrated more deeply into mass consciousness
etc, I would agree.

(Hall 1986, p. 50)

But for the most part Hall conceives of postmodernism and
postmodernity in terms of a 'new kind of absolute rupture', as
representing a break with modernism and modernity, and thereby as
a necessary (and easy) target of criticism. In particular it is over the
'question of the political possibilities of the masses' that the sharpest
contestation with postmodernism arises for Hall.

I have implied above that Hall's critique of Baudrillard misses its
target on the question of the masses. This arises primarily from an
unaddressed difference between their respective conceptions of the
masses. Hall conceives of the masses, the silent majority, as a socially
constituted potential unity, whereas Baudrillard argues that it is 'not
something to do with the "millions of individuals"' but is a kind of
inertia, a 'mode of circulation and inertia' (1984a, p. 23). Within
Hall's remarks there is the clear implication of 'the masses' acting,
transforming and struggling. References slide from the masses,
popular masses, social movements, a movement of people, to 'social
forces, classes, groups, political movements etc'. These are clearly not
equivalents, but are presented, by implication, as related social entities
with the potential as subjects (and objects) to act, to engage, to
reorganise and to transform. For Baudrillard the masses are neither a
'group-subject' nor an object. The term has 'no sociological
reality . . . nothing to do with any *real* population, body, or specific
social aggregate' (1983b, p. 5). It is an imaginary referent, a
simulation. Here lies the critical difference between the two views,
and it has less to do with 'postmodernism' *per se* and rather more to
do with different modes of conceptualisation and different
interpretations of the present, relatively quiescent, *Western* European
political scene. For Hall the political possibilities of the masses remain
open, a matter of struggle, for Baudrillard the 'indifference of the
masses is their true, their only practice' and it constitutes 'an explicit
and positive counter strategy' (1983b, p. 14: p. 11). Where Hall
continues to find ambiguity and contradictory plurality in cultural
production and associated events, and in consequence a remaining
potential for ideological struggle, Baudrillard considers 'the more

general promise of a relationship of forces . . . has vanished. Everywhere, always, the system is too strong: it is hegemonic' (1984b, p. 39). In consequence Baudrillard suggests that if the system is to be checked, it is necessary to push it to its limit(s) and to achieve this end it is necessary to substitute a fatal theory for critical theory.

IN THE SHADOW OF CRITICAL THEORY

With the emergence of a third order of simulacra the idea that images refer to a real world of real objects and 'reproduce something which is logically and chronologically anterior to themselves' (Baudrillard 1988b, p. 13) is not sustainable. Citing Benjamin as a precursor who recognised the significance of transformations in the order of (re)production Baudrillard comments that 'in the dialectical relation between reality and images . . . the image has taken over and imposed its own immanent ephemeral logic; . . . a logic of the extermination of its own referent, a logic of the implosion of meaning' (Baudrillard 1988b, p. 23). This does not mean that events have become insignificant or meaningless, rather that under the logic of simulation they are preceded by models with which they can only coincide. Given an effacement of the sovereign difference between 'the real' and 'simulation models', the liquidation of referentials, or practical impossibility of isolating the 'process of simulation' and the 'process of the real', the conventional aim of critical theorising and analysis, to reveal the deep meanings buried beneath the surface appearance of things, to disocclude, demystify, and discover the 'objective' reality or order of things, becomes highly problematic, if not inconceivable.

Baudrillard argues that just as the chief accomplishment, the true revolution, of nineteenth-century modernity might be regarded as 'the immense process of destruction of appearances' in favour of meaning (representation, history, criticism, etc.), so the twentieth-century 'revolution' of postmodernity has been synonymous with an 'immense process of the destruction of meaning, equal to the earlier destruction of appearances' (1984b, pp. 38–9). It is in this context that the question of critical theory needs to be reconsidered. Has critical theory been overtaken by events associated with the emergence of a third order of simulacra? Baudrillard argues that the possibility for a transgression or subversion of codes has been lost. There are no longer any symbolic referents or 'lost objects' to be recovered. Our present situation has become one in which the destiny of the object has effectively displaced the desire of the subject. In consequence the aim of theory has changed, no longer is it to 'be the reflection of the real, to enter into a relation of critical negativity with the real' (1988a, p. 97). Rather theory becomes a challenge to the real, its goal being not *effets de vérité*, but to force things into an 'over-existence', literally to their limits and beyond. Indeed given an 'enigmatic bias in the order of things', the indifference of the world to our explanations and solutions, the status of theory can only be that of a challenge to the real. Here Baudrillard seems to have returned us to something like the position to which Horkheimer became resigned in an earlier context, where the prospects for radical politics seemed poor, if not non-existent. The significant difference was that for Horkheimer critical theory constituted an appropriate and relevant focus for intellectual activity, for Baudrillard it is merely a residual form of theorising which belongs to an earlier second order of simulation, one synonymous with the industrial reproduction of a series of mass objects. The transition to a neo-capitalist cybernetic order of simulation requires the substitution of a 'fatal' form of theory for critical theory.

Baudrillard's analysis of the world's indifference to our explanations and endeavours betrays traces of Weber's more sober conception of the unintended consequences of human action, as well as Foucault's more rigorous notion of the lack of correspondence between programmes, practices and effects. Just as for Weber and Foucault it is the elusive complexity of social and cultural forms which continually haunts and limits our analyses, so for Baudrillard it is necessary to come to terms with the enigmatic and fatal quality of things. This means addressing 'the objective irony of things caught in their own devices' (1988a, p. 83). It involves a recognition of the 'intensifying spiral', acceleration, saturation, and increasing excess to which things have become subject, tendencies which it has become impossible to reverse or slow down. In turn this leads to a view of our present condition as one not of growth but excess, and of our societies as incessantly developing in a disorganised way, with no prospect of many of the manufactured products and functions serving any useful purpose. Baudrillard expresses amazement at the congestion and 'obesity of all current systems . . . represented by our means of communication, memory, storage, production, and destruction, means that have been expanded and overburdened so much that their uselessness is a foregone conclusion' (1989, p. 30). In short, there is too much information, too many messages, too many signals. The alleged information revolution is certainly not the subject of celebration; on the contrary Baudrillard muses on the possible need for an 'information dietetics' and/or 'institutions to uninform' (Poster 1988, p. 190). But if the excessive expansion of information and communications systems is the target of criticism, the impression continues to be conveyed that the processes to which we are subject are irreversible, that the corollary of over-production and an excess of information and communication is exhaustion and inertia, in short that the political game of hope and promise is over. The impression given is that

> we are settling into a *modus vivendi* without illusion, without bitterness, and without violence. The issue is not resignation since there is no alternative phantasm. That is just the way it is; that is the way of life. *Modus vivendi* . . . And the same goes for the general political cycle – a lethargic relationship between the masses and power. One refuses to change the form that it assumes, for any alternative illusion is dead.
>
> (Baudrillard 1989, p. 42)

Statements such as this confirm Baudrillard's credentials as the *homme fatal* of (post)modern social theory.

FATAL STRATEGIES, FATAL FLAWS

The idea that different times call for different explanations, analyses, theories, and strategies for action is not contentious. The question of whether present times are different, or at least significantly so, is contentious. Accepting for one moment that Baudrillard's account of the present provides a convincing version of the way things *really* are, a paradoxical consequence for a theory which claims an end to the possibility of differentiating reality from simulation, there remains the question of the strategy recommended, the strategy required for the times in which we live. Basically Baudrillard's position is that 'when all critical radicalism has become pointless, when all negativity is resolved in a world that pretends to be fulfilled' (Poster 1988, p. 205), it is necessary to go over to 'the side of the object', effectively to turn the system's own logic against it, to 'push the simulation machine to its limit, to a point of non-return' (Chen 1987, p. 85). But what does this necessitate? And how is it to be achieved?

Baudrillard's work has come under considerable criticism for its inconsistencies and its analytic and political consequences.[11] But is it fatally flawed? The biggest problem with Baudrillard's analysis arises from its central claim concerning the end of 'the real', for as Morris has effectively demonstrated the work is 'absorbed by the mystery of correspondences between discourse and the world' (1988, p. 191). Baudrillard seems to want to be read 'telling it like it is', yet the tale, ironically, is that such 'true stories' can no longer be told. We are apparently unable to decipher 'reality' from 'simulation'. Had Baudrillard taken a little more care with his exploration of McLuhan's work he might well have avoided an unnecessary lament over a lost 'reality'. One might well ask of Baudrillard 'when was the real?' Before the advent of electronic simulation? Surely not, for then there was already mechanical reproduction. Even if we move further back to the first order constituted by Baudrillard, that of the 'original' and the 'counterfeit', we encounter problems, for we remain in an environment of language, words, and speech and, as McLuhan notes, the

> spoken word was the first technology by which [woman] man was able to let go of [her] his environment in order to grasp it in a new way. Words are a kind of information retrieval . . . [they] are a technology of explicitness. By means of translation of immediate sense experience into vocal symbols the entire world can be evoked and retrieved at any instant.
> (McLuhan 1973, pp. 67–8)

In brief, Baudrillard's 'real' has always lacked a clear referent and in consequence it has continually constituted a dilemma.

The 'real' has not come to an end, other than in the sense that it is increasingly difficult to disentangle 'event' from media constituted 'representation'. To an extent the representation or, as Baudrillard has it, the simulation is the event, it is what is known of the event, it becomes virtually synonymous with the event. Here we are on the terrain of Baudrillard's 'hyperreal', that is 'the meticulous reduplication of the real, preferably through another, reproductive medium' (Poster 1988, p. 144). The key point is that there no longer exists an unmediated 'reality' as the potential object of representation; the real has become 'that which is always already reproduced' and to that extent hyperreal. Where once there 'existed a specific class of objects that were allegorical . . . , such as mirrors, images, works of art (and concepts?) . . . Today the real and the imaginary are confounded in the same operational totality' (Poster 1988, p. 146). Undoubtedly this means an end to the idea of an external independent 'reality' which might constitute the measure or reference point for representations, the fount from which simulations spring. But this is by no means a novel position. What we take to be reality is, as Eco has reminded us, necessarily 'always already made by other messages' (1978, p. 79).

In conditions of modernity the relationship between social analysis and social reality, as Giddens cogently observes, 'has to be understood . . . in terms of the "double hermeneutic"' (1990, p. 15). But this does not mean an end of the real, rather that social reality is necessarily or unavoidably reflexive. In short, 'we are abroad in a world which is throughly constituted through reflexively applied knowledge' (Giddens 1990, p. 39), a world in which certitude is subverted and significant levels of indeterminacy and contingency seem to prevail. The complex and diverse consequences of this contemporary condition have, in turn, led to speculations concerning the possible emergence of a postmodern order. Premature, paradoxical, or persuasive, the idea of the postmodern has become a prominent focus of analysis and debate.

5

THE POSTMODERN PARADOX

If there is a degree of agreement amongst analysts and commentators that the present era constitutes a significant moment in history, a time of radical change, there nevertheless remain substantial differences in respect of both conceptualisation and explanation of changes identified. Of the range of terms introduced to analyse the various signs of transformation evident in the present, two sets of conceptual distinctions have become particularly prominent and influential, namely those of 'industrial' and 'postindustrial' society and the 'modern' and 'postmodern' respectively. As I have explained above, the controversial and ambiguous conceptual distinction between 'industrial' and 'postindustrial' society has been invoked to describe a complex range of changes in social and economic life, changes considered to be closely associated with, if not ultimately determined by, innovations in technology and the effects of their deployment, the latter, in turn, generally being analysed in abstraction from a prevailing, increasingly global, capitalist mode of production and an associated military–industrial complex. The second even more nebulous conceptual distinction, between the 'modern' and the 'post-modern', has been employed in an extensive range of analyses of changes identified in social, political, and cultural life, in aesthetics, architecture, communications, science, epistemology, morality and ethics.

The question of the possible emergence of postmodern forms of life, of a condition of postmodernity, seems to have displaced the former preoccupation with the prospect of a transition to postindustrial society at the centre of intellectual debate in the West. This possibly reflects the widespread sense that Western civilisation, its cultural forms and practices, are undergoing an accelerating process of irreversible transformation. Subject to uncertainty, question, and

141

challenge 'the West' no longer represents, or for that matter conceives of itself, as the universal, the model for emulation, or the paradigm for 'progress'. Indeed the very project upon which the hegemony of the West has been predicated is now in question in the debate over the possible closure or 'end of modernity'. It is this possibility to which the awkward and ambiguous term 'postmodernity' refers.

In so far as postmodern forms of life, or a condition of postmodernity, are conceived to be articulated with radical transformations in the structure and organisation of Western economies, the introduction of new information and telecommunications technologies, and related changes in culture and society, the idea of postindustrial society has continued to remain on the agenda for discussion and analysis. Indeed a number of contributors to the debate over the nature of present conditions suggest a degree of correspondence, if not a close articulation, between postmodern and postindustrial forms. The most obvious example is to be found in Lyotard's agenda-setting report on the postmodern condition of knowledge. Lyotard suggests that 'the status of knowledge is altered as societies enter what is known as the postindustrial age and cultures enter what is known as the postmodern age' (1986, p. 3). And subsequently that, 'in contemporary society and culture – postindustrial society, postmodern culture – the question of the legitimation of knowledge is formulated in different terms' (Lyotard 1986, p. 37). A second, somewhat different, example is present in Frankel's critical analysis of the concept of postindustrial society. Frankel notes that the contemporary discussion of modernity and postmodernity 'has in many ways become an explicit debate over the nature of culture and social production in the emerging "postindustrial" society' (1987, p. 10). Then, in the context of a brief address of the complex issues involved, he adds that the various discourses on modernity and postmodernity in the realms of 'aesthetics, the future of society and the confrontation with the Marxist tradition, have overlapped with one another and with the whole discussion of postindustrialism' (Frankel 1987, pp. 179–80). Further allusions to the possible articulation of postindustrial and postmodern forms are present in Burger (1984/85), Miyoshi and Harootunian (1989), and Karatani (1989).

Alternatively the social, economic, and technological changes and developments frequently identified with the emergence of postindustrial society, and the associated constitution of postmodern forms of life, might be conceptualised as symptoms of another cycle or process of structural transformation under way within the capitalist mode of production. For example, Jameson rejects the idea of postindustrial society, yet simultaneously embraces the idea of postmodernism as an appropriate way of conceptualising the cultural space of 'late' capitalism. Jameson comments that rather than

> denounce the complacencies of postmodernism as some final symptom of decadence, or . . . salute the new forms as the harbingers of a new technological and technocratic Utopia, it seems more appropriate to assess the new cultural production within the working hypothesis of a general modification of culture itself within the social restructuration of late capitalism as a system.
>
> (Jameson 1984a, p. 63)

Broadly comparable positions are outlined by Lash and Urry (1987) and Harvey (1989). Lash and Urry find that the 'breakdown of older organised capitalist forms' is accompanied by the emergence of a postmodernist cultural sensibility, and Harvey argues that the various changes identified signify a transition 'from Fordism to flexible accumulation' within the capitalist mode of production, and that this process has as its cultural and experiential correlate the constitution of a condition of postmodernity. However, before adequate consideration can be given to the difficult issues which arise in connection with the key question of the complex forms of articulation that might exist between a late twentieth-century (post)industrial capitalism and postmodern cultural forms and practices, it is necessary to devote attention to the theoretical and analytical problems which are associated with the modern and postmodern conceptual configurations.

ON THE QUESTION OF MODERNITY

An analysis of the modern and postmodern problematics encounters a number of acute difficulties. To begin with there is the problem of the presence of a constellation of related terms all lacking in specificity (Featherstone 1988). Distinctions drawn between the 'modern', 'modernism', and 'modernity', and the 'postmodern', 'postmodernism', and 'postmodernity' appear at times to fluctuate from one analyst to another. A related difficulty arises with the question of historical periodisation. Specifically there is, as will become apparent below, a marked variation in conceptions of the

143

modern age and the historical circumstances in which it is considered to have emerged and developed. Further problems and confusions arise from the existence of a number of conceptual distinctions drawn between 'positive' and 'negative' manifestations of respectively modern and postmodern forms (Graff 1973). But alongside such differences there are also similarities and common reference points. For example, it might be argued that the various reflections on the modern and postmodern constellations signify a process of 'desynonymisation of "modern" and "contemporary"' (Calinescu 1977, p. 86), and recall earlier debates over Apollonian and Dionysian tendencies in cultural history, as well as the more pertinent *querelle des anciens et des modernes*. At the very least, the analyses to be considered here share a common preoccupation with the question of present conditions and a mutual interest in the fate of modernity, albeit articulated at times in different ways.

From the eighteenth century European social thought has displayed a concern with the question of the emergence and development of various social practices, institutions, relationships, and experiences considered to be constitutive of a distinctively different form of life – modernity (Bierstedt 1979, pp. 21–2; Habermas 1987, pp. 6–7). In their various idiosyncratic ways the respective works of Marx, Weber, Durkheim and Simmel provide an analysis of the transformations of values, beliefs, practices, and patterns of organisation and interaction in socioeconomic, cultural and political life arising from the emergence of modernity. However, precisely when the modern age or modern chapter of Western history might be considered to have commenced has remained a matter of debate. Advocates and antagonists of the idea of *post*-modernity seem to concur that a necessary first step is to reconsider what is meant by the modern age, by the idea of modernity. From a position broadly sympathetic to the idea of postmodernity Kroker and Cook (1988) place emphasis upon the emergence of a distinctive physics, logic, and ethics held to be constitutive of the modern experience. In their view the modern age began with Augustine's break with the classical conception of reason and reconstitution of the discourse of Western metaphysics. Kroker and Cook argue that '[with] Augustine's "registration in consciousness" of the *analyticus* of being/will/intelligence and with his ethical defence of the "will to truth" as a historical *and* moral necessity, the modern age is suddenly upon us – in the fourth century after Christ' (1988, p. 72). Hence their call to rethink the crisis of the modern age in relation to the metaphysics of classical Antiquity and early Christianity. Analysts sceptical about the idea of postmodernity have argued in a similar vein for a reconsideration of the meaning of the modern age, whilst simultaneously emphasising its persisting vitality (Burger 1984/85); its continuing impact on human experience (Berman 1983); and, as yet, its incomplete fulfilment and unrealised potential or promise (Habermas 1981).

Although there has been a tendency to equate the emergence of modernity with the advent of a 'tradition of reason' at the turn of the eighteenth century, what is generally identified as 'the Enlightenment', it is clear that other historical moments have been identified as marking the beginning of the modern age. Certainly Kroker and Cook locate the dawn of the modern age well before the 'rationalist calculus of the Enlightenment'. However, a more frequent reference is to a series of events which occurred in the course of the fifteenth and sixteenth centuries, namely the 'discovery of the "new world", the Renaissance, and the Reformation' (Habermas 1987, p. 5). These events set Western European societies on a distinctively different developmental path, one which culminated in the eighteenth century in political, economic, and intellectual transformations from which modern society and a self-consciousness of the present as a 'new age', modernity, developed. The idea of modernity as a distinctive era of history is explicitly addressed by Toynbee (1954a) and Berman (1983). In a wide-ranging historical survey Toynbee locates the beginning of the modern age of Western history in a series of developments which occurred around the turn of the fifteenth and sixteenth centuries amongst the peoples on the Atlantic seaboard of Europe. Notably, there was the emergence of a form of 'cultural pharisaism' and a mastery of oceanic navigation techniques, which allowed Western peoples to discover new continents and cultures and to constitute themselves as different, as superior, a corollary of which has been the identification of the form of life considered peculiar to the modern West with the value of 'civilisation'.[1]

A different analysis of the idea of modernity as an era of history is offered by Berman. In a discussion of the modern experience – 'of space and time, of the self and others, of life's possibilities and perils' – Berman distinguishes between three distinctive historical phases in the development of modernity, that 'paradoxical unity, . . . unity of disunity . . . [which] pours us all into a maelstrom of perpetual disintegration and renewal, of struggle and contradiction, of ambiguity and anguish' (1983, p. 15). The first phase identified in the development of modernity extends from the beginning of the sixteenth to the end of the eighteenth century, a period in which people are just beginning to encounter the initial manifestations of modern forms of life. The second phase opens with the French Revolution and the upheavals in social, political, and personal life associated with 'the great revolutionary wave' of the late eighteenth century. Berman comments that 'the nineteenth century modern public can remember what it is like to live, materially and spiritually, in worlds that are not modern at all. From this inner dichotomy, this sense of living in two worlds simultaneously, the ideas of modernisation and modernism emerge and unfold' (Berman 1983, p. 17). The third phase is synonymous with the global diffusion of the process of modernisation which, in turn, precipitates more turmoil in social and political life, more uncertainty and agitation. In this final, contemporary phase,

> as the modern public expands, it shatters into a multitude of fragments, speaking incommensurable private languages; the idea of modernity, conceived in numerous fragmentary ways, loses much of its vividness, resonance and depth, and loses its capacity to organise and give meaning to people's lives. As a result of all this, we find ourselves today in the midst of a modern age that has lost touch with the roots of its own modernity.
>
> (Berman 1983, p. 17)

One obvious sign of this loss of touch for Berman is the contemporary preoccupation with the 'mystique' of the postmodern, to which his analysis of the phenomenal forms of modernity is, in part, a critical response.

Although the idea of a distinctively modern age, an epoch of modernity, emerging around the turn of the sixteenth century, was only fully conceptualised in the course of the eighteenth century, the root idea of the 'modern' may be traced further back to the late fifth-century Latin form 'modernus' (Calinescu 1977 p. 14; Habermas 1981 p. 3). Habermas contends that the term was initially employed to distinguish an officially Christian present from a pagan past, and that subsequently 'modern' was employed to situate an existing epoch in relation to the past of antiquity – appearing and reappearing 'exactly during those periods in Europe when the consciousness of a new epoch formed itself through a renewed relationship to the ancients' (Habermas 1981, pp. 3–4). With the late seventeenth century *querelle des anciens et des modernes* antiquity no longer constituted the unquestioned reference point or model for knowledge and taste. The blind veneration of classical Antiquity was brought to a close by changes in the condition of knowledge, by a growing sense that 'in *any* . . . temporal relationship of two branches of the human race, the later in time *must* have advanced in mental development beyond the earlier in time' (Bock 1979, p. 50). From here a conception developed of modernity as a distinctive and superior period in the history of humanity. The old metaphor of 'modern' dwarfs standing on the shoulders of 'ancient' giants was displaced by a new and powerful alternative in which 'a temporal–psychological contrast is called upon to convey a sense of progressive development by which modernity is completely vindicated' (Calinescu 1977, p. 24). Henceforth Greek and Roman antiquity is conceived to be the dawn of civilisation, synonymous with infancy, inexperience and naivety, and it is the present, modernity, that is accorded the status of wisdom and experience.[2] Such a revised relationship between antiquity and modernity is clearly articulated by Marx in a number of brief reflections on the paradox of the continuing appreciation of Greek art. Marx argues that the conception of natural and social phenomena which informs and structures the imagination and artistic endeavour of classical Antiquity, that is, mythology, is displaced by the growth of the rational modern scientific world-view associated with the development of the forces and social relations of production. But if Greek art is a product of an earlier stage of social and economic development how is it that it continues to provide aesthetic pleasure? Marx's modern answer is that it is no surprise that art produced in the 'historical childhood of humanity' (1976, pp. 44–5) should continue to exert an eternal charm. Indeed its charm is considered to derive indirectly from the 'immature social conditions' which constitute its foundation.

On a number of counts, in relation to knowledge, aesthetic expression and appreciation, 'the moderns' considered themselves to be more advanced, more refined, and in possession of more profound truths than 'the ancients'. However, if the transformation in the idea of being modern, and its subsequent association with 'the infinite progress of knowledge and . . . the infinite advance towards social and moral betterment' (Habermas 1981, p. 4), was initially inspired by scientific and technological superiority, the questioning of the contemporary relevance and superiority of ancient forms and practices was initially most clearly articulated in the sphere of aesthetic discourse. During the eighteenth century the moderns questioned the idea of timeless aesthetic norms and began instead to think in terms of a 'relative and historically immanent beauty' (Calinescu 1977, p. 36; Habermas 1987, p. 8). The absence of timeless or universal criteria meant that modernity, constituted through a process of disarticulation from antiquity, had to confront the problem of grounding itself, of creating its own criteria of normativity. This general problem is first addressed in the realm of aesthetic criticism, and in particular in the work of Baudelaire, which is frequently cited as a turning point in the development of an understanding of the experience of modernity. Baudelaire is credited with indicating 'the price for which the sensation of the modern age may be had' (Benjamin 1973, p. 196); with illuminating the complexities and conditions of modern life by drawing attention to a 'new private and public world at the very moment when it is coming into being', and thereby making 'the men and women of his century aware of themselves as moderns' (Berman 1983, pp. 152: 132); with being 'one of the first artists to oppose aesthetic modernity . . . to the practical modernity of bourgeois civilisation' (Calinescu, 1977, p. 4); and finally for recognising that modernity 'can no longer gain its self-consciousness from opposition to an epoch rejected and surpassed' (Habermas 1987, p. 9).

As the comments offered above suggest, a definitive idea of the modern age, of modernity, has proven elusive. Modernity has been identified with ephemerality and contingency, with a radically different consciousness of time, a rebellion against normative standards, and a constitution of the 'new'. Of course these are not unrelated attributes, as Habermas suggests in a series of comments on the unfolding of modernity in various avant-garde movements, 'these forward gropings, this anticipation of an undefined future and the cult of the new, mean in fact the exaltation of the present' (1981, p. 5). However, if our ideas about the modern have been powerfully informed and influenced by the development of art, it is nevertheless evident that analysis of modernity through the discourse of aesthetic criticism constitutes merely one possible way of proceeding. Indeed it might be argued that '"the project of modernity" only comes into focus when we dispense with the usual concentration upon art' (Habermas 1981, p. 8). The project of modernity is traced by Habermas back to the attempts of the eighteenth-century Enlightenment philosophers to cultivate objective scientific inquiry and knowledge, universal morality and law, and autonomous art according to their respective inner logics, the principal objective being to achieve a 'rational organisation of everyday social life', to facilitate control of natural and social phenomena and forces, enhance understanding, promote progress, and increase the happiness of humanity. Modernity in this context is synonymous with the goals and values typical of the Western world, with the Western pattern of development as the norm and model to be emulated. It is coterminous with a conception of history as the progressive unfolding of Occidental rationality, with the ultimate

> victorious struggle of Reason against emotions or animal instincts, science against religion and magic, truth against prejudice, correct knowledge against superstition, reflection against uncritical existence, rationality against affectivity and the rule of custom. Within such a conceptualisation, the modern age defined itself as, above all, the kingdom of Reason and rationality.
>
> (Bauman 1987, p. 111)

This has constituted the most basic conception and self-definition of modernity, the most persistent understanding of the modern age. It receives its most celebrated elaboration in Weber's reflections on the distinctive features of the process of progressive rationalisation associated with the Occident (Habermas 1984; Bauman 1987, p. 112). Although this too has proven to be a controversial matter in so far as Weber's views on modernity are fragmentary, scattered throughout his work, and open to a number of interpretations (Roth 1987).

Alongside the various celebrations of modernity there have been a number of more sober reflections which have questioned both the feasibility and desirability of the project. The assumption of an increasing growth of rationality and its equation with a conception of historical progress began to be questioned towards the end of the nineteenth century, as did the costs and problems which were increasingly recognised to be a corollary of the benefits. For example, Freud drew attention to the discontents and ailments synonymous with the development of modern civilisation; Nietzsche depicted the modern age as one of struggle in which the outcome could not be guaranteed, and where the aftermath would include both victors and vanquished; and Simmel drew attention to the complex contradictions endemic in modern urban forms of social life (Bauman 1987, pp. 113–14). An additional set of doubts and criticisms of the various transformations associated with socioeconomic and technological modernity are articulated in the discourse of aesthetic modernity to which I have already briefly referred. Calinescu suggests that these two modernities are quite distinct and 'bitterly conflicting'. One expounds a doctrine of progress, emphasises the virtues and benefits of science and technology, and equates increasing rationality with freedom; the other, 'radical antibourgeois' form of modernity, rejects middle-class values and attempts to negate existing cultural forms and practices. A comparable contrast is developed in Bell's (1976) analysis of the cultural contradictions besetting contemporary (postindustrial) capitalism. The difference between the two analyses is that Bell bemoans the advent of adversarial cultural forms and worries about the threat to the middle-class value system.

What worries Habermas is that the spirit of aesthetic modernity is on the wane, that 'this modernism arouses a much fainter response than it did fifteen years ago', and, more seriously, that throughout the 'entire Western World a climate has developed that furthers capitalist modernisation processes as well as trends critical of cultural modernism' (1981, pp. 5:13). Although we have far from finished with the question of modernity, it is clear that some consideration needs to be given to the conceptualisation of modernism.

ON MODERNISM

In response to the confusing profusion and conflation of references to the modern age and modernism Lash (1987) has proposed that our age, the 'modern', should be understood not as 'modernity', but rather in terms of 'modernism'. The argument is that modernity is generally considered to have been inaugurated in the sixteenth and seventeenth centuries and 'modern*ism* is usually taken as a paradigm change in the arts which began at the end of the nineteenth century' (Lash 1987, p. 355). Lash proposes that the concept of modernism be extended to encompass contemporary social and cultural practices, practices which have, at times, been treated as an exemplification of the emergence of *post*-modern forms. However, such observations beg the question of the meaning or, rather, meanings of modernism, and it is to this matter that our attention should first be directed.

Modernism was initially employed in the eighteenth century by defenders of the classical tradition antagonised by the claims advanced by 'moderns' during the course of the infamous *querelle*. The term only began to be used in a positive sense to describe an aesthetic or cultural movement towards the close of the century, the first approving references appearing in Dario's praise of the work of the Mexican author Ricardo Contreras and, subsequently, in 1890, in the constitution of *modernismo* as a movement in Latin America for cultural emancipation from Spain. Hispanic modernism constitutes a synthesis of all the significant late nineteenth-century French literary and cultural movements or tendencies, a distillation of the radical innovative tendency or spirit common to the various 'conflicting schools, movements, or even sects (*"Parnasse"*, *"décadisme"*, "symbolisme", "école romane", etc)' (Calinescu 1977, p. 70). However, barely two decades later criticisms were being expressed that the term meant something different to each analyst using it, that it referred to no specific school or movement, and at best represented an ambiguous periodising term. For many critics of the time the term was deemed to serve no useful purpose, merely reflecting a passing fad or fashion. Calinescu's response to the reduction of modernism to the status of a temporary fad takes the form of an argument that the phenomenon is of broader significance, that Hispanic modernism shares a number of distinctive elements with other Western cultures encountering modernity. Modernism is described as a common feature of Western culture during the late nineteenth and early twentieth centuries. Not a school or a movement, but rather something of the order of a cultural *mentalité*. An appropriate example of such a position is provided in the work of Federico de Onis. Seeking to salvage the concept of modernism from its critics, de Onis argues that there is an indissoluble connection between the ideas of modernism and modernity. Modernism is conceptualised as 'the search for modernity' and, given the specificity or difference of the latter is constituted through its opposition to, or break with, the traditional, modernism effectively becomes an 'antitraditional tradition'. For de Onis the discourse of Hispanic modernism constitutes a specific instance of a 'universal literary and spiritual crisis . . . manifesting itself in art, science, religion, politics and, gradually, in all other aspects of life' (quoted in Calinescu 1977, p. 76). Essentially modernism is deployed by de Onis as a broad period concept to analyse a series of changes and developments in the production of literary works. These include a late nineteenth-century stage of transition from romanticism to modernism, the subsequent 'triumph of modernism', a postmodern reaction, and finally the emergence of ultramodernism. Underlying each of these respective stages is the common denominator of modernity, which by definition, and in contrast to the persisting forms and practices associated with tradition, is considered to be constantly in flux. Many of the arguments and positions outlined above return in contemporary debates over the alleged development of a 'postmodern condition' and associated emergence of 'postmodernity'. These will be considered below.

However, before proceeding to a discussion of the postmodern constellation a more detailed consideration needs to be given to the question of modernism. One response to the idea of *post*-modernism, shared by a range of analysts, has been to return to the question of the history of modernism. The principal focus of such works falls upon the relationship between sociocultural, political, and economic changes associated with the capitalist mode of production, and various manifestations and transformations identified with the idea of modernism (Bell 1976: 1980; Berman 1983; Habermas 1981; Williams 1989; Harvey 1989). Although there are evident differences in conceptualisation and periodisation in the analyses of modernism to be considered below, there is a common denominator, namely the presence of a broadly comparable antipathy to the idea of the *post*-modern.

In an analysis of contemporary capitalism American sociologist Daniel Bell argues that there is a growing disjunction between economic and cultural forms of life that derives primarily from the transformation of modernism. Bell rejects the holistic view of society. In its place he introduces a conception of contemporary society as a problematic amalgam of three quite distinctive realms or spheres, namely social structure, culture, and polity. It is a perceived disjunction or lack of fit between these three realms, with their own distinctive rhythms of change, patterns of legitimation and characteristic forms of conduct, that Bell believes is responsible for the social tensions and conflicts which have become an increasing feature of Western societies over the past 150 years. In particular it is transformations in the realms of social structure (defined in terms of the economy, technology, and occupational system) and culture that are considered to be the principal source of tensions in the present. Bell argues that the economic and cultural impulses which drove both entrepreneurs and artists relentlessly to 'search out the new, to rework nature, and to refashion consciousness' (1976, p. 16) began as aspects of the same surge towards modernity and modernism. However, in the course of their development the economic and cultural impulses of modernism came to be antagonistic. Within Western societies a radical individualism in economics, and a predisposition towards the displacement of traditional social practices and relations by modern forms has been accompanied by an opposition to, if not a fear of, forms of radical experimental individualism in the sphere of culture. On the other hand, modernists in the cultural sphere, whilst being well disposed towards exploration and experimentation in various areas of aesthetic experience and expression, have been critical of the utilitarian, materialistic, and excessively disciplined forms considered typical of 'bourgeois life'. The outcome is a disjunction which is considered to be the principal source of the cultural contradictions besetting contemporary (post)industrial capitalism. In brief, Bell comes to the conclusion that the traditional cultural source of legitimation of capitalism has been eroded and ultimately undermined. Ascetic Protestant values which have promoted self-restraint, discipline, and the idea of work as a calling have been lost as a consequence of developments internal to the capitalist mode of production itself – the introduction of the instalment plan, instant credit, mass production and consumption – and the subversion of bourgeois forms of life by modernist culture.

Modernism is described by Bell as a cultural temper or mood, one which is present in all the arts. Although modernist aesthetic forms appear to lack a single unifying principle, it is argued that they share a number of important features. These include a tendency to be 'wilfully opaque' and 'self-consciously experimental', the objective of which is to create in the reader–observer–audience a sense of unfamiliarity, disturbance and shock. Modernism in this sense constitutes a response to late nineteenth-century transformations in sense perception and self-consciousness, which arose from two principal sources. The first source concerns changes in space–time orientations associated with major innovations in communication and transportation, the second is the 'crisis in self-consciousness' arising from an erosion of the beliefs and values, guarantees, securities or certainties associated with religious world-views. With modernism the emphasis is upon movement and flux, on the absolute present, 'now', if not the future *as* present. Modernism is synonymous with discontinuity, with a constant struggle against, and attempted negation of, all that has gone before. It is, in brief, characterised by a 'refusal to accept limits, the insistence on continually reaching out . . . [to] a destiny that is always *beyond*: beyond morality, beyond tragedy, beyond culture' (Bell 1976, p. 50). One important implication of this is that modernism constitutes an adversary culture, one which seeks to 'negate every prevalent style, including, in the end, its own' (Bell 1976, p. 47).

In Bell's view the high point of modernism as an innovative and effective adversarial cultural form now lies in the distant past.[3] Although a modernist artistic syntax which eclipses the distance between artist and spectator, or art work and aesthetic experience, is conceived to be increasingly apparent from the mid-nineteenth century, it is the period from 1890 to 1930 that Bell regards as the high point of exploration and experiment in style and form. The suggestion is that after this time there has scarcely been any innovation of any significance or value in the realm of culture, a claim which leads to the conclusion that 'today modernism is exhausted'. The exhaustion of modernism is associated with the development of mass cultural forms and practices, and their associated industries. Innovative and creative impulses are held to have been dissipated or rendered predictable through the increasingly extensive and flexible processes of accommodation and institutionalisation associated with the growth of mass communication and culture. In effect modernism has become familiar, accepted, and, to some at least, pleasing. The upshot has been that the disturbing and shocking no longer disturbs or shocks, and anti-bourgeois rebellious impulses have become standard fare, part of the mainstream. In brief, 'experimental forms have become the syntax and semiotics of advertising and haute couture' (Bell 1976, p. 20), a development which parallels the increasing significance accorded to consumption, the commodity as sign, and signs as commodities within the contemporary capitalist mode of production (Baudrillard 1981).

The tenor of Bell's comments on modernism is generally critical. The qualification is important, for Bell does briefly introduce a distinction between 'traditional' modernism and postmodernism, describing the former as 'within the constraints of art . . . [and] on the side of order', whereas the latter, in contrast, is considered to overflow 'the vessels of art' (1980, p. 288: 1976, p. 51). But for the most part there is little sign that the possible exhaustion of modernism is to be lamented. To the contrary, it is the apparent erosion of the traditional bourgeois organisation of life, with its associated forms of rationality and sobriety, that represents the primary focus of concern. The scenario outlined is of contemporary capitalist society in crisis as a consequence of a lack of regulation, or an absence of adequate restraint, on conduct, desires, and appetites. The condition is a product of the pursuit of hedonism in the economic sphere and modernism in the cultural sphere. But if the former is viewed with regret, and is regarded as a significant contributor to the growing imbalance of 'private appetite and public responsibility', it is the cultural mode of modernism which ultimately constitutes the target of Bell's criticisms. A strong sense of disapproval of the moral temper and culture of modernism is conveyed in a series of comments. For example, Bell refers to 'the overturn of the "rational cosmology" which shaped Western thought from the fifteenth century on: the sequence of time . . . the interior distance of space . . . and the sense of proportion and measure that united both in a single conception of order' (Bell 1976, pp. 118–19); the emphasis within modernist culture on 'anti-cognitive and anti-intellectual modes', 'apocalyptic moods and anti-rational modes of behaviour' (1976, p. 84); the promotion of 'pre-rational spontaneity' in place of reason (1976, p. 143); and the pursuit of excess and release without 'any sure moral or cultural guides as to what worthwhile experiences may be' (1976, p. 145). Although modernism as an *innovative* cultural force is considered, on the one hand, to be exhausted, it is evident that, on the other hand, Bell believes its effects continue to contribute to the cultural contradictions of contemporary capitalism.

As I have implied above, Bell's most critical comments are reserved for a cultural configuration which carries 'the logic of modernism to its farthest reaches' (1976, p. 51: 1980, p. 288), that is, postmodernism. The emergence of a powerful current of postmodernism is associated with a number of events and developments which are traced to the 'permissive' decade of the 1960s. Bell describes postmodernism in a number of negative ways. It is said to be exemplified by 'porno-pop culture'; an evaluation of the instinctual over the 'aesthetic justification for life'; a dissolution of the distinction between art and life; and ultimately with a position in which 'reason is the enemy and the desires of the body the truth' (1980, p. 288). In brief, postmodernism seems to constitute evil incarnate for Bell, nothing less than 'the psychological spearhead for an onslaught on the values and motivational patterns of "ordinary" behaviour, in the name of liberation, eroticism, freedom of impulse, and the like' (1976, p. 52).

The idea that 'the postmodern' constitutes a cultural development which remains broadly within the logic of modernism is a position shared by a diverse range of analysts and commentators. However, before turning to the ambiguities, idiosyncrasies, and insights which have been a feature of the debate over the postmodern condition, there are additional analyses of the question of modernism that need to be briefly explored, analyses which situate modernism and its transformations within the context of a broader process of 'societal modernisation' (Habermas 1981). Whereas Bell analyses modernism as a virtually autonomous cultural phenomenon, Berman and Harvey attempt to situate it in relation to the development of the capitalist mode of production, and associated social and economic processes of 'modernisation'. Specifically, both Berman and Harvey argue that the transient, fleeting, and contingent character of modernism, the feeling and experience of insecurity, and the transitoriness of things associated with modernity, derive in the final instance from the 'desperate pace and frantic rhythm that capitalism imparts to every facet of modern life' (Berman 1983, p. 91), from 'the changing meaning of space and time which capitalism has . . . wrought' (Harvey 1989, p. 283). Similarly, both regard modernism as a complex and contradictory phenomenon, a phenomenon with an interesting history and continuing contemporary relevance. However, there are a number of differences between their respective positions. Berman seems to equate modernism with a perpetual process of upheaval, destruction, and renewal, a process in which the forms and practices of the past are continually overturned in the course of an endless pursuit of new 'forms of reality, of beauty, of freedom, of justice' more appropriate to, or compatible with, the turbulent experiences of personal and social life synonymous with modern times. The implication is that the modern world has changed and will go on changing, whilst nevertheless remaining quintessentially modern. In other words,

> the culture of modernism will go on developing new visions and expressions of life: for the same economic and social drives that endlessly transform the world around us,both for good and evil, also transform the inner lives of the men and women who fill this world and make it go.
>
> (Berman 1983, p. 348)

A corollary of this is that a periodising conception of the postmodern appears to be, at best, excessively premature. As Berman comments, 'those who are waiting for the end of the modern age can be assured of steady work' (1983, p. 347). One might ask, is it at all conceivable, within Berman's terms of reference, for there to be an end to the modern age? Or do we encounter here an alternative conception of the 'end of history'?

In contrast, Harvey is both more sensitive to significant transformations of modernism and more open to exploring the possibility that a number of developments in intellectual, aesthetic, and cultural life reveal the emergence of *post*-modern forms, or a condition of *post*-modernity. To a considerable degree Harvey endorses many of the elements identified by Berman in his analysis of the experience of modernity. For example Harvey comments that 'the only secure thing about modernity is its insecurity' (1989, p. 11), and subsequently proceeds to draw attention to the way in which 'the commodification and commercialisation of a market for cultural products during the nineteenth century . . . was bound to reinforce processes of "creative destruction" within the aesthetic field itself (1989, p. 22). However, if Harvey, like Berman, ultimately treads 'the path of the moderns', the journey as a whole includes a serious exploration of the postmodern terrain. But before proceeding to an analysis of reactions and responses to the postmodern, it is necessary to trace briefly the various transformations to which modernism has been subject, 'if only to help understand what kind of modernism the postmodernists are reacting against' (1989, p. 27). Harvey distinguishes between five broad phases in the development of modernism. The first is synonymous with the Enlightenment and the assumption that 'the world could be controlled and rationally ordered if we could only picture and represent it rightly'. This hope begins to fall apart after 1848 with the beginning of a second phase, in which accelerating industrialisation, massive urbanisation, and political dissension precipitate an increasing diversity of forms of experience, systems of thought, and representation. Harvey notes that a 'furore of experimentation resulted in a qualitative transformation in what modernisation was about somewhere between 1910 and 1915' (1989, p. 28). The transformation of forms of representation and knowledge, of literary texts, art, music, linguistics, and science, derived from a growing disenchantment with Enlightenment thought and the associated promise of progress. In the interwar years 'modernism took a strongly positivist turn', exemplified by the practices of modernist architecture, science, and technology. During this third phase modernist and realist art was dominated by the myth of the machine. Simultaneously the philosophical ground was being prepared for a fourth phase, which began after 1945 and led to the emergence of 'high' modernism. In the post-war period,

High modernist art, architecture, literature etc, became established arts and practices in a society where a corporate capitalist version of the Enlightenment project of development for progress and human emancipation held sway as a political–economic dominant.

(Harvey, 1989, p. 35)

However, such a process of incorporation is not necessarily synonymous with the exhaustion of modernism. Harvey argues that although modernism has been absorbed into 'official and establishment ideology' it has not thereby become a spent force. It remains a powerful aesthetic form even if it has lost its revolutionary appeal. The emergence of a diverse range of cultural forms, practices, and movements in response to the existence of 'high' modernism constitutes the final phase identified by Harvey. Once again it is with the appearance of a range of cultural phenomena in the late 1960s that the first traces of a 'subsequent turn to postmodernism' are identified.

The difficulty of deciding exactly what modernism might refer to has led to a number of different responses from other analysts, whose work might also be located within the generous parameters of historical materialism occupied by Berman and Harvey (cf. Anderson 1984; Williams 1989). For example, Anderson argues that the aesthetic forms of modernism have a temporal and spatial specificity, and that Berman's 'perennialist' conception is misguided. Describing modernism as an aesthetic form which is 'generally dated precisely *from* the 20th century', and whose geographical distribution is uneven, Anderson proposes 'a *conjunctural* explanation of the set of aesthetic practices and doctrines subsequently grouped together as "modernist"' (1984, p. 104). The cultural force field of modernism is constituted, in Anderson's view, by three coordinates, namely a highly formalised and institutionalised 'academicism' in the arts; the emergence of 'the key technologies or inventions of the second industrial revolution: telephone, radio, automobile, aircraft, and so on' (1984, p. 104); and finally a pervasive sense that, within Europe, a social revolution is a distinct possibility. Each of these coordinates contributed to the constitution of modernism. Official academicism provided a common critical focus for a range of aesthetic forms and practices possessing little or no unity, and to that extent it was constitutive of 'modernism'. New technological innovations, the subsequent development and effects of which were unknowable, provided a powerful stimulus to the imagination. And lastly 'the haze of social revolution drifting across the horizon of this epoch gave it much of its apocalyptic light for those currents of modernism most unremittingly and violently radical in their rejection of the social order as a whole' (Anderson 1984, p. 105).

However, the historical conditions which were constitutive of modernism were destroyed by World War II. The old aristocratic order, which had constituted a critical reference point and resource for the diverse aesthetic practices of modernism, disappeared with the universalisation of bourgeois democracy. The advent of mass production, mass consumption, and an associated monolithic industrial capitalist order resolved doubts and erased hopes about the form socioeconomic and technological developments might assume in the future. Finally the post-war settlement, the 'onset of the Cold war and the Sovietisation of Eastern Europe' put paid to the hopes for social revolution. It is in this context, where the conditions necessary to ensure the vitality of modernism have ostensibly disappeared, that Anderson locates the emergence of 'the ideology and cult of modernism', the contemporary preoccupation with modernism. If modernism serves to identify *provisionally* a cultural force field peculiar to the European or Western world during the first half of the twentieth century, further consideration suggests to Anderson that in fact it is now 'the emptiest of all cultural categories . . . It designates no describable object in its own right at all: it is completely lacking in positive content' (1984, pp. 112–13). Describing modernism as a 'portmanteau concept' which conceals a diverse range of, at times, incompatible aesthetic forms and practices, Anderson concludes on a note which ironically is reminiscent of Bell's observations on the current fate of modernism. Anderson comments that,

> There is no other aesthetic marker so vacant or vitiated. For what once was modern is soon obsolete. The futility of the term, and its attendant ideology, can be seen all too clearly from current attempts to cling to its wreckage and yet swim with the tide still further beyond it, in the coinage of 'post modernism'.
> (Anderson 1984, p. 113)

Like Bell, Anderson laments the absence of 'creative' contemporary cultural forms and practices, a condition which is presented as a corollary of the emergence of a monolithic industrial capitalist civilisation. Similarly, they share a strong antipathy to the idea of postmodernism. However, given their contrasting theoretical orientations and analytic preferences it is no surprise to find them advocating quite different responses to present conditions and problems.

159

Whereas Bell recommends a 'return in Western society of some conception of religion' (1976, p. 29) as a potential solution to the crisis of modernity, Anderson continues to cling to an unexplicated conception of socialist revolution, the vocation of which is 'neither to prolong nor to fulfil modernity, but to abolish it' (1984, p. 113). This of course leaves open the complex and contentious matter of the (necessary) relationship between the enthusiasm for socialist revolution and the experience of modernity designated for abolition. Furthermore, the positive benefits and developments ascribed to a 'genuine socialist culture' by Anderson bear more than a passing resemblance to some of the characteristics outlined in 'positive' or 'progressive' versions of the postmodern condition (Foster 1985). For example, the idea of a culture which multiplies 'the different, in a far greater *variety* of concurrent styles and practices than have ever existed before', and in addition institutes 'diversity founded on the far greater plurality and complexity of possible ways of living' (Anderson 1984, p. 113), not subject to divisions of gender, race, or class, might well be equated with a number of 'progressive' conceptions of postmodernism, as we will see.

Anderson's critical analysis of modernity and modernism is effectively endorsed in Williams's (1989) reflections on the emergence, development, and subsequent integration of modernism within the new international capitalism. The canonisation of modernism within the gallery–academy–exhibition circuit in the post-war period, and the compatibility of its perpetually changing forms, styles, and techniques with the demands of the market for novelty – new commodities, signifying systems, and desires – leads Williams to conclude that 'the innovations of what is called Modernism have become the new but fixed forms of our present moment' (1989, p. 35). To escape what is described as the 'non-historical fixity of *post*-modernism' Williams argues that it will be necessary to articulate an alternative tradition, one able to address itself 'to a modern *future* in which community may be imagined again' (1989, p. 35). With this we are returned to a familiar but nevertheless problematic scenario, one in which the clear implication is of some form of 'socialist alternative' reconstituted around 'new kinds of communal, cooperative, and collective institutions' (Williams 1985, p. 123). The idea that modernity and modernism are concepts which lack specificity is endorsed, albeit in a radically different manner, by Foucault. Responding to a series of questions about the relationship between his work and contemporary social thought, Foucault comments that he is not sure what is meant by either modernity or postmodernity, that it is not clear what kinds of problems the two terms refer to.[4] In response to the ambiguous idea of modernity as an historical epoch 'preceded by a more or less naive or archaic premodernity and followed by an enigmatic and troubling postmodernity' Foucault proposes an alternative, namely to conceive of modernity as an attitude rather than an historical era, as

> a mode of relating to contemporary reality; a voluntary choice made by certain people; . . . a way of thinking and feeling; a way, too, of acting and believing that at one and the same time marks a relation of belonging and presents itself as a task . . . And consequently, rather than seeking to distinguish the 'modern era' from the 'premodern' or 'postmodern' . . . it would be more useful to try to find out how the attitude of modernity, ever since its formation, has found itself struggling with attitudes of 'countermodernity'.
>
> (Foucault 1986, p. 39)

An attitude or ethos of modernity, one which involves a permanent critique of ourselves and our era, continues to link us with the concerns of the Enlightenment. By this Foucault does not mean that we have to declare ourselves either 'for' or 'against' the Enlightenment. It is not a question of either remaining 'within the tradition of its rationalism' or, alternatively, of trying 'to escape from its principles of rationality' (1986, p. 43), but rather of recognising that how we think about ourselves and the present era continues, to a degree at least, to be determined by the Enlightenment. Specifically, it is the existence and relevance of a form of analysis which is simultaneously critical, historical, and experimental – the aim of which is to problematise our relationship to the present, illuminate through historical analysis the limits to which we are subject, and thereby open up the possibility of transgression – that is considered by Foucault to constitute the most significant element connecting us to the Enlightenment. Such an analytic attitude or ethos of critique, directed towards a 'permanent creation of ourselves in our autonomy', is presented as a definitive feature of modernity, rather than as a symptom of an emerging 'postmodern condition'.

The analyses considered briefly above illustrate the range of views which have been expressed on the subject of modernism and modernity. Although there are a number of significant differences between the respective analyses, there are also some interesting similarities, the most relevant to present concerns being the expression of a generally sceptical and/or critical response to the idea of the postmodern.

THE END OF MODERNITY?

One of the key figures in the debate over modernity and the idea of *post*-modernity has been Habermas. In a series of essays and articles Habermas has sought to counter the critical response to the 'project of modernity' associated with the postmodern configuration. For Habermas the issue appears to be quite clear. Postmodernism is identified as one of the major forms in which conservative responses to the apparent shortcomings of the project of modernity have been articulated. The idea of the postmodern signifies for Habermas 'the end of the Enlightenment' or, more precisely, it constitutes a movement 'beyond the horizon of the tradition of reason in which European modernity once understood itself' (1987, p. 4). As such, postmodernism appears to be synonymous with anti-modernism and a critique of reason *tout court*.

Although Habermas accepts the validity of some of the limitations attributed to modernism by 'postmodern' social theorists, he rejects the idea that the 'project of modernity' should be abandoned. Habermas acknowledges that the Enlightenment hope that development of 'objective science, universal morality and law, and autonomous art, according to their inner logic' (1981, p. 9) would facilitate a more rational organisation of everyday social life has yet to be fulfilled. As the spheres of science, morality, and art have become increasingly differentiated from one another, they have become the exclusive province of professionals and experts, and thereby further removed, if not entirely divorced, from the forms of understanding and communication intrinsic to everyday life. In short, increasing rationality has not been synonymous with an enhanced understanding of self and others, or the promotion of moral progress and human happiness. But for Habermas this does not mean that we should give up 'modernity and its project as a lost cause' (1981, p. 11). Depicted as a 'postmodern' reaction, the latter is considered to be a far from appropriate or necessary response, for it constitutes a 'totalising repudiation of modern forms of life' that is 'insensitive to the highly *ambivalent* content of cultural and social modernity' (Habermas 1987, p. 338). However, if Habermas is justified in drawing attention to both the continuing promise of modernity and the diversity of modern forms of life, his conceptualisation and understanding of what has been termed postmodernity, or postmodernism, is problematic, if not 'insensitive' to the range of different views and positions outlined on the subject of a possible postmodern condition. It is to a consideration of different conceptions and analyses of postmodernity and postmodernism that I now propose to turn.

The postmodern condition, and its associated cluster of terms, is no less ambiguous than the modern and its corollaries. If the roots of a postmodern critique of 'Occidental rationalism' may be traced to Nietzsche's address of the discourse of modernity (Habermas 1987, pp. 74:83–105), a qualitative transformation or transcendence of the modern by *post*-modernism is first identified within aesthetic discourse, in debates over the emergence of ostensibly novel cultural and literary forms. An early trace is present in the analysis by Federico de Onis of the poetry of Spanish and Latin-American writers. Describing modernism as a broad period concept, de Onis situates the emergence of postmodernism in the first decade of the twentieth century, and considers it to be 'a conservative reaction within modernism itself, when the latter settles down and becomes rhetorical like any literary revolution that has won out' (quoted in Calinescu 1977, p. 77). As will become evident below, postmodernism and postmodernity are rarely rigorously differentiated from modernism and modernity, indeed within aesthetic, philosophical, and sociological discourse there has been a marked tendency to conceptualise the *post*-modern as a part of the modern. For example, Lyotard talks of the postmodern as 'undoubtedly a part of the modern' (1986, p. 79); Graff argues that 'postmodernism should be seen not as breaking with romantic and modernist assumptions but rather as a logical culmination of the premises of these earlier movements' (1973, p. 385); and Raulet suggests that 'post-modernity is not necessarily the impasse of a decomposition that abolishes reason . . . [it] could be a renewed modernity, not in the sense of a repetition and an intensification of the modern failure, but of a new start' (1986, p. 162).

If a conception of postmodernism was first articulated in a literary context, to denote a conservative reaction within modernism, it was in an architectural setting that postmodernism initially became most publicly visible, when 'an eclectic collage of contrasting architectural styles pillaged from disparate periods of history, together with borrowings from the contemporary vernacular, came to disturb the austerely elegant functionalism of the International Style' (Burgin

1986, p. 45). But the term has also been employed in a number of other contexts, in relation to a broader range of forms, discourses, and sensibilities. The postmodern problematic has been invoked to distinguish an historical period, an aesthetic style, and a change in the condition of knowledge; to conceptualise difference – a distinctive form beyond the modern – as well as similarity – a variant of the modern, or its limit form; and to describe affirmative or reactionary and critical or progressive discourses and movements.

The idea of a postmodern historical era is introduced by Toynbee in a contrast drawn between a 'modern' chapter of Western history, dating from approximately the end of the fifteenth century to the beginning of the twentieth century, and a subsequent 'post-Modern age'. Toynbee suggests that it is the prevalence of middle-class forms of life that constitutes *modern* Western culture and civilisation. In effect, that 'Western Communities became "modern" . . . just as soon as they had succeeded in producing a bourgeoisie that was both numerous enough and competent enough to become the predominant element in society' (1954a, p. 338). However, a number of events, including the rise of an industrial urban working class, have led, in Toynbee's view, to the emergence of a postmodern chapter in Western history, and by implication to a displacement or dissolution of revered middle-class forms of life. The scenario outlined is of an unprecedentedly prosperous, comfortable, and overcomplacent late nineteenth-century Western middle class, which had begun to lose the necessary fund of creative psychic energy required to drive the industrial capitalist system (1954b, p. 576). Imagining that history had reached its end, that a 'safe, satisfactory Modern life had miraculously come to stay as a timeless present (1954b, p. 421), the Western middle classes were ill-prepared for the advent of a postmodern age. It is the beginning of World War I, 'the first post-modern general war' (Toynbee 1954b, p. 422), that disrupted the cosy complacency and fragile security of the Western middle classes. This event and its sequel, the second act which began in 1939, are considered by Toynbee to have brought into focus a series of problems specific to Western civilisation, unprecedented problems arising from the accelerating pace of technological change, the impact of associated innovations, and the persistence of political and economic inequalities which had become, in principle at least, remedial. In Toynbee's view such problems raised the spectre of the mortality of Western civilisation, if not, in the case of the destructive use of atomic energy, the entire human species.[5]

The unparalleled predicament confronting Western civilisation emanates from an increasing lack of correspondence between powerful and rapid developments in technology and slower, more uneven changes in the spiritual, moral, and political capacities of humanity. Technological developments may have dramatically increased 'the extent of the mastery that a Late Modern and post-Modern Western Man had acquired over Non-Human Nature', and have made a significant contribution to 'the constantly accelerating rapidity of the process of social change in the Western World' (Toynbee 1954b, p. 465), but the ability to relate to one another, and the capacity to cope with moral and political problems and conflicts has not kept pace. The pursuit of technological mastery over nature and an accelerating rate of social change have been longstanding features of Western civilisation, constitutive of the modern age, of modernity. However, Toynbee argues that unprecedented increases in the power of technological innovations have precipitated a qualitative transformation in human affairs. Innovations in the power of production technologies have fundamentally transformed experiences of space and time. Just as 'the invention of the steamship, the railway train, and the motor-car had "annihilated distance" for travellers . . . [so] telegraph, telephone, gramophone, radio, television, and radar had "annihilated distance" in a fourth dimension by enabling human beings to communicate with one another instantaneously round the whole circumference of the globe' (1954b, p. 467). The scale and pace of such social and technological changes are presented as problematic, as virtually 'beyond the adaptational capacity of a single life', a view which receives a subsequent endorsement in Toffler's (1971) conception of the experience of 'future shock' arising from rapid 'postindustrial' forms of change. The problems of coping with the scale, pace, and moral and political impact of socioeconomic and technological changes are exacerbated, in Toynbee's view, by a further event, namely the deployment towards the close of World War II of the 'titanic force of atomic energy', a force unleashed on the citizens of Hiroshima and Nagasaki.[6]

The scale, pace, and impact of 'postmodern' forms of social and technological change are ultimately lamented by Toynbee because of the corrosive effects they are alleged to have had on the hegemony of the 'North-Western European middle class'. The post-war scenario outlined is of middle class political and economic power being conceded, both at home and abroad. At home it is portrayed as concessions to 'the industrial workers', a corollary of which is a significant shift on the part of the middle class away from the pursuit of 'personal economic profits to the altruistic motive of serving the public interest' (Toynbee 1954b, p. 572). A redirection of the 'creative psychic energy' of the middle class away from private enterprise and towards a growing public sphere – a 'ponderous public administration' – which threatens, in Toynbee's view, to spell capitalism's doom, and raises in turn the question of the prospects for Western civilisation as a whole. The concessions abroad, to 'Asiatic dominions' and 'new supra-national Great Powers', are considered to be further evidence of a postmodern relocation of the economic and political epicentre of Western civilisation, away from North-western Europe and towards America. Ironically, a quarter of a century later Daniel Bell articulates a similar nostalgic conservative concern about the postmodern cultural contradictions besetting middle-class values and life-styles, but in this instance it is American hegemony that is in question.

A number of parallels may be drawn between the respective works of Toynbee and Bell. Both identify a comparable time or age of transition; the undermining of a way of life, if not a civilisation; and an erosion of the creative energy or zest for work associated with the development of Western capitalism. Both appear to regret the displacement of 'high' and/or 'traditional' cultural forms, and to view with concern, if not contempt, the impact of new 'mass' forms of cultural production and consumption associated with economic and technological innovations. Furthermore, they each identify the public sphere, or public household, and its relationship to private interests and enterprise as an increasingly critical problem within Western capitalist social formations. However, it is their mutual understanding of the crisis of postmodern Western civilisation as essentially one of the absence or loss of spiritual values and belief that constitutes the most significant parallel between their respective analyses. Where Toynbee suggests that the predicaments confronting Western civilisation in a postmodern age might be alleviated through a transfer of energy from economics to religion (1954b, p. 641), Bell argues that a return to religion in Western civilisation is required if postmodern problems arising from the existing 'shambles of appetite and self-interest and . . . destruction of the moral circle which engirds mankind' (1976, p. 171) are to be resolved. It is evident that for both the concept of the 'postmodern' carries strong negative connotations but, as I have demonstrated above, a critical response to the postmodern problematic is by no means a monopoly of cultural conservatives. However, responses to the postmodern problematic within social, cultural, and literary theory and analysis extend beyond the narrow range of positions considered above, to encompass other sociocultural, intellectual, and political positions and movements, of which some at least might be regarded as positive or progressive.

Although I have suggested that there are parallels between particular aspects of the respective works of Toynbee and Bell on the possible emergence of a 'postmodern' age or era, it is evident that the family of terms associated with the modern and the postmodern have had a significantly different trajectory in continental European and American contexts.

(POST)MODERNITY IN THE OLD AND NEW WORLDS

Postmodernity and postmodernism have achieved a high profile, they have 'taken off' (Hall 1986, p. 45). But postmodernism first achieved public prominence in America in the 1960s, in criticisms of the institutionalisation of 'high' culture and the incorporation of modernism within the mainstream (Howe 1971). The criticisms advanced of the political incorporation and economic institutionalisation of art within the culture industry parallel, to a degree, the concerns articulated by the European avant-garde earlier in the century. Indeed it might be argued that the emergence of postmodernism in the 1960s, articulating opposition to the neutralisation of modernism's critical potential, to its domestication or transformation into a form of affirmative culture, compensated for the absence of an indigenous avant-garde in the United States.

The relationship between the emergence of an American postmodernism, the European avant garde, and 'the international tradition of the modern' is explored by Huyssen (1981: 1984a). Huyssen attributes four major characteristics to American postmodernism in the 1960s, namely a strong spatiotemporal imagination; an attack on the institution of art; technological optimism; and a vigorous cultural populism. In so far as it displays a 'powerful sense of the future and of new frontiers, of rupture and discontinuity, of crisis and generational conflict'; attacks the tradition and institutional practices of high art; and manifests an 'exuberant technological optimism', it is suggested that 1960s American postmodernism is reminiscent of an earlier European avant-garde (1984a, pp. 20–3). But if it constituted a form of avant-garde, Huyssen adds that it 'must be seen as the endgame of the avant-garde and not the radical breakthrough it often claimed to be' (1981, p. 31). Just as the European avant-garde was ultimately undermined when it was recognised to be 'artistically significant by the same class whose values it so drastically rejected' (Calinescu 1977, p. 120), so postmodernism has been exhausted by the capacity of a 'technologically and economically fully developed media culture' to turn even the most serious challenges into marketable commodities or pleasing entertainments (Huyssen 1981, p. 32). Deprived of its avant-garde rhetoric, postmodernism has been described as a logical culmination of the premises of romantic–modernist traditions; as a reactionary tendency which 'reinforces the effects of technocratic bureaucratic society' (Graff 1973, p. 385); and as a style which emphasises diversity, displays a penchant for pastiche, and adopts an 'inclusivist' philosophy, advocating eclectic use of elements from the past (Ghirardo 1984/85, p. 189). One implication of this is that the apparently limitless assimilative capacity of contemporary society, exemplified by its ability both to convert attacks upon its values into 'pleasing entertainments' and neutralise opponents and critics with the rewards of 'success' (Howe 1971, pp. 16:224), leads postmodernism to suffer the very same fate as the avant-garde. But this is not the end of the story. For as the prospects and rhetoric of avant-gardism declined in the course of the 1970s, so a 'genuinely post-modern and post-avantgarde culture' (Huyssen 1984a, p. 24) developed. At the centre of this genuinely postmodern culture is a dissolution of the distance between 'high' and popular, or 'low' culture intrinsic to modernism. In other words,

> the great divide that separated high modernism from mass culture and that was codified in the various classical accounts of modernism no longer seems relevant to postmodern artistic or critical sensibilities.
>
> (Huyssen 1984a, p. 26)

A further manifestation of the transformation of postmodernism is the shift towards theory. Since the 1970s there has been a proliferation of theorising on the subject of postmodernism. Reflecting on the increase in postmodern literary theory and criticism Huyssen speculates that it may well signify a 'falling rate of artistic and literary creativity' (1981, p. 34), and/or, in the case of the turn by American critics to 'exotic' continental, primarily French, forms of social theory, a desperate attempt to salvage a vestige of avant-gardism.[7]

Ironically some of the key French texts which have featured prominently in debates over the ideas of postmodernism and postmodernity, for example the respective works of Derrida, Barthes, Foucault, Deleuze and Guattari, might more appropriately be read as analyses of modernism or modernity. Once again history appears to have repeated itself, for just as late nineteenth-century modernism was constituted from a range of literary tendencies and movements present in France, so 1970s postmodernism seems to have derived its principal impetus from French analyses which are primarily concerned with modernism and modernity. An example of the way in which European analyses of modernism and modernity have been read in the American context as contributions to an analysis of postmodernism and postmodernity is provided by the reception Foucault's work has received. As I have noted above, Foucault is critical of the notion of the postmodern, and argues that his analyses remain firmly within the threshold of modernity, focused on modern forms of knowledge and relations of power, as well as on the techniques and practices through which the modern subject is constituted. However, the analyses have been both criticised for the contribution they have made to the generation of a 'post-modern mood' or temper (Bell 1976), as well as celebrated for the significant contribution they make to an understanding of the 'postmodern scene' (Fekete 1988) and the '"strange loop" of postmodern power' (Kroker and Cook 1988).

It is only since the emergence, at the end of the 1970s, of Lyotard's report on the postmodern condition of knowledge that postmodernism and postmodernity have found a prominent place on the European intellectual agenda. However, the issues raised in debates over the possible development of postmodern conditions, for example the question of the crisis of modernity, if not its possible closure, have a longer history, extending back at least to the works of Nietzsche and Heidegger at the turn of the century (Vattimo 1988).

THE POSTMODERN CONDITION

If the notions of modernism and modernity seem to lack specificity, then postmodernism and postmodernity are equally, if not more, deficient. To some degree the lack of specificity associated with these terms might be considered perfectly consistent with the complex and changing realities they seek to designate. The very experiences and realities which the terms 'modernity' and 'postmodernity' attempt to address, namely on the one hand turmoil and flux, perpetual disintegration and renewal, struggle and contradiction, and increasingly rapid and at times cataclysmic forms of change, and on the other a qualitative transformation in the experience of space and time, an exponential increase in the pace of social and economic life, and a growing sense of fragmentation and discontinuity, render specification problematic. To clarify the central themes and issues which have been raised in connection with the possible emergence of postmodern forms of life it is appropriate, if not necessary, to turn to the work of Lyotard (1986: 1989).

In a report on the changing condition of knowledge 'in the most highly developed societies', prepared for the Conseil des Universités of the Government of Quebec, Lyotard comments that the term postmodern 'designates the state of our culture following the transformations which, since the end of the nineteenth century, have altered the game rules for science, literature, and the arts' (1986, p. xxiii). The principal transformation identified is in the way in which forms of knowledge are legitimated. The question of changes in the conditions of knowledge and social life is approached through an analysis which places emphasis upon the growing importance of language in a sociocultural and economic context transformed by the increasing prominence of information and communication. In its simplest form the thesis suggests that the modern pursuit of legitimation through references to metadiscourses or appeals to grand narratives has become problematic. The emergence of a postmodern condition of knowledge, of 'incredulity toward metanarratives', is presented by Lyotard as an outcome of a complex process of sociocultural and economic development, a process in which three factors predominate. The first concerns the development, since the end of World War II, of postindustrial techniques and technologies, which have contributed to the shift of emphasis away from questions concerning the intrinsic value of forms of knowledge, and the ends or goals of human conduct, and towards the promotion of knowledge as simply a means for optimising the efficiency of the performance of various systems, the rationales for which remain unquestioned. The second factor identified is the regeneration of the capitalist mode of production, in the form of a 'renewal that has eliminated the communist alternative and valorised the individual enjoyment of goods and services' (Lyotard 1986, p. 38). However, if the advent of a consumer capitalism promising ever increasing prosperity and the development of disorienting postindustrial forms of technology have affected the condition of knowledge, Lyotard argues it has only been possible because of the presence of the third factor, namely 'the seeds of "delegitimation" and nihilism that were inherent in the grand narratives of the nineteenth century' (1986, p. 38). Although Lyotard makes reference to the articulation between 'what is known as the postindustrial age' and the emergence of a postmodern condition, it would be inappropriate to read into this an endorsement of the various associated developments. Equally it is misleading to suggest that in Lyotard's view 'modernism has changed because the technical and social conditions of communication have changed' (Harvey 1989, p. 49). The latter contribute to transformations in the condition of knowledge, but the crucial factor is internal to the development of scientific knowledge itself.

Lyotard argues that postindustrial technological transformations have affected both scientific research and 'the way in which learning is acquired, classified, made available, and exploited' (1986, p. 4). The implication is that, given such wide-ranging transformations, knowledge itself cannot remain unchanged, that increasingly the determinant of new research initiatives and directions, not to mention funding, will be the facility with which research programmes and results can be translated into computer language. Lyotard comments that 'along with the hegemony of computers comes a certain logic, and therefore a certain set of prescriptions determining which statements are accepted as "knowledge" statements' (1986, p. 4). Associated with this process is a shift in the principle of legitimation of knowledge, away from the narratives of speculative self-legitimation and emancipation or liberty, that is from predominantly philosophical and political forms, and towards the invocation of performativity, or techno-economic forms of legitimation. As this has occurred the process of knowledge production and use has been increasingly subject to commodification, and the idea of science and knowledge for its own sake, for its intrinsic value, has been steadily eroded. In other words, with the accelerating mercantilisation of knowledge, research has become increasingly oriented towards the needs of clients, and knowledge, in turn, has been produced in order to be sold, produced for its exchange-value.

Legitimation through performativity arises not only from the increasing articulation of technological innovation with 'progress' in knowledge, which develops from the moment that science becomes a force of production within the capitalist mode of production, it also grows out of a process of delegitimation, out of a 'crisis' of scientific knowledge. Specifically the crisis of science is synonymous with the growing problem of determinism precipitated by an increasing recognition of forms of instability and undecidability. Lyotard comments that the crisis of legitimation affecting scientific knowledge,

> signs of which have been accumulating since the end of the nineteenth century, is not born of a chance proliferation of sciences, itself an effect of progress in technology and the expansion of capitalism. It represents, rather, an internal erosion of the legitimacy principle of knowledge. There is erosion at work inside the speculative game, and by loosening the weave of the encyclopedic net in which each science was to find its place, it eventually sets them free.
>
> (Lyotard 1986, p. 39)

In a sense Lyotard is revisiting here an analysis of the condition of knowledge articulated by Durkheim (1964) at the end of the nineteenth century. The key difference is that for Durkheim the 'anomic' condition of modern forms of knowledge – the growing specialisation and fragmentation of the sciences, the difficulty of unifying methods that are 'immanent in the . . . sciences', the erosion of 'grand generalisations', and the increasing inability of philosophy to assure the unity of science, to be the 'collective conscience of science' – is destined to resolve itself. In short 'the unity of science will form of itself' (Durkheim 1964, p. 371). For Lyotard the 'initial' conditions have been further aggravated or transformed by a series of additional major developments within the field of knowledge, notably a questioning of the boundaries and a concomitant increase in overlaps between sciences, the disappearance of disciplines, the emergence of new analytic spaces and territories, and a collapse of the 'speculative hierarchy of learning'. Developments such as these have contributed to the emergence of a postmodern condition of knowledge, one in which speculative forms of legitimation have become problematic.

The erosion of speculative narratives is paralleled by a decomposition of emancipatory narratives of legitimation. In the case of the latter form of narrative, knowledge achieves validity in a practical or prescriptive context, its 'distinguishing characteristic is that it grounds the legitimation of science and truth in the autonomy of interlocuters involved in ethical, social, and political praxis' (Lyotard 1986, pp. 39–40). The problem increasingly encountered in this context is that of reconciling denotative statements possessing cognitive value with prescriptive statements containing practical value. In brief, Lyotard argues that a descriptive statement may be 'true', but it does not follow that a prescriptive statement predicated upon it is 'just'. Given the distinction between theoretical and practical reason, and the respectively different sets of rules defining relevance and competence, it follows that science 'has no special calling to supervise the game of praxis . . . The road is then open for an important current of postmodernity: science plays its own game; it is incapable of legitimating the other language games' (1986, p. 40). It is in this context, where philosophical and political legitimatory narratives have become problematic, that performativity or 'context control' has effected a form of legitimation. In postindustrial capitalist social formations there is an increasing emphasis upon performativity, which within science enhances the ability both to produce proof and to be 'right'. The articulation of science, technology, and context control or performativity is described by Lyotard in the following terms:

> since 'reality' is what provides the evidence used as proof in scientific argumentation, and also provides prescriptions and promises of a juridical, ethical, and political nature with results, one can master all of these games by mastering 'reality'. That is precisely what technology can do. By reinforcing technology, one 'reinforces' reality, and one's chances of being just and right increase accordingly. Reciprocally, technology is reinforced all the more effectively if one has access to scientific knowledge and decision-making authority.
>
> This is how legitimation by power takes shape. Power is not only good performativity, but also effective verification and good verdicts. It legitimates science and law on the basis of their efficiency, and legitimates this efficiency on the basis of science and law. It is self-legitimating, in the same way a system organised around performance maximisation seems to be. Now it is precisely this kind of context control that a generalised computerisation of society may bring.
>
> (Lyotard 1986, p. 47)

The promotion of performativity has an impact upon both knowledge production and transmission. In respect of research the tendency increasingly is to fund projects that optimise system performance and to abandon those that do not. Likewise, education and learning have become much more subject to the demands of system performance, more oriented towards the provision of 'training' and the inculcation of 'skills', and rather less concerned with what are increasingly denigrated as 'liberal' values and ideals.

The delegitimation of metanarratives and the proliferation of performativity criteria constitute two inter-related aspects of the postmodern condition of knowledge. However, there is a third and final aspect considered by Lyotard which questions the appropriateness and the adequacy of maximised performance as a model of legitimation for science. The counter-argument is that 'science does not expand by means of the positivism of efficiency' (1986, p. 54), or by the direct pursuit of performativity. Rather science develops through the invention of counter-examples, by 'looking for a "paradox" and legitimating it with new rules in the games of reasoning' (1986, p. 54), rules that derive from a discourse that is immanent to science itself. There are possibly parallels here with Kuhn's (1970) conception of the development of scientific knowledge. Kuhn describes 'normal' science as puzzle elaborating work conducted within an agreed paradigm, one which is shared by the community of practising scientists until it is challenged by the eruption of a scientific 'revolution'. One implication of this is that a condition or state of consensus is reached in science, but that it is merely provisional or temporary, because it is bound to be disturbed or questioned and ultimately overturned. Focusing on the pragmatics of scientific knowledge Lyotard takes the view that consensus is never fully realised or achieved, that it constitutes a perpetually receding horizon for science. This does not mean that there are no agreements or shared understandings within the scientific community. To the contrary, Lyotard quite explicitly acknowledges the presence of shared understandings and agreements within scientific work, but argues that

> research that takes place under the aegis of a paradigm tends to stabilise; it is like the exploitation of a technological, economic, or artistic 'idea'. It cannot be discounted. But what is striking is that someone always comes along to disturb the order of 'reason'.
>
> (Lyotard 1986, p. 61)

In brief, within the pragmatics of scientific knowledge consensus is not the end of discussion.

In contrast to theorists who place emphasis upon the stability of systems and legitimation through performance, Lyotard comments that in its postmodern condition science is concerned 'with such things as undecidables, the limits of precise control, conflicts characterised by incomplete information, "fracta", catastrophes, and pragmatic paradoxes . . . [with] theorising its own evolution as discontinuous, catastrophic, nonrectifiable, and paradoxical' (1986, p. 60). Legitimation in this context derives not from the former grand narratives of the 'dialectic of Spirit' or emancipation, nor from the techno-administrative criterion of system performativity, but from *paralogy*, from the generation of new statements, new locally determined norms of understanding or rules delineating new fields of investigation, which mark a 'difference from what is already known'. In brief, legitimation is bound up with 'the little narrative [petit récit] . . . the quintessential form of imaginative invention, most particularly in science' (1986, p. 60), that is, with the generation of new ideas and new statements.

At various points in Lyotard's discussion of the postmodern condition of knowledge a critical concern with the present order and its development becomes explicit. The prospect of technocratic context control, the arrogance of decision makers, threats to the imaginative development of knowledge, and the possibility that 'the computerisation of society' will only enhance efficiency of control and regulation are each subjected to criticism, but not from an oppositional position promising emancipation. Lyotard argues that the complex articulation of a postmodern condition of knowledge, accelerating technological innovation, 'economic "redeployment" in the current phase of capitalism', and changes in the institution of the state, make necessary a serious reconsideration of alternative positions and strategies, the apparent objective being to outline a conception of 'a politics that would respect both the desire for justice and the desire for the unknown' (1986, p. 67). To clarify the conception of a 'postmodern' politics implied in this statement it is necessary to elaborate further on Lyotard's conceptualisations of the postmodern.

Lyotard (1989) distinguishes between three connotations of the term 'postmodern'. First there is an aesthetic sense of the term, postmodernism employed with reference to developments in the arts, architecture, and painting. Here postmodernism signifies a break or rupture with modernism, and as such it constitutes a periodising term, and implies succession. Lyotard's response to this connotation of the term is unequivocal:

I take the term in a sense which is completely different from that which is generally accepted in these matters [American literary criticism and the crisis of modernism in the Arts], from its designation as the end of modernism. I have said and will say again that 'postmodern' signifies not the end of modernism, but another relation to modernism.

(Lyotard 1988, p. 277)

A second sense of the term is outlined at some length in deliberations on the current condition of knowledge. Reflecting on this second sense of the postmodern, Lyotard comments that the association of increases in rationality, of developments in the arts, the sciences, and technology with 'progress', with increasing freedom and happiness for humanity as a whole is no longer sustainable. The 'modern' promise of universal emancipation no longer seems remotely feasible; on the contrary, it might be argued that in some respects our condition has deteriorated, that the accelerating 'development of techno-sciences' is aggravating rather than alleviating our difficulties, introducing a destabilising 'obligation to complexify' that is unrelated to the needs and demands of individual and social life. The problem of excessive complexity, to which one part of humanity, predominantly the 'first-world', has subjected itself, constitutes a major element of the failure of the modern project. Its corollary, Lyotard argues, is the terrible and ancient burden of survival to which the majority of humanity remains sentenced.

The third and final sense of the term outlined is of a somewhat different order. It constitutes a response to the political implications of the end of avant-gardism, the erosion of the legislative role of the intellectual, the collapse of the grand narratives of emancipation and progress, and the associated problem of the absence of a safe space or secure site from which to constitute oppositional forms of thought and politics. In short, it represents an attempt to preserve the possibility of opposition and criticism through a conception of postmodernism as a 'politics of resistance'.[8]

THE POLITICS OF POSTMODERNISM – RESISTANCE AND REACTION

Within contemporary social theory, cultural analysis, and philosophy a concept of postmodernism has been invoked to delineate the limits and limitations of the project of modernity. Postmodernism signifies incredulity towards metanarratives in general, and towards the grand narrative of emancipation in particular. The principal implication is that the promise of the project of modernity to facilitate 'the emancipation of humanity from poverty, ignorance, prejudice, and the absence of enjoyment' (Lyotard 1988, p. 302) no longer seems to be feasible. Such grand hopes associated with global or totalising forms of social theory and, not infrequently, a politics of 'revolution', have been diminished by the realisation that forms of knowledge, socioeconomic, cultural and political conditions, human experiences, and subjectivities, and their respective complex forms of articulation with one another, are not as they were once thought, or assumed, to be. Briefly, the grand old narratives of modern social theory and philosophy have been rendered inoperative, they have lost their credibility. An analysis of this order, which problematises emancipatory narratives, may seem to undermine the prospects for criticism, opposition, and resistance; certainly, that is the conclusion reached by analysts who equate postmodernism and postmodernity with a form of neo-conservative politics (Habermas 1981; Berman 1983).

In contrast to the conception of postmodernism as 'conservative' an alternative might be articulated, not of a postmodernism which effaces 'the older (essentially high-modernist) frontier between high culture and so-called mass or commercial culture' (Jameson 1984b, p. 54), only to become infatuated with the culture industry, but rather of an oppositional or critical postmodernism, a postmodernism of resistance. A distinction between 'oppositional' and 'affirmative' forms of postmodernism, between a postmodernism which attempts to deconstruct modernism, and challenge or criticise the status quo, and 'a postmodernism which repudiates the former to celebrate the latter' is articulated by Foster (1985 pp. xi–xii). Countering the conflation of postmodernism with eclecticism, populism, and a principle of 'anything goes', which is taken to be synonymous with both a general decline in creativity and an acceptance, if not a celebration, of the prevailing order of things, Foster argues for an oppositional postmodernism, for postmodernism

> as a counter-practice not only to the official culture of modernism but also to the 'false normativity' of a reactionary postmodernism. In opposition (but not *only* in opposition), a resistant postmodernism is concerned with a critical deconstruction of tradition, not an instrumental pastiche of

177

pop- or pseudo-historical forms, with a critique of origins, not a return to them.

(Foster 1985, p. xii)

A comparable conception of a postmodern politics of resistance is developed by Lyotard.

Accepting that there has been an erosion of foundational thought and a collapse of the 'grand narratives' of liberalism and Marxism, Lyotard nevertheless considers that there remains scope for a politics of resistance. One important focus for resistance is the preservation of elementary liberties, basic freedoms, which prescribe the limits of sociopolitical fashioning or fabrication – 'our clear duty there is to intervene when they are at stake' (1988, p. 302). But there is another more 'pertinent' and specific form of resistance to which our attention is drawn. Given the decomposition of emancipatory metanarratives and the associated displacement of the universalising, legislative role of the intellectual, Lyotard argues that:

> The real political task today, at least in so far as it is also concerned with the cultural . . . is to carry forward the resistance that writing offers to established thought, to what has already been done, to what everyone thinks, to what is well known, to what is widely recognised, to what is 'readable', to everything which can change its form and make itself acceptable to opinion in general. The latter, you understand, always works with what is taken for granted and with what is forgotten as such . . . 'Culture' consists as 'activity' and 'animation', in introducing all that into the order of writing in the wide sense, into literature, painting, architecture and so on.

(Lyotard 1988, p. 302)

It is this form of resistance that is most often implied by the idea of an oppositional or critical postmodernism.

The conception of postmodernism as embodying a politics of resistance is open to a good deal of misunderstanding, particularly given the associated denial of emancipatory narratives and politics. To clarify the idea it is helpful to recall that the concept of the 'postmodern' refers not to a transcendence, or 'critical overcoming' of the modern, nor to an historical period after modernity, or a 'temporal overcoming' of the modern, rather it signifies a new relationship with the modern. Postmodernism as resistance attempts 'to question rather than exploit cultural codes, to explore rather than

178

conceal social and political affiliations' (Foster 1985, p. xii). It constitutes a distinctive mode of analysis of the presuppositions and forms of life of modernity, a form of reflecting back on modernity through a process of 'anamnesis' (Lyotard 1988, p. 302: 1989, p. 10). In this sense the idea of the postmodern is both 'something new in relation to the modern, but also . . . a dissolution of the category of the new' (Vattimo 1988, p. 4). An oppositional postmodernism, a postmodernism of resistance, does not threaten, or promise, to overturn modernity, rather it allows analysis to achieve a critical distance from the present, from the central presuppositions of the project of modernity. In turn it offers an analysis of both the pervasive contemporary Western experience of *post-histoire* and the routin-isation and subsequent dissolution of the idea of progress. Finally it allows consideration to be given to the prospect that 'late modernity is the place [time] where, perhaps, a different possibility of existence . . . emerges' (Vattimo 1988, p. 11).

Ranged against the idea of postmodernism as resistance is a critique of postmodernism as reaction, a position economically outlined by Jameson, for whom postmodernism represents the cultural correlate of late, consumer, multinational capitalism. In a series of papers Jameson has sought to reconstitute the credentials of Marxist analysis as the sole remaining viable grand narrative by arguing that postmodern cultural forms replicate, reproduce, and in the final instance serve to reinforce the logic of consumer capitalism. The implication is that any former vestige of autonomy, or 'semi-autonomy', possessed by the cultural sphere has been eroded by the process of increasing commodification associated with the development of the capitalist mode of production. But the upshot of this is not that culture has been marginalised. To the contrary, Jameson emphasises that there has been a fundamental cultural muta-tion, a 'prodigious expansion' throughout the whole social realm, the principal effect of which has been that 'everything in our social life – from economic value and state power to practices and to the very structure of the psyche itself – can be said to have become "cultural" in some original and as yet untheorised sense' (1984b, p. 87). Albeit through a process initiated and fashioned by the 'logic' of late capitalism!

Although critical of postmodern cultural forms Jameson is not entirely dismissive of them. Whilst he rightly rejects the idea of their enthusiastic espousal as 'harbingers of a new technological or technocratic Utopia', he wisely refrains from an endorsement of their denouncement as decadent. Although the terms in which he has expressed his position have varied, he has consistently argued that new, postmodern forms of cultural production need to be located within a 'general modification of culture itself within the social restructuration of late capitalism as a system' (1984a, p. 63).[9] As such, postmodernism is not merely a 'style', one option among many, but rather the cultural dominant of the logic of late capitalism. However, as I have suggested above, such a conclusion does not mean that postmodernism is to be completely written off as reaction(ary). Rather it suggests that Jameson is casting around for a functional alternative to an older, now sadly compromised modernism, a modernism that once was 'critical, negative, contestatory, subversive, oppositional and the like' (1985, p. 125). In Jameson's work there is a clear recognition of the uniqueness and the originality of post-modern space, 'of the suppression of distance . . . and the relentless saturation of any remaining voids and empty places to the point where the postmodern body . . . is now exposed to a perceptual barrage of immediacy from which all sheltering layers and intervening mediations have been removed' (1988, p. 351). But if there is an evident willingness to consider the emergence of spatial peculiarities as possible 'symptoms and expressions of a new and historically original dilemma', Jameson is not yet convinced that whilst post-modernism reinforces the logic of consumer capitalism it may also contain the potential to resist it.

It is how the postmodern condition is conceived that determines its appropriateness or relevance for an analysis of the present. Without doubt, major differences over the conceptualisation of the postmodern, and the associated question of its relationship to the project of modernity, are behind the contrasting judgments made of its political import. Setting postmodernism up as 'anti-rational' and '(neo)conservative' makes it a relatively simple target for criticism. But postmodernism cannot be disposed of so readily. The opposition to 'reason' frequently attributed to 'postmodern' analyses is, to be more precise, an opposition to a totalising idea of reason, hence the association of reason and terror. There is no 'postmodern' opposition to rationality *per se*. Rather it is the existence of a plurality of 'rationalities which are, at the least, respectively theoretical, practical, aesthetic' (Lyotard 1988, p. 279) that constitutes the necessary focus for 'postmodern' critical theorising and analyses. It is in this respect that the postmodern condition constitutes a contemporary diagnosis of the near century-long 'crisis' to which scientific forms of rationality have been subject. In other words, the postmodern condition does not signify an abandonment of rationality, but rather a 'critical interrogation of reason' or, to be more specific, a critical reflection on the project of modernity and its rationalities. It is worth emphasising that it is equally problematic simply to dismiss postmodernism as conservative or reactionary, for there are a number of different strands of postmodern thought, some of which, as I will attempt to show, have been interwoven with Marxism.

Writing in the 1950s, the American Marxist sociologist Wright Mills (1970) suggested that the 'modern age' was being succeeded by a 'post-modern period', in which the post-Enlightenment assumption of an increasingly close correlation of freedom and reason had become questionable. The increasing rationalisation of modern Western society could no longer 'be assumed to make for increased freedom' in Wright Mills's view. Increasing doubts about the values and assumptions of the Enlightenment, for example 'progress by reason' and 'faith in science', along with the evident emergence of new structures which seemed to resist analysis in terms of 'modern "ideals"' lead Wright Mills to conclude that, 'in our time these two values, reason and freedom, are in obvious yet subtle peril' (1970, p. 186). It is this potentially perilous condition that is identified as postmodern. Subsequently the concept of the 'postmodern' has been further 'invested with theoretical and activist critiques of technological civilisation and of its prevailing paradigm of conquest and domination' (Huyssen 1984b, p. 622). Given the above it makes little sense simply to equate postmodernism *per se* with reactionary or affirmative forms of analysis, for it is evident that there are forms of postmodernism which are critical, in short that there is a 'postmodernism of resistance . . . that refuses to simply redecorate the cracking walls of capitalist culture' (Huyssen 1984b, p. 623). But this does not resolve the postmodern paradox, or the paradox of postmodernity.

A range of significant forms of change have been identified since the end of World War II. In addition to the changes in sociocultural and intellectual life implied above, references have been made to the dispersal and deterritorialisation of economic production within an increasingly global economy (Aronowitz 1987/88); an erosion of the sovereignty of the nation-state and national politics (Rose 1988); a proliferation of new political movements, and an increase in 'insecurity' and 'terrorism' (Eco 1987; Baudrillard 1983b); as well as an associated dissolution of the 'unity' of society (Touraine 1984:

1989; Bauman 1988a: 1988b). The question is, what are we to make of these various contributions to an understanding of present conditions? Should they be seen, as Giddens suggests, 'as the first real initiatives in the ambitious task of charting the cultural universe resulting from the ever-more complete disintegration of the traditional world' (1987, pp. 28–9)? In other words, as contributions to an understanding of the continuing development of modernity, perhaps of its 'radicalisation' (Giddens 1990). Or do they constitute symptoms of the emergence of a postmodern order?

The idea of the postmodern is now firmly on the agenda for debate. Diverse and at times conflicting references to postmodernism and postmodernity are to be found in a growing number of disciplinary fields. But this should not occasion 'panic', even if panic is conceived to be 'the key psychological mood of postmodern culture' (Kroker *et al.* 1989, p. 13). Neither does it necessitate an unqualified endorsement of the polymorphous perversities sometimes associated with manifestations of the postmodern. Rather the critical implication is that complex transformations, questions, and problems deemed to be constitutive of the present are not adequately articulated in prevailing modern forms of theory and analysis. That is the 'rational' kernel of the postmodern challenge to which a considered response is necessary.

6

MARXISM AND POSTMODERNISM

Major changes in production and consumption, communications and culture, and knowledge and information confirm that the process of constant revolutionising, uninterrupted disturbance, uncertainty, and agitation, identified by Marx and Engels in *The Communist Manifesto* has far from abated. Indeed, it might be argued that subsequently the process of change has gathered momentum, if not increased in scale, scope, and intensity (Berman 1983). However, if the present is broadly agreed to be a time of transition, a time of increasing change, there nevertheless remains substantial disagreement over the question of the impact, or effect, of contemporary forms of change, their political implications and explanation.

A prominent focus of debate within contemporary social theory has been on a series of developments which have been conceptualised as manifestations of a 'postmodern condition' (Lyotard 1986), a 'postmodern situation' (Arac 1989), or a 'condition of postmodernity' (Harvey 1989).[1] As I have indicated, there are a number of positions outlined on the subject of a possible postmodern condition, or condition of postmodernity. In its paradigmatic form the thesis on the postmodern condition of knowledge suggests that it is no longer possible to generate universal solutions or answers to problems and questions concerning contemporary forms of life from within, what might be termed, a conventional 'modern' problematic. In short, that the analyses, understandings, goals, and values which have been a central feature of Western European civilisation since the Enlightenment can no longer be assumed to be universally valid or relevant. The 'project of modernity' is unfinished or incomplete, because its completion is inconceivable, and its value is increasingly open to question. One critical corollary of this is that we can no longer have recourse to 'grand narratives', guarantees, or secure foundations, for either our analyses, or our political strategies. Conversely, conceptualised as an epiphenomenal form of a, by implication, longer-standing and broader process of economic rationalisation, the 'condition of postmodernity' is presented as a more limited cultural corollary of 'late' developments in the capitalist mode of production towards more flexible modes of accumulation (Jameson 1984b; Harvey 1989). One implication of such an analysis is that a radically abbreviated postmodern condition leaves at least one of the 'grand narratives' of contemporary social analysis relatively unimpaired. That narrative is of course Marxism.

The idea of an emerging postmodern condition, or condition of postmodernity, has been addressed in a number of different ways within the broad parameters of historical materialism, within the terms of reference of the most prominent of the 'grand narratives'. A distinction may be drawn between four distinctive categories of response to the idea of a postmodern condition within Marxist discourse. To begin with there is a broadly based categorical rejection of the conception as of little or no analytic relevance, or political significance, or worse, as a symptom of political and cultural conservatism (Habermas 1981; Berman 1983; Anderson 1984; Williams 1989). Second, there is a recognition of postmodernism as a cultural form precipitated by the development of 'consumer or multi-national capitalism' (Jameson 1985), or as a cultural condition which crystallises with the 'transition from Fordism to flexible accumulation' (Harvey 1989). Third, there is a more responsive or accommodating critical reading of postmodernism which attempts, in a radical manner, to explore the implications for Marxism, a reading which opens up Marxism to 'a necessary and overdue spatialisation, to a materialist interpretation of spatiality that would match its magisterial historical materialism' (Soja 1989, p. 40), and in another version leads to the notion of a Marxism 'without guarantees' (Hebdige 1988). Finally there is a response which involves a more radical theoretical reconsideration of Marxism, one predicated on an 'avalanche of historical mutations' and a 'whole series of positive new phenomena'. Although it is not explicitly articulated in terms of the emergence of a possible postmodern condition, the form of theoretical reflection and reconsideration concerned clearly embraces a number of prominent and significant postmodern features in the course of the constitution of what has been termed a 'post-Marxist' analysis (Laclau and Mouffe 1985: 1987).

I have already commented on some of the ways in which the

concept of the postmodern has been rejected because of its lack of analytic significance, or surfeit of conservative political resonance. The focus of the discussion in this chapter will be on analyses which attempt to incorporate the idea of postmodernism, or a condition of postmodernity, within the existing parameters of Marxism; explore the implications of postmodern conditions for Marxism; and finally develop a postmodern form of Marxism, or a 'post-Marxist' analysis, in order to more adequately address changing social, cultural and political conditions.

POSTMODERNISM, POSTMODERNITY AND MARXISM

Typically within a Marxist analysis both postmodernism and postmodernity are viewed, in some sense, as manifestations of transformations in the capitalist mode of production. Two different yet broadly compatible analyses of postmodernism and postmodernity from within the parameters of an unquestioned Marxist analysis are provided by Jameson (1984a: 1984b: 1985: 1988) and Harvey (1989).

Jameson is in no doubt that 'we are *within* the culture of postmodernism to the point where its facile repudiation is as impossible as any equally facile celebration of it is complacent and corrupt' (1984a, p. 63). The requirement now is to submit it to analysis, attempt to understand or explain its emergence and development, and consider its impact or effect, particularly on social and political life. Postmodernism is analysed as a cultural form which emerged in response or, perhaps more appropriately, in reaction to various manifestations of high modernism. In architecture, art, music, film and literature Jameson (1985) argues that most of the manifestations of postmodernism constitute reactions against well established forms of high modernism. For example, within architecture postmodernism is synonymous with criticism of both high modernism, 'the destruction of the fabric of the traditional city and of its older neighbourhood culture', and associated forms of elitism and authoritarianism. In contrast to modernism, postmodernism challenges the distinction between 'high' and 'mass' or 'commercial' culture, and attempts to present itself as a form of aesthetic populism. The latter is presented as a 'fundamental feature of all postmodernisms' (Jameson 1984b, p. 54).

Postmodernism does not simply represent another cultural style or movement in Jameson's view, rather it constitutes a 'cultural dominant', a corollary of the latest stage in the development of the capitalist mode of production. Following Mandel's (1980) conception of the stages of capitalist development – market capitalism, monopoly capitalism, and 'late' or multinational capitalism – Jameson proposes a parallel cultural periodisation in the form of realism, modernism, and postmodernism. An important implication of which is that postmodernism is not to be conceived as 'little more than one more stage of modernism proper', but rather as a periodising term which allows reference to be made to the emergence of historically distinctive dominant cultural forms, practices, and experiences. Now there are a number of potential objections to such a conception of which Jameson is aware, and to which he attempts to respond. The two most critical objections are that a periodising hypothesis constitutes historical periods as homogeneous, and to that extent occludes significant internal forms of cultural difference, and, as a corollary, diminishes the significance of similarities or continuities between modernism and postmodernism. Two clarificatory observations are appropriate in this context. First, there is no suggestion in Jameson's work that all contemporary cultural production is postmodern; rather the emphasis placed upon the latter is intended to signify that it constitutes the 'dominant cultural logic, or hegemonic norm'. As for the possible existence of continuities or similarities between modernism and postmodernism, it is argued that

> even if all the constitutive features of postmodernism were identical and continuous with those of an older modernism – a position I feel to be demonstrably erroneous . . . – the two phenomena would still remain utterly distinct in their meaning and social function, owing to the very different positioning of postmodernism in the economic system of late capital, and beyond that, to the transformation of the very sphere of culture in contemporary society.
>
> (Jameson 1984b, p. 57)

To clarify Jameson's position it is necessary to both delineate the distinctive features attributed to postmodernism and enlarge upon the question of its articulation with 'late' capitalism.

The key features attributed to the cultural dominant of postmodernism include a 'new depthlessness', evident in contemporary theory and cultural life in general in the preoccupation with interpretation, surfaces, images and simulacra; 'a consequent weakening in historicity'; a decentring of the subject and associated changes in emotional tone and intensity; and broad changes in the experience of space and time, associated with 'a whole new technology, which is itself a figure for a whole new economic world system' (Jameson 1984b, p. 58). Elaborating on these features of postmodernism Jameson argues that it is categories of space rather than time that increasingly dominate our daily life and our experiences and, further, that we lack the perceptual equipment to match the new form of postmodern space which has opened up around us. Our minds and imaginations find it difficult to grasp 'the whole new decentred global network of the third stage of capital' (1984b, p. 80). At present we seem to lack the capacity, as Jameson puts it, 'to map the great global multinational and decentred communicational network in which we find ourselves caught as individual subjects' (1984b, p. 84). Curiously, to compensate for this lack, it is an analysis of postmodernism as a *historical* phenomenon that is proposed, an analysis which it is implied will constitute a contribution to a *social cartography* of the current conditions in which we find ourselves, and to which we are subjected.

The principal objective then appears to be to generate an analysis of postmodernism as a historical phenomenon, rather than to engage in positive or negative moral judgments of its worth. Indeed, there is an explicit recognition of the corrosive effect that the emergence of a postmodern condition has had on the 'luxury of the old-fashioned ideological critique, the indignant moral denunciation' (Jameson 1984b, p. 86). However, it is evident that the effects of the postmodern condition are not considered to extend to totalising forms of analysis, or emancipatory narratives on the subject of socialism. In consequence, as the 'abolition of critical distance' and the process of mutation of the cultural sphere under late capitalism is outlined, the impression is simultaneously conveyed of the existence of another space or place, outside and beyond the sphere of influence described, from which, by implication, a privileged analysis can continue to be conducted. Although reference is made to the possibility that 'cherished and time-honoured radical conceptions' may have become outmoded, and that 'distance in general (including "critical distance" in particular) has very precisely been abolished in the new space of postmodernism' (1984b, p. 87), Jameson remains confident that new cultural forms and associated transformations in the experience of space and time can be adequately theorised in terms of a global and totalising analysis of the development of multinational capital. Furthermore, such a development and its politically 'progressive' corollary, namely the constitution of a 'new and more comprehensive socialism', made possible through 'the invention and elaboration of an internationalism of a radically new type' (1984b, p. 88), are presented as outcomes perfectly consistent with, if not actually anticipated in the classical analyses, or master narratives, produced by Marx and Lenin.

Proceeding from Mandel's model of the historical development of the capitalist mode of production, Jameson argues that at each stage a unique type of space has been generated as a 'result of discontinuous expansions or quantum leaps in the enlargement of capital, in the latter's penetration and colonisation of hitherto uncommodified areas' (1988, p. 348). Briefly, the respective stages are as follows. First with the advent of classical or market capitalism space is reconstituted in the form of 'geometrical and Cartesian homogeneity'. Heterogeneous space is subjected to the logic of the grid. Jameson comments that although problems of representation or 'figuration' are associated with the emergence of geometric space they are not crucial. With the passage to a second stage, of monopoly capital, problems of figuration become more significant and acute. It becomes increasingly difficult to articulate the connection(s) between lived experience, or the phenomenological experience of the human subject, and the increasingly complex structural coordinates and conditions through which experiences are effectively constituted. In short, *figuring* the relationship between structure(s) and experience(s) becomes increasingly problematic. Jameson comments that 'this new situation poses tremendous and crippling problems for a work of art' and that it is in response to 'this dilemma that modernism, or perhaps better, the various modernisms as such emerge' (1988, p. 349). It is also, of course, a source of major problems for an emancipatory grand narrative which needs to articulate its analysis of the 'real' structural conditions of existence with the equally 'real' forms in which those conditions are lived, experienced, and rationalised. The irruption of a third stage, of late capitalism – synonymous for Mandel with an extension of industrialisation to all branches of the economy, the development of a 'permanent pressure to *accelerate technological innovation*' (1980, p. 192), and a growing intensification of the mode of production as a whole, including its contradictions – is the moment to which Jameson traces the emergence of postmodernist space, a new space which 'involves the suppression of distance (in the sense of Benjamin's aura) and the relentless saturation of any remaining voids and empty places' (1988, p. 351).

Jameson's conception of the three historical stages of capitalism, paralleled by cultural periods, and distinctive forms of space, bears a number of striking similarities to Baudrillard's (1983a) discussion of three historical orders of simulacra (Smart 1990). Of particular relevance in this context is the conception outlined by Baudrillard of a third order of simulacra peculiar to our 'postmodern' present. Baudrillard's view is that in a context where the real world is increasingly constituted in and through models, the relationship between images, codes, subjects and events is fundamentally transformed. In brief it is no longer possible simply to appeal to a 'real' referent, for the trusted distinctions between representations and their objects have become problematic. Indeed it is suggested that such distinctions can no longer be sustained effectively in a world where simulation models predominate. This is the 'new and historically original dilemma' that Jameson associates with postmodernism. It is a dilemma with which we are struggling to get to grips, 'one that involves our insertion as individual subjects into a multidimensional set of *radically discontinuous realities*, whose frames range from the still surviving spaces of bourgeois private life all the way to the *unimaginable decentring of global capital* itself' (1988, p. 351: emphasis added). It is a dilemma which is experiential, analytical, and political. In response to the existence of such a postmodern dilemma Jameson argues that what is required is a form of cognitive mapping of the new conditions to which we are now subject. In the final instance this means a cognitive map of 'the social and global totality', or more precisely (and predictably), a cognitive mapping of 'the totality of class relations on a global (. . . multinational) scale' (1988, p. 353). The latter specification raises the spectre, once again, of the incorporation or subordination of different forms of subjectivity and political expression within a class analysis, and to that extent it displays a lack of both imagination and understanding, in effect a preference for a 'nostalgic' mapping. In sum, an ambiguous proposal of 'the need for class consciousness of a new and hitherto undreamed of kind' (Jameson 1989, p. 44). As a conclusion it follows irresistibly from the initial conception of postmodernism as 'unthinkable without the hypothesis of some fundamental mutation of the sphere of culture in the world of late capitalism' (1984b, p. 86).

It is argued by Jameson that there is a need to generate new forms of representation appropriate to the global space of multinational capital. But it is less clear that individuals and collective subjects lack forms of representation through which to make sense of their positions and so 'regain a capacity to act and struggle which is at present neutralised by our spatial as well as our social confusion' (ibid., p. 92). Has a capacity to act and struggle been lost? Are we spatially and socially confused? It might be argued that political action and struggle has not ceased or been lost, but rather has increasingly assumed 'inconvenient' non-class forms. This suggests that it is the dearth, if not absence, of social class forms of political struggle that Jameson has in mind, and that it is the apparent erosion of these specific forms that is equated with an incapacity to act and struggle, an incapacity explained, in turn, by socio-spatial 'confusion', a condition which begins to look suspiciously like 'false consciousness' in postmodern dress. Of course, Jameson does not go so far as to deny the existence of the political struggles of new social movements (e.g. feminist, sexual rights, environmental, peace, ethnic and religious constituencies, etc.). Furthermore, we are assured that 'it is not a question of substituting a total class/party politics for the politics of new social movements' (1988, p. 360). But what is presented as necessary, if struggle is not to be doomed or limited in success to reform, is that 'local struggles involving specific and often different groups' are articulated within a common project, a project which Jameson describes as socialism, or 'a *total* transformation of society'. Quite what this might mean, or involve, is not at all clear. By what mechanism(s) might a common project be constituted from the diverse 'local' struggles and interests of a plurality of social and political movements? Does the adoption of the term 'socialism' betray the persistence of 'orthodox' assumptions about the form any 'common' project needs must take? In the absence of any consideration of what the vacant category 'socialism' might comprise in a postmodern context, statements about a total transformation of society represent merely empty slogans. Ironically, an attempt to engage radically with the social and political dilemmas implied above is made from within a discursive form which Jameson derides, one which, however, constructively confronts the weaknesses and limitations of Marxist analysis and political strategy. I have in mind the controversial subject of 'post-Marxism' of which, paraphrasing Lyotard (1986), it might be said that it is not necessarily Marxism 'at its end but in the nascent state', a 'postmodern' Marxism relieved of the burden of the dead-weight of its own long and uneven history.

The question of the emergence and complex articulation of postmodern cultural forms with developments in the capitalist mode of production is explored in greater depth and detail by Harvey

(1989). However, if both Jameson and Harvey approach modernism and postmodernism as cultural forms, sensibilities, and practices which, in the final instance derive from, or correspond to, the changing conditions of capitalist modernisation, there nevertheless remain differences between their respective analyses, differences of analytic focus and conceptualisation. There are two particular differences that might be noted at this point. The first is a matter of focus and concerns the question of the historical moment at which postmodernism, or a condition of postmodernity, emerged. There is a degree of ambiguity over this question in Jameson's work. The emergence of postmodernism is traced both to the development after World War II of a new stage of the capitalist mode of production ('late, consumer, or multinational'), and more precisely to the moment, in the early 1960s, when high modernism was institutionalised within the academy, when high modernism became mainstream, relatively safe, and a 'good' investment (Jameson 1985).

Harvey nominates a later moment, and argues that the 'counter-cultural and anti-modernist movements of the 1960s' were in fact preparing the ground for the emergence of postmodernism 'as a full-blown though still incoherent movement' (1989, p. 38) somewhere between 1968 and 1972. If one moment is selected, then it generally tends to be 15 July 1972, when at 3.32 p.m. the Pruitt–Igoe 'modernist' public housing complex in St Louis was demolished. It is this event that is frequently cited as the moment at which modernism perished, at least in its architectural guise, and a 'postmodern' movement emerged (Gardner 1989, p. 55). Although Harvey refers to the demolition of 'a prize winning version of Le Corbusier's "machine for modern living"' (1989, p. 39) as the moment high modernism gave way, the emergence of postmodernism, or a condition of postmodernity, is identified with a pervasive process of transformation in the political economy of capitalism, with the growing problems of 'Fordism–Keynesianism' and a process of transition to flexible forms of accumulation under way within the capitalist mode of production since 1973. In brief the difference between the two positions is that Jameson identifies the emergence of postmodernism with the 1960s and the advent of consumer capitalism, but fails to acknowledge that the decade identified constitutes 'merely the superheated summit of the postwar boom' (Davis 1985, p. 108). In contrast Harvey traces the emergence of a condition of postmodernity to the critical moment at which the boom went bust, to the break-up of the 'Fordist–Keynesian' post-war configuration after 1973, an episode which 'inaugurated a period of rapid change, flux, and uncertainty' (1989, p. 124).

The second difference worthy of note in this context concerns their respective conceptualisations of the distinctions between modernism and postmodernism. Although Jameson acknowledges the possible existence of common features and even continuities between modernism and postmodernism his argument is that the latter constitutes a quite distinctive cultural 'force field', and that we now live in a postmodern 'period' or 'era'. Harvey is far more circumspect and, whilst he employs a conception of postmodernism, reference is simultaneously made to the persistence of Fordist–modernist forms and the question of their complex modes of articulation with 'flexible postmodernism'. There is an explicit address in Harvey's work of the question of time–space compression, and many of the other elements of a postmodern condition identified by Jameson (e.g. new types of consumption; planned obsolescence; the mobilisation of mass fashion; developments in communications media, etc.). But Harvey, unwittingly endorsing Lyotard's line on the question of postmodernism, suggests that the uniqueness and newness attributed to the 'postmodern' experience is exaggerated, that 'stressful though the current condition undoubtedly is, it is qualitatively similar to that which led to various modernist reconceptualisations of space and time' (Harvey 1989, p. 305). This does not represent a denial of the existence of postmodern conditions, but it does constitute a significant challenge to the idea that we are now living in a postmodern era.

Although the diagnosis that there is 'an omnipresent danger that our mental maps will not match current realities' (Harvey 1989, p. 305) is endorsed, it is clear that Harvey, like Jameson, does not consider the danger to extend to the map of historical materialism. The existence of a distinctive, 'somewhat special' condition of postmodernity, exemplified by a dramatic intensification of time–space compression, and a marked increase in the ephemerality and fragmentation of personal, social and political life, is categorically affirmed. But it is considered only as a manifestation of a 'history of successive waves of time–space compression generated out of the pressures of capital accumulation with its perpetual search to annihilate space through time and reduce turnover time' (Harvey 1989, p. 306–7). Placing the condition of postmodernity within range of a historical materialist analysis does indeed generate an understanding of some aspects of the present, but it certainly does not exhaust the possible implications of the emergence of a postmodern condition for the present. In particular the question of the possible impact of the condition of postmodernity on knowledge and political forms of life has been left relatively unexplored, if not, in the specific instance of Marxist analysis and political strategy, neglected altogether. Both Jameson and Harvey avoid any serious engagement with such matters. The closest Jameson comes to acknowledging that there might be a case to answer is in a series of very brief comments directed towards what is described, with unintended irony, as 'the taboos and shibboleths of a faddish post-Marxism' (1988, p. 353), a discursive formation encompassing a range of texts and analyses which problematise several of the foundational assumptions of Marxism, including the pivotal concept of the social totality. Given a serious interest in transgressing 'taboos' and deconstructing 'shibboleths' it would be appropriate for Jameson to look closer to home, beginning perhaps with the 'holy trinity', the assumed articulation of a 'conception of the social totality' and a transformation of the whole social system, with a 'properly socialist politics' (1988, p. 355). A more extensive and detailed, but equally predetermined and, to that extent, closed analysis of a range of parallel aspects of the postmodern condition is provided by Harvey.

Harvey acknowledges that in so far as postmodernism is concerned with difference, communication difficulties, and the peculiar complexity and specificity of interests, cultures and places, 'it exercises a positive influence' (1989, p. 113) and has a potentially radical edge. But the potential positive influence of postmodernism is said to be threatened, if not effectively compromised and undermined, by a range of serious weaknesses and inconsistencies. These include an exaggeration of both the differences with, and the deficiencies of modernism; an excessive preoccupation with the deconstruction and delegitimation of arguments and validity claims; and either the absence of any 'coherent politics', or the traces of a 'reactionary neoconservativism' manifest in an accommodation with the market and an associated celebration of entrepreneurial culture. As I have indicated, it is very debatable whether the weaknesses and inconsistencies noted above necessarily apply to the fabricated 'unity' postmodernism. For example, the idea that there is 'more continuity than difference' between modernism and postmodernism, and that it is more appropriate to conceive 'the latter as a particular kind of crisis within the former' (Harvey 1989, p. 116) is arguably already an integral feature of Lyotard's thesis on postmodernism. In the case of 'deconstruction' a parallel misunderstanding is evident. The objective of deconstruction is to seek out the presuppositions that we take for granted in analysis, to investigate all the traces or sediments deposited within our analytic positions, or formulations, by the history of metaphysics (Derrida 1981). As a sceptical mode of thought deconstruction also challenges 'the "taken-for-granted" rhetoric of Marxist theory' (Norris 1982, p. 89). So, instead of viewing deconstruction as a threat to the possibility of 'reasoned action', it might be received, and welcomed, as an attribute of critical thought necessary for combating the claims of spurious forms of objectivity, one that provides an opportunity to examine the analyses, actions, and forms of rationality in play, not least of all in the conceptualisation of a 'coherent politics'.

What appears to emerge from Harvey's work is a choice between an, at best, ambiguous postmodernism and an unquestioned historical materialism, and that in effect constitutes no contest. Postmodernism is held not only to deny 'that kind of meta-theory which can grasp the political–economic processes (money flows, international divisions of labour, financial markets . . .) that are becoming ever more universalising in their depth, intensity, reach and power over daily life' but, even worse, to have acknowledged the authenticity of other political voices only to deprive them of 'access to more universal sources of power' (1989, p. 117). This is a curious statement, for in respect of the first point there is no denial, from a postmodern position, of the continuing 'regional' relevance of a Marxist analysis for generating an understanding of aspects of current developments in the capitalist mode of production. Although there might be arguments at the margins about the depth, intensity, and reach of political–economic processes over daily life, it is clear that for Lyotard the postmodern condition of knowledge is articulated with developments in the capitalist mode of production. What is denied, however, are the assumptions of 'universality' and 'totality', as well as associated emancipatory claims, which are insinuated along with the analysis of existing conditions. There is also a denial of the related assumption that there exists a privileged political site or space, albeit 'temporarily' vacant, which might empower all currently 'disempowered' voices. Harvey contends that 'postmodernism is dangerous for it avoids confronting the realities of political economy and the circumstances of global power' (1989, p. 117) A more appropriate comment would be that postmodernism is disconcerting in so far as it subjects the assumed realities of political economy to question.

The various postmodernisms do not claim to be providing a competing global theory which attempts to encompass the 'social totality'. To the contrary, the idea of 'the social' as a totality is itself deconstructed within such analyses. Furthermore, the realities of political economy are not absent from analyses of the postmodern condition. The question of the relationship between developments in contemporary capitalism and transformations in the condition of knowledge is addressed, but it is not the sole analytic preoccupation.[2] More importantly, there is no recourse to a 'grand narrative', and that is the disturbing difference which arises with the postmodern condition.

Lyotard's work does not constitute an occasion, or an opportunity, for a critical (re)consideration of possible changes in the condition of knowledge for Harvey; rather it becomes a target for an exercise in parody, perhaps best exemplified by a series of comments on the closing paragraphs of *The Postmodern Condition*. Proceeding on the assumption that there is very little to reconsider as far as changes in the conditions of knowledge are concerned, and that *the* emancipatory narrative is still intact, Harvey offers a (per)version of Lyotard's work that effectively renders it not worthy of serious consideration. The story is that Lyotard presents a silly 'radical proposal', namely that opening up computer data banks to everyone would represent a 'prologue to radical reform' (Harvey 1989, p. 117). Such a 'proposal' is described as instructive because it demonstrates that postmodernists are faced with 'making some universal gesture (like Lyotard's appeal to some pristine concept of Justice)' (Harvey 1989, p. 117) or, alternatively, with remaining politically silent like Derrida. Political 'silence' in this context seems to mean not only abstaining from pronouncements about 'what should be done', but by implication, that there is no politics of, or for that matter in, deconstruction.

If we turn to Lyotard's closing remarks on the postmodern condition it is apparent that the principal concern is with the implications of the idea of an incommensurability of language games, and an associated absence of the possibility of universal or common metaprescriptives. Lyotard comments that

> There is no reason to think that it would be possible to determine metaprescriptives common to all of these language games [denotative, prescriptive, performative, technical, evaluative etc.] or that a revisable consensus like the one in force

at a given moment in the scientific community could embrace the totality of metaprescriptions regulating the totality of statements in the social collectivity.

(Lyotard 1986, p. 65)

It is in this context, of an absence of grand narratives of legitimation, that Lyotard locates the emergence and development of an increasingly cynical systemic emphasis upon criteria of performativity, and expresses concern about the possible consequences of an associated 'computerisation of society'.

One possible consequence of the computerisation of society identified by Lyotard is the institutionalisation of an 'instrument for controlling and regulating the market system . . . governed exclusively by the performativity principle . . . [which] would inevitably involve the use of terror' (1986, p. 67). This is a conceivable scenario of concern to a diverse range of theorists, including many working from within a Marxist problematic (Noble 1983: 1984; Webster and Robins 1986; Robins and Webster 1989). In response to this troubling scenario Lyotard notes another possibility, that computerisation might 'aid groups discussing meta-prescriptives by supplying them with the information they usually lack for making knowledgeable decisions'. But for this prospect to become a possibility, it is necessary to 'give the public free access to the memory and data banks' (1986, p. 67). It is this brief comment that Harvey translates into a 'radical proposal', and then inflates into a prologue for radical reform. To conceive of Lyotard's position in such terms is effectively to miss the point, for it suggests the presence of a hidden alternative technocratic agenda, and an associated conflation of differences 'between denotative, or knowledge, games and prescriptive, or action, games' (Lyotard 1986, p. 64). The contrary is the case, it being consistently argued that a prescriptive statement or a command 'cannot find its justification in a denotative statement' (Lyotard and Thébaud 1985, p. 22), and moreover that what might hold for the relative simplicity of the pragmatics of science cannot be assumed to extend to the much greater complexity of social pragmatics.[3]

Whilst Harvey goes a long way towards recognising various manifestations of a condition of postmodernity, ultimately developments are conceived solely in terms of the process of capital accumulation-circulation and its consequences. Changes in the experience of space and time, increases in ephemerality and fragmentation, a proliferation of images, and erosion of 'confidence in the association between scientific and moral judgments' are accepted to be significant transformations, but ultimately to lie well within the grasp of a form of Marxist, historical materialist analysis. Addressing postmodernity as a 'historical–geographical' condition allows Harvey to generate a range of interesting insights and ideas concerning the complex forms of articulation which exist between contemporary social, cultural, political, and economic practices. However, the corollary, namely an exploration of the impact of postmodern forms of life on knowledge and politics in general, and Marxist forms in particular, receives short shrift.

Where consideration is given to the question of a potential crisis of historical materialism it takes the form of a series of brief reflections on the responses of the New Left to the limits and limitations of 'traditional communist parties and "orthodox" Marxism'. Harvey argues that from its inception the New Left has placed emphasis upon cultural practices and politics, has embraced the new social movements, and thereby has effectively contributed to the 'turn to aesthetics that postmodernism has been about' (1989, p. 354). But whilst a move away from the limitations of old style left politics might have been necessary, Harvey clearly considers the New Left has gone too far in abandoning

> its *faith* both in the proletariat as an instrument of progressive change and in historical materialism as a mode of analysis . . .
> The New Left thereby cut itself off from its own ability to have a *critical perspective on itself* or on the social processes of transformation that underlay the surge into postmodernist ways of thought. In insisting that it was culture and politics that mattered, and that it was neither reasonable nor proper to involve economic determination even in the last instance (let alone involve theories of capital circulation and accumulation, or of necessary class relations in production) it was unable to stop its own drift into ideological positions that were weak in contest with the new-found strength of the neo-conservatives.
> (Harvey 1989, p. 354: emphasis added)

Interestingly the evidence which has led analysts to question the idea of a politics predicated on the 'messianic' agency of the proletariat is not considered; rather criticisms and doubts about the historic mission accorded to this problematic social constituency are equated with a loss of faith, a condition no doubt aggravated, if not precipitated, by the accumulation of 'disenchanting' signs of emerging postmodern political forms and movements (Aronowitz 1987/88). But given Harvey's critical diagnosis of the postmodern condition of the New Left, only one remedy is really conceivable, namely a 'renewal' of historical materialism. However, renewal requires more than a restatement of analytic and political certitudes. It necessitates, to begin with, an acknowledgement of the limits and limitations of the existing paradigm, and as a corollary a degree of deconstruction of Marxist categories and assumptions. This is something Harvey appears unwilling to contemplate.

Proceeding from a broadly comparable analytic orientation Soja (1989) and Hebdige (1988) engage more openly than either Jameson or Harvey with the question of the possible emergence of a postmodern condition. In consequence they are able to devote more serious consideration to the question of the potential implications of an emerging condition of postmodernity for historical materialism, critical modes of thought and analysis, and radical politics.

WITHOUT FAITH OR GUARANTEES – MARXISM AFTER POSTMODERNISM

Postmodernism challenges Marxism on a number of counts. It questions its generalising aspirations, its totalising claims, and its emancipatory scenario(s). It problematises its conception of both history and politics, and raises doubts about the pivotal move within Marxist discourse from denotative, or knowledge, statements – explanations and interpretations of the world – to prescriptive or political statements – proposals for changing the world. This does not mean that nothing can, or should, be changed, but rather that questions of politics and ethics cannot simply be resolved through scientific knowledge or 'correct' theory (Lyotard and Thébaud 1985). Marxist responses to the postmodern challenge have been described as 'disturbing and unsatisfactory' in so far as they involve a retreat into 'the arms of orthodoxy . . . [and] much moral finger-wagging (postmodernism is decadent, self-indulgent, irresponsible, a subterfuge of late capitalist imperialism) which dismisses any genuine theoretical debate' (D'Amico 1986, p. 136). If this represents an appropriate comment on some responses offered to the postmodern 'threat', it is completely inadequate to describe the different ways in which both Soja and Hebdige have responded to the growing signs of change associated with the reality, if not the 'promise', of postmodern conditions.

Soja and Hebdige offer significantly different, yet complementary, approaches to the realities and possibilities contained within the postmodern condition. Both approach postmodernism, at least in the first instance, through the process of capitalist modernisation, but do so without reducing it to an epiphenomenal, or derivative, set of forms. Furthermore, they each present postmodernism as a terrain to be contested, rather than abandoned, one within which it is both possible, and necessary, to constitute a postmodern politics of diversity, resistance, and demystification, to counter existing reactionary forms of postmodern politics. But their respective analyses of postmodernism display important differences in both emphasis and focus. Soja, paralleling Harvey's reflections on the condition of postmodernity, gives analytic priority to the question of space, or rather the effects of spatialisation synonymous with the emergence of a postmodern condition, and the onset since the late 1960s of a new crisis-induced phase of capitalist modernisation. The central thesis is that the radical forms of restructuring currently occurring constitute a fourth modernisation of capitalism, a new phase which 'cannot be practically and politically understood only with the conventional tools and insights of modern Marxism or radical social science' (Soja 1989, p. 5).[4] The implication is clear – existing concepts and forms of analysis need to be adapted, not abandoned. It is not a question of either Marxist analysis or a form of post-structuralist deconstruction, but rather in Soja's view of recognising the emergence of a postmodern discourse that is 'seeking not to dismiss Marxism as a critical theory but to open it up to a necessary and overdue spatialisation, to a materialist interpretation of spatiality that would match its magisterial historical materialism' (Soja 1989, p. 40). In short for Soja postmodernism offers the possibility of a deconstruction and reconstitution of Marxism. In contrast Hebdige is more directly concerned with the various manifestations of postmodernism and less explicitly preoccupied with revising or adapting Marxism.

In a series of cultural studies Hebdige confronts the diversity of forms and practices associated with the complex and ambiguous configuration of postmodernism. Acknowledging that the term postmodern is used to describe a wide range of objects, texts, practices, experiences, and conditions – everything from

> the decor of a room, the design of a building, . . . the construc-
> tion of a record, . . . an anti-technological tendency within
> epistemology, . . . the collective chagrin and morbid

projections of a post-War generation of baby boomers confronting disillusioned middle age, . . . a new phase in commodity fetishism, [to] the 'decentring' of the subject, an
'incredulity towards metanarratives', [and] a sense . . . of
'placelessness' . . . or (even) a generalised substitution of spatial
for temporal coordinates.

(Hebdige 1988, p. 182)

Hebdige expresses a similar opinion to Soja, namely that the postmodern should not be simply dismissed as meaningless or reactionary,
but rather explored and examined.

If Hebdige appears to be less concerned with reconstituting
Marxism, it is ultimately because the neo-Gramscian line adopted is
considered to share 'historical and intellectual ground' with the more
critical versions of the postmodern condition subjected to analysis.
The question of the relationship between postmodernism and
Marxism is not absent from Hebdige's deliberations, but it does
assume a different form from the postmodern problem of spatial
reorganisation identified by Soja as a neglected dimension within the
Marxist tradition of analysis. Both Soja and Hebdige approach the
subject of postmodernism with caution, place emphasis upon
continuities between modernity and postmodernity, and endorse a
sceptical or critical orientation towards many aspects of the
postmodern condition. But, as I have indicated, they each stop well
short of a dismissal of postmodernism as an irretrievably reactionary
tendency, and ultimately endorse its relevance for understanding new
forms of spatialisation and the pressing analytic problems and political
predicaments encountered in the present. Specifically, Soja refers to
the 'emergence of a new, postmodern culture of space and time', and
to the relevance of postmodernism for understanding 'changes in the
way we think about and respond to the particularities – the perils and
the possibilities – of the contemporary moment via science, art,
philosophy, and programmes for political action' (Soja 1989, p. 62).
For his part Hebdige acknowledges that the range of conditions
encompassed by the term postmodernism is not entirely novel, and he
endorses Hall's view that the 'old certainties began to run into trouble
from the 1900s onwards' (1986, p. 47). However, there does now
appear to be a significant difference, namely a growing realisation that
'we must learn to live without the kinds of guarantee which have
sometimes seemed to underwrite the human project' (Hebdige 1988,
p. 240).

The complex forms of societal restructuring associated by Soja with a fourth phase of capitalist modernisation have transformed economic, political, cultural, ideological, and intellectual patterns and practices. Simultaneously, prevailing forms of analysis and political strategy have been exposed as deficient and inappropriate. The emergence of new forms, forces, and combinations and the increasing inappropriateness of theoretical and political responses to the 'peculiarities of "late capitalism"' lead Soja to argue that a restructuring of Marxism is long overdue. As I have noted, for Soja the key restructuring issue concerns the theorisation of space or spatiality, and the principal focus of the analysis of the postmodern condition consequently falls on the question of whether, or not, it is possible to find a place for a 'theoretically meaningful spatial dimension' within a reconstituted Marxism. It is not enough simply to attempt to incorporate yet another new variable within an existing, unquestioned and unchanged master narrative, rather 'Marxism itself . . . [has] to be critically restructured to incorporate a salient and central spatial dimension' (Soja 1989, p. 59). This necessarily involves a process of radical deconstruction of 'historical materialism and its despatialising master narratives', the aim being to generate a mode of analysis, and a political culture, relevant to the 'postmodern capitalist landscape'.

There are already traces of a spatial analysis, or perspective, within the Marxist tradition, in the form of theories of imperialism, the existence of a movement in the USSR, between 1917 and 1925, to institute a 'new socialist spatial organisation', indirect references to spatial relations present in Gramsci's work, and more significantly, an explicit address by Lefebvre of 'the importance of spatiality and the existence of an intrinsic spatial problematic in the history of capitalism' (Soja, 1989, p. 50). But if the question of spatiality has been pivotal in various encounters between modern geography and Western Marxism since the early 1970s, and has in turn led to the 'formation and reformation of Marxist geography', it remains open, a continuing matter of debate. The question of spatiality remains contentious, in good part because of the persistence and continued defence of the modern intellectual division of labour. However, in the midst of various forms of intellectual retrenchment, confrontation, and confusion, Soja argues that 'a more reconstructive postmodern critical human geography' has begun to emerge, a form of flexible specialisation which lies outside the parameters of both modern geography and Western Marxism. The approach outlined has a number of postmodern features, notably a resistance to 'paradigmatic closure and rigidly categorical thinking', rejection of totalising visions, 'suspension of epistemological formalism', and openness towards new ways of interpreting the empirical world. But to achieve the objective of a 'politically charged . . . spatio-temporal perspective on society and social life' (Soja 1989, p. 73), radical deconstruction alone is not sufficient. If the emerging discursive formation is to make a contribution to the development of a 'radical postmodernism of resistance' it must also be responsive to the political and theoretical demands of the present, be able to 'encompass all the scales of modern power', and be critically attuned to both the political struggles of the peripheralised and oppressed, as well as the complexities of 'contemporary restructuring processes and emerging regimes of "flexible" accumulation and social regulation' (Soja 1989, p. 74).

The task is to get to grips with the 'passage to postmodernity', which has opened up since the late 1960s and the end of the post-war boom in the global capitalist economy, to achieve an understanding of the emerging new culture of time and space, and related transformations in forms of knowledge and experience in the (post)-modern world. Given such an agenda, it becomes necessary to move

> beyond rigorous empirical descriptions which imply scientific understanding but too often hide political meaning; beyond a simplistic anti-Marxism which rejects all the insights of historical materialism in the wake of an exposure of its contemporary weaknesses and gaps; beyond the disciplinary chauvinisms of an outdated academic division of labour desperately clinging to its old priorities; beyond a Marxist geography that assumes that a historical geographical materialism has already been created by merely inserting a second adjective.
>
> (Soja 1989, p. 75)

It is by proceeding in these terms that Soja suggests a radical and resistant political culture of postmodernism might be developed.

The question of the implications of the various manifestations of the postmodern condition for Marxism is also an integral feature of several of Hebdige's essays. Postmodernism is presented as antagonistic to the generalising aspirations and universalistic claims of the traditions of inquiry which have developed in the West since the Enlightenment, as sceptical of teleological forms of explanation, and as opposed to the associated technocratic planning, programming, and engineering of global/collective solutions/destinations. And, as such, it is antithetical to many of the accepted features of Marxism. The threat and promise of postmodernism for Marxism draws a range of responses from Hebdige, everything from barely concealed antagonism to grudging accommodation, acceptance, and affirmation.

The symptoms associated with the postmodern condition include a displacement of the universalising intellectual, the legislator–prophet, by the specific intellectual, the partisan facilitator–interpreter; accumulating doubts about universal validity claims; opposition to centralised, bureaucratically organised forms of politics; and the emergence of new collectivities and forms of subjectivity which reveal the limits and limitations of existing critical discourses and radical political strategies. These developments have contributed to a 'crisis of representation' that encompasses both the domain of politics and the terrain of analysis, and extends to the whole post-modern naturalisation of the hyperreal, sheltered as Baudrillard would have it, 'from any distinction between the real and the imaginary' (1983a, p. 4). A crisis which is associated with an increasing erosion of the binary structures of reality–appearance, real and phenomenal forms, science and ideology, consciousness and the unconscious, and with growing doubts about analytic claims to reveal hidden truths. The erosion of 'critical distance and the depth model' is particularly problematic for Marxist critical practice for it makes it

> no longer possible to speak of our collective 'alienation' from
> some imagined (lost or ideal) 'species being'. Without the gaps
> between say perception, experience, articulation and the real
> opened up by the modernist master categories of ideology and
> alienation, there is no space left to struggle over, to struggle
> from.
>
> (Hebdige 1988, p. 192)

The difficulties identified are further exacerbated by the decentring of the subject, the disarticulation of the idea of the unitary subject, and the increasing inconceivability of any ultimate resolution to the problems, conflicts, and struggles deemed to be synonymous with the 'history of all hitherto existing society' (Marx and Engels 1968). The promise of an end to that particular history has not so much been broken, as finally recognised to have been, all along, a simulation, a quasi-secular transposition of an older 'grand (Hebraic) narrative . . .

(Armageddon, the Apocalypse, Socialism: end of class struggle)' (Hebdige 1988, p. 194). The upshot is not the disappearance or absence of alternatives, but rather that 'resolutions', in their turn, in their space and time, reveal their structurally induced problems and dangers, their typical struggles and conflicts. As Hebdige economically observes, 'postmodernity is modernity without the hopes and dreams which made modernity bearable' (1988, p. 195).

At several points an understandable tension is evident in Hebdige's reflections, a tension between an acknowledgement, even an acceptance, of the existence of changed circumstances and conditions which might be described as 'postmodern', and an antagonism to the same which gets displaced onto a cluster of analysts who approach the problems and possibilities associated with the conditions identified without the conceptual tools (baggage) and commitments (obligations) of Marxism. It is a tension which appears to derive from Hebdige's conviction that we now seem to be 'strung out on the road to nowhere', whilst simultaneously wishing to be heading somewhere in particular. This is most evident in a series of comments directed, once again, at the work of Lyotard, who at times is mistakenly represented as an *advocate* rather than an *analyst* of the postmodern condition. Notwithstanding a disclaimer to the contrary, there is in Hebdige's work a polarising of positions between the adopted neo-Gramscian Marxist line and Lyotard's approaches to the question of the postmodern condition. As a lapsed Marxist Lyotard is assumed to be an antagonist, and in consequence his work is presented as antithetical to the kind of project that might be derived from a process of deconstruction–reconstitution of Marxism. Hebdige refers to Lyotard's 'explicit renunciation of Marxism'; rigorous exclusion of 'any aspiration to "present the unpresentable" through politics'; recommendation that we 'should instead think of the human project in terms of "the infinite task of complexification"' (1988, p. 199); and subsequent equation of 'the claim for simplicity' with barbarism. Such a reading of Lyotard's work is more than playful; it exemplifies a cavalier attitude of 'anything goes', including, in places, what appears to be blatant misrepresentation. It is a puzzling reading because it unnecessarily fabricates problems and differences, and thereby impedes one of the chief objectives, namely of thinking through the implications of the postmodern condition for a form of reconstituted Marxism.

The comments on Marxism, politics, and the present made by Lyotard are less contentious than Hebdige is willing to recognise or allow. Marxism is not so much renounced as qualified, circumscribed, and limited in its relevance to an understanding or analysis of the development of capitalism.[5] However, when Lyotard proceeds to question the existence of observable 'working classes' and the 'proletariat' as 'the name of an Idea of Reason, the name of a subject to be emancipated' (1989, pp. 23–4), he is, as Hebdige notes, reminding us of the difficulty (impossibility?) Marxism has encountered in reconciling theory and praxis, a difficulty which grows out of the overinflated contrast drawn in the 'eleventh thesis' on Feuerbach between interpretations of the world and actions directed to its transformation. The eleventh thesis has much to answer for. It has in too many instances served to legitimate concealed moves from the analytic terrain to the political domain, by insinuating that 'just' political prescriptions can be drawn from a 'description that is true, in the sense of "correct"' (Lyotard and Thébaud 1985, p. 23). But equally, if not more significantly, it has contributed to the generation of a significant misunderstanding about the relationship between social knowledge and social life. Knowledge or interpretations of the social world alter the world, but not according to a preconceived design. Under current conditions knowledge 'does not simply render the social world more transparent, but alters its nature, spinning it off in novel directions' (Giddens 1990, p. 153). Given 'the reflexivity or circularity of social knowledge' identified by Giddens, it no longer makes much sense to continue indicting analysts for *only* interpreting the world rather than changing it. Interpretations, understandings, and knowledges of the social world contribute to its transformation, but not under conditions entirely within our control, nor in the ways, or directions, we might intend. It is for 'these reasons [that] we cannot seize "history" and bend it readily to our collective purposes' (Giddens, 1990, p. 153).

Likewise, Lyotard's comments on 'complexification' and 'simplicity' need to be placed in their appropriate context, namely of a discussion of the effects of the development of 'techno-sciences' and 'new technologies'. Technological development, not to be equated with 'progress', seems according to Lyotard virtually to have a momentum of its own, literally *appears* to 'be taking place by itself'. In consequence the possibility that technological innovation, development, and complexification is a result of the development of capitalism *alone* is questioned. An additional, more tentative hypothesis is proposed, namely, isn't it more something of an obscure desire which produces this development of techno-science: an obscure desire towards extra-sophistication? . . . We can perhaps consider human history as a series of attempts at organising human society and minds, *not* in order to achieve freedom or happiness or anything like that . . . but just to achieve the infinite task of complexification.

(Lyotard 1989, pp. 21–2)

But far from recommending this scenario Lyotard is quite explicitly critical of it, commenting that such developments (of techno-sciences) have constituted a 'means of increasing disease, not of fighting it', and have destabilised 'human entities (individual or social)'. Hence the conclusion:

Our demands for security, identity and happiness, coming from our condition as living beings and even social beings appear today irrelevant in the face of this sort of *obligation to complexify*, mediate, memorise and synthesise every object, and to change its scale. We are in this techno-scientific world like Gulliver: sometimes too big, sometimes too small, never at the right scale. Consequently, the claim for simplicity, in general, appears today that of a barbarian.

(Lyotard 1989, p. 9: emphasis added)

This impasse and its corollary, the subjection of other human communities to the 'terrible ancient task of survival', is presented as 'a major aspect of the failure of the modern project (which was in principle, valid for mankind as a whole)' (1989, p. 10). This is hardly the substance of which recommendations are made; on the contrary, Lyotard's comments have more in common with those of a range of radical critics of the 'technological infatuation' (Roszak 1986), 'cultural fetishisation of technology' (Noble 1984), and 'technical fixes' (Robins and Webster 1989) afflicting contemporary forms of life.

What ultimately emerges from Hebdige's meandering journey through the postmodern landscape is a confirmation of a Gramscian line. To paraphrase Hall (1988), it is a case of 'Gramsci and no further'! However, several of Hebdige's comments on the Gramscian approach, notably the commitment to local forms of radical politics, flexible strategies, and decentralisation, and in particular the fact that nothing is anchored to the *grands recits*, to master narratives, to stable (positive) identities, to fixed and certain meanings: all social and semantic relations are contestable, hence mutable; everything appears to be in flux: there are no predictable outcomes.

(Hebdige 1988, p. 206)

suggest the absorption or adoption of postmodern positions. The imminent prospect of a postmodern Marxism prompts Hebdige to seek refuge in qualification, notably that there are 'crucial differences between the two sets of orientations' associated with postmodernism and a neo-Gramscian line. But it is not entirely clear what these crucial differences amount to, beyond a few rhetorical flourishes concerning the need to engage with the multiple axes and forms of articulation of both power and the popular, 'with the popular as constructed and as lived', and with the 'issues, problems, anxieties, dreams, and hopes of real (i.e. actually existing) men and women' (1988, pp. 203–4). Moreover the differences referred to are themselves controversial, for they are already the focus of 'postmodern' approaches to social enquiry (Bauman 1988a; Heller and Feher 1988). What is clear is that there is a willingness to accommodate, if not embrace postmodernism if it means

the opening up to critical discourse of lines of enquiry which were formerly prohibited, . . . the opening up of institutional and discursive spaces within which more fluid and plural social and sexual identities may develop; . . . the erosion of triangular formations of power and knowledge with the expert at the apex and the 'masses' at the base, if in a word, it enhances our collective (and democratic) sense of *possibility*.

(Hebdige 1988, p. 226)

It is not then a matter of modernity or postmodernity, Marxism or postmodernism, but rather of reflecting on the impact of postmodern conditions on modernity and Marxism. The terrain is moving, the foundations which may once have seemed secure have slipped (again), and in the case of Marxism the conventional and seemingly reliable reference points of scientificity, laws of history, proletariat, revolution, and socialism have become problematic, if not anachronistic in some instances.

In circumstances where 'totalizing representations have been identified as critical components of power' characteristic of a discredited modernity, and radical transformations in the societies of Eastern Europe have been described as possible signs of 'a "post-modern" revolution' (Sayer 1991, p. xi), it is not surprising to find that Marxism is again a focus of critical reflection. What is emerging, as Hebdige has cogently observed, is a 'Marxism without guarantees'. It is a Marxism which has to cope without its teleological infra-structure, a Marxism which has lost its 'guaranteed philosophical and epistemological underpinnings' (Hall 1988, p. 73). Although this does not signal the end of Marxism, it does suggest the prospect of a more radical process of deconstruction and reconstitution, a process which leads in one direction to 'the emergence of a post-Marxism or a postmodern Marxism' (Laclau 1988, p. 72).

THE LAST POST?

In one form or another Marxism has been in crisis almost from its inception.[6] Given the central objective has been an intellectual and political engagement with a dynamic, increasingly changing mode of production, and with parallel transformations in social, cultural, and political life, the intermittent recurrence of a sense of crisis in Marxism is hardly surprising; indeed it might be considered a necessary feature, even a positive sign. The history of Marxism is punctuated with crucial debates, turning points, repeated calls for clarification and revision, as well as reinterpretations and reformu-lations following critical reflections on changes in socioeconomic circumstances and developments in theory and analysis. The idea of a postmodern Marxism, or post-Marxism, belongs in that broad con-text in so far as it constitutes a response to changes in social, political and theoretical conditions.

Post-Marxism is a contentious idea, one which has been equated with an anti-Marxist stance (Frankel 1987), described as 'faddish' (Jameson 1988), and criticised for abandoning the core of the Marxist project, and thereby for lacking any sense of political direction (Geras 1987: 1988; Burawoy 1989). But it has also been identified as a necessary development, an appropriate response to the changed circumstances we encounter (Laclau and Mouffe 1985: 1987; Hall 1986: 1988; Emmison et al. 1987/88). In debating terms the contrast is effectively between post-Marxism as simply another form of 'revisionism', a form of analysis which institutes a dangerous, heretical, and unnecessary departure from the 'correct' understanding of Marx's work (Geras 1987: 1988; Burawoy 1989), and post-

Marxism as a necessary movement beyond conceptions of laws of history, a reductionist understanding of the significance of economic relations, and the assumption of a close articulation between class subjects and political agents. In other words the contrast is between a 'business-as-usual' Marxism and a perceived necessity to break with some of the cherished features of Marxism, in order to develop an understanding of 'the transformations of the world in which we live' and their implications for theory and politics (Giddens 1987; Poster 1990; Sayer 1991).

The most sustained address of the need to move beyond a Marxism with lapsed guarantees is provided by Laclau and Mouffe in *Hegemony and Socialist Strategy*. Laclau and Mouffe argue that a range of socioeconomic and political transformations, and associated developments in critical thinking, have placed left-wing thought 'at a crossroads':

> The 'evident truths' of the past – the classical forms of analysis and political calculation, the nature of the forces in conflict, the very meaning of the Left's struggles and objectives – have been seriously challenged by an avalanche of historical mutations which have riven the ground on which those truths were constituted.
>
> (Laclau and Mouffe 1985, p. 1)

Although no explicit reference is made to either postmodernism or postmodernity in the description and analysis of the historical mutations which have contributed to the fragmentation of the epistemological foundations of classical forms of analysis and political calculation, the changes referred to closely resemble those identified by Lyotard as symptomatic of the emergence of a postmodern condition. The various historical transformations described by Laclau and Mouffe include the failures and disappointments associated with actually/formerly existing socialism; structural transformations within the capitalist mode of production which have led to the emergence of 'postindustrial' forms of life, and an associated relative decline of the classical working class in first world, Western societies; and the emergence of 'post-liberal', 'post-Marxist', and 'postmodern' social and political movements, conflicts, and forms of protest (Aronowitz 1987/88). The evidence of an extension of forms of social conflict and struggle, around ecology, sexuality, ethnicity, religion, and the plight of national minorities, encourages the view that an established and unquestioned conception of socialism, predicated upon the pivotal role of what is assumed to be a potentially radical working class, possessing an enthusiasm for revolution, which will constitute 'the founding moment in the transition from one type of society to another' (1985, p. 2), cannot continue to be sustained.

Socialism now seems to be a concept with very little, if any, content. Given the fate of socialism in the twentieth century, the 'possibility needs to be faced, even by those persuaded of the validity of Marx's indictment of capitalism, that something may be awry in the very idea of socialism itself . . . Invidious as capitalism might be, the moral superiority of socialism can no longer be presumed a priori' (Sayer 1991, p. 147). In such circumstances a reconsideration of possible alternative positive social futures and associated political strategies would appear to be not only desirable, but unavoidable. If, as Burawoy contends, such a response 'softens Marxism's hard core' it is surely timely, because petrification is an obstacle to both analysis and understanding. Marx's thoughts were not, after all, inscribed in stone. If aspects of an analysis become an encumbrance, both to understanding the present and acting effectively within it, then they need to be jettisoned. To understand the 'durability of capitalism, the mollification of class struggle, [and] the failure of socialism' (Burawoy, 1985, p. 245) requires something more than a return to a diet of 'plain Marxism', that way surely lies analytic and political malnutrition.

The political imaginary at the centre of Marxism now seems completely at odds with the (dis)order of the (post)modern world. Ideas of 'universal' subjects, the singularity or 'unity' of history, and '"society"' as an intelligible structure that could be intellectually mastered on the basis of certain class positions and reconstituted, as a rational, transparent order, through a founding act of a political character' (Laclau and Mouffe 1985, p. 2), have been dissolved by the emergence of a plurality of social and political movements, and diverse associated forms of struggle. To analyse such contemporary social and political struggles in their specificity it is necessary to abandon the classical Marxist conception of 'history and society as intelligible totalities constituted around conceptually explicable laws' (1985, p. 3), and to employ a conception of 'hegemony', a conception which introduces both a 'logic of the social' and historical contingency into considerations of the political. The objective is to contribute to the development of a 'new politics for the Left based upon the project of a radical democracy'. It is a task which necessitates a deconstruction of Marxist categories which have promised to disclose the 'real', a recognition that the reign of normative epistemologies and universal discourses has ended. One obvious implication of such postmodern conditions of knowledge is of a break with other key features of the modern Marxist problematic, notably 'the conception of subjectivity and classes, . . . vision of the historical course of capitalist development, . . . [and] conception of communism as a transparent society from which antagonisms have disappeared' (1985, p. 4). The postmodern Marxist project is concerned, in part, to delineate the limits and limitations of Marxist analysis, but it simultaneously attempts to recover and develop traces and elements relevant to an understanding of present conditions and conducive to a 'radicalization of democracy' (Heller and Feher 1988, p. 34).

The project belongs, at one level at least, within the history of Marxism, for it is concerned with the question of the recurring discrepancy between the historical development of capitalism and analytically constituted normative expectations. But if Laclau and Mouffe begin from a reconsideration of the various attempts which have been made from within the Marxist tradition to respond to the growing 'opacity of the social, . . . the complexities and resistances of an increasingly organised capitalism; and the fragmentation of the different positions of social agents which, according to the classical paradigm, should have been united' (1985, p. 18), they ultimately argue that it is necessary to go beyond the theoretical and political horizon of modern Marxism. Their response to the various ways in which the evident limitations of the conceptions of historical necessity, economic reductionism, and the working class as a revolutionary political subject have been addressed within the Marxist tradition rotates around the concept of hegemony. Although Gramsci's (1976) adoption and development of the concept of hegemony represents a crucial moment in the constitution of a new political logic, there remains a problem. Namely the persistence in Gramsci's work of a residual essentialism which surfaces in the central privileged articulatory role assigned to the working class. This causes Laclau and Mouffe to comment that,

> Gramsci's thought appears suspended around a basic ambiguity concerning the status of the working class which finally leads it to a contradictory position. On the one hand, the political centrality of the working class has a historical, contingent character . . . On the other hand, it would seem that this articulatory role is assigned to it by the economic base – hence, that the centrality has a necessary character.
>
> (1985, p. 70)

To overcome this impasse it is necessary to pursue further the 'deconstructive logic of hegemony' left relatively underdeveloped in Gramsci's work. Effectively what this amounts to is a critical analysis of the last base of essentialism, namely a 'naturalist vision of the economy' and an associated tendency towards reductionism.

The argument is that analytic assumptions concerning the economy at the heart of modern Marxism cannot be sustained. The economy is not a 'self-regulated space subject to endogenous laws'; social and political constituencies do not have an essential 'class core' or base; and there is no necessary relationship between social class positions and 'interests'. In short 'fundamental interests in socialism cannot be *logically* deduced from determinate positions in the economic process' (Laclau and Mouffe 1985, p. 84). The consequences to be drawn from this are, first that social identities are purely relational, a consequence of 'articulation within a hegemonic formation', rather than an effect of any necessary class belonging, and that 'as this system of relations has itself ceased to be fixed and stable – thereby making hegemonic practices possible – the sense of every social identity appears constantly deferred' (1985, p. 86). Second, that the diverse range of contemporary forms of social and political protest or struggle are not subordinate to a priori class struggles and demands. In brief, the latter have no first claim, or privileged access to radical political practices and objectives. Finally, given the genealogy of the concept of hegemony, its emergence within the history of Marxism as a possible resolution to the problem of the 'hiatus that has opened in the chain of historical necessity', Laclau and Mouffe submit that it too should be deconstructed, and theoretically reconstituted.

The theoretically reconstructed 'non-essentialist' conception of hegemony which emerges from the process of deconstruction refers to a type of political relation in which social identities remain open or incomplete, and subject to articulatory practices in a field traversed by antagonisms. Laclau and Mouffe comment that it is,

> the presence of antagonistic forces and the instability of the frontiers which separate them . . . the presence of a vast area of floating elements and the possibility of their articulation to opposite camps – which implies a constant redefinition of the latter – . . . [that] constitutes the terrain permitting us to define a practice as hegemonic.
>
> (1985, p. 136)

A formulation of this order avoids the twin elements of essentialism present in Gramsci's work, namely the conflation of hegemonic subjects with 'fundamental' social classes, and the idea that there is a 'single hegemonic centre' in every social formation. Specifically it is a formulation which abandons the idea of a single constitutive principle through which the field of social differences might be fixed, one which problematises 'the premise of "society" as a sutured and self-defined totality' (1985, p. 111), and places emphasis upon the unstable and changing conditions in which contemporary political struggles and movements emerge and develop. Hence the connection identified between the emergence of relatively fluid new social and political movements, and the associated predominance of a hegemonic form of politics, with increases in the 'open, non-sutured character of the social' (1985, p. 138).

The new social movements, antagonisms, and forms of social conflict representing new forms of political subjectivity and expressing antagonism to new relations of subordination are conceived to be extensions of the 'democratic revolution'. The context in which new relations of subordination and associated expressions of antagonism, resistance, and opposition have arisen since World War II has been one of increasing change and growing complexity, involving significant economic, political, and cultural transformations. In terms of economic transformation there has been a process of diffusion of capitalist relations of production to more and more areas of social life. The process of commodification and the logic of capitalist accumulation now seem to have no bounds, and extend to virtually every domain of individual and collective life ('culture, free time, illness, education, sex, and even death'). However, paralleling the increasing diffusion of capitalist relations and the associated development of new types of pleasure and subordination, numerous new forms of struggle and resistance have developed, for example around concerns over waste, pollution, and the depletion of natural resources (ecology movements), the use and development of 'social space' ('urban' protest movements), and the rights of various 'minorities' and marginalised constituencies.

Likewise, the political development of an interventionist Keynesian Welfare State has had complex and uneven effects, including the provision of conditions necessary for a new regime of capitalist accumulation; the cultivation of a new type of right, 'social rights'; the constitution of new forms of subordination; and associated antagonisms and forms of struggle. Reflecting on developments such as these Laclau and Mouffe argue that, 'given the bureaucratic character of state intervention, . . . [the] creation of "public spaces" is carried out not in the form of true democratisation, but through the imposition of new forms of subordination. It is here that we have to look for the terrain on which numerous struggles emerge against bureaucratic forms of state power' (1985, p. 162). Finally, there is the question of cultural transformations, in particular the rapid growth of means of mass communication which have stimulated the development of new cultural forms and practices. As with the economic and political changes briefly noted above, the consequences of cultural transformations are both complex and ambiguous. On the one hand they seem to have precipitated 'massification', 'uniformisation', and pacification, yet on the other, there are signs of a democratisation of forms of consumer culture, evident for example in the 'emergence of new struggles which have played an important part in the rejection of old forms of subordination' (1985, p. 164).

The new forms of antagonism and struggle have tended to express themselves through an affirmation of 'liberalism' rather than in terms of collective struggle, primarily because they constitute forms of resistance to accelerating social processes of commodification, bureaucratisation, and homogenisation. To that extent the emergence of new forms of struggle and political subjectivity may indicate an extension of the democratic revolution. Common to all the new forms of struggle is the constitution of a social identity, which simultaneously introduces a division into social space, a division predicated upon attributed relations of equivalence and difference, through which political identity and opposition are formed. An analysis that takes account of the proliferation of political antagonisms allows a radically different approach to be taken to the question, which has been continually posed within the Marxist tradition, of the absence of a political identity, or unity, of the working class: namely, that 'unsuccessful' strategies for (re)constituting a form of working class unity, if inverted, make possible a recognition of 'the plurality of the social, and the unsutured character of all political identity' (1985, p. 166). Such an 'inversion' allows existing alternative forms of social solidarity and radical political strategy to be analysed in their own right, rather than as signs of an absent 'coherent', collective class politics.

One frequent response to the existence of new social and political movements and struggles has been to dismiss them as 'liberal', or to portray them as inevitably doomed to be incorporated and neutralised. From such a standpoint 'real' change necessitates a recuperation of what are taken to be aberrant forms of struggle within the overall framework of 'historical materialist enquiry . . . and class politics (with its emphasis upon the unity of the emancipatory struggle)' (Harvey 1989, p. 355). However, the implied concept of a unified class subject is a problem, because it obscures the processes of discursive constitution through which the existing multiplicity of political subjectivities are constituted, and thereby it impedes the development of a radical and plural democracy. Once the problematic category of the unified subject is abandoned it becomes possible to recognise the range and variety of forms of antagonism and resistance which have been continually conflated within the category 'workers' struggles. Specifically it allows other occluded or subordinated social relations and forms of subjectivity, which may, or may not, be implicated in specifically work-place or work-based struggles, to be identified. In sum there is no basis for privileged forms of subjectivity or struggle, no foundation for guaranteed causes or outcomes. As Laclau and Mouffe comment:

> There is no *unique* privileged position from which a uniform continuity of effects will follow, concluding with the transformation of society as a whole. All struggles, whether those of workers or other political subjects, left to themselves, have a partial character, and can be articulated to very different discourses. It is this articulation which gives them their character, not the place from which they come. There is therefore no subject – nor further, any 'necessity' – which is absolutely radical and irrecuperable by the dominant order, and which constitutes an absolutely guaranteed point of departure for a total transformation. Equally, there is nothing which permanently assures the stability of an established order.
>
> (1985, p. 169)

References to increases in contingency, pluralism, fragmentation, discursively constituted forms of subjectivity, the 'open, non-sutured character of the social', the significance of transformations in economic, political, and cultural life after World War II, and the absence of guarantees or secure foundations for analysis and political strategy, indicate that the provisional proposal for a radical and plural democratic politics advanced by Laclau and Mouffe exemplifies a radical or critical postmodern position.

ANALYSIS AND POLITICS UNDER POSTMODERN CONDITIONS

The idea of a postmodern condition of knowledge and its corollary, the notion of an emerging social and political condition of postmodernity, present a direct challenge to modern Marxism. It is, as Jay remarks, as if 'the spectre of detotalisation and disintegration, which haunted the bourgeois *fin-de-siècle*, has returned to chill the socialist movement . . . of our own day' (1988, p. 2). Chilled and stirred by the emergence of postmodern conditions, Marxism encounters difficulties on a number of fronts. Analytically and politically there are major problems, problems which indicate that the intellectual tradition of Marxism is in need of revitalisation, that, once again, it is necessary to draw upon a range of intellectual currents that lie beyond its shores, hence the ambiguous notion of post-Marxism. Recourse to 'alien' philosophies is of course nothing new – it has been a longstanding feature of the Marxist tradition. However, whereas earlier engagements with phenomenological and existential philosophies and subsequent structuralist analyses served ultimately to reaffirm the central tenets and premises of Marxism, recourse to poststructuralist forms of analysis and accommodation to postmodern conditions raises the prospect of embracing analytic and social developments which extend well beyond the conventional theoretical and political parameters of modern Marxism.

One of the problems with the idea of 'post-Marxism' is that it implies a final settling of accounts, a 'going beyond' in the sense of 'taking leave'. But just as the idea of the postmodern does not signify a transcendence of the modern, so the idea of post-Marxism does not necessitate an abandonment of the Marxist tradition. On the contrary, '"post-marxism" is not an "ex-marxism" ' (Laclau 1988, p. 77); rather, it represents an accommodation of Marxist analysis to postmodern conditions, and an associated reconstruction of radical politics. It is the development of 'postmodern' social and political conditions, and parallel transformations in the field of knowledge, which have made necessary the deconstruction and reconstitution of Marxism. And it is from this process of deconstruction–reconstitution that a 'Marxism without guarantees' has emerged, a Marxism which, to that extent, is *post*-modern. Such a position contrasts starkly with that of the self-appointed guardians of the word, whose mission appears to be to continually subordinate the increasingly complex and changing realities of the world to the inviolable tenets of a chosen version of Marxism (Geras 1987: 1988; Callinicos 1989). It is not difficult to appreciate why Marx was moved to comment, 'all I know is that I am not a Marxist' (Marx and Engels 1975, p. 393).

There are three key issues on which Marxism has been shown to be vulnerable. Philosophically there has remained an 'essentialist apriorism', that is a 'conviction that the social is sutured at some point, from which it is possible to fix the meaning of any event independently of any articulatory practice' (Laclau and Mouffe 1985, p. 177), the corollary of which is a privileging of particular antagonisms ('classism'), strategies ('economism'), and mechanisms ('statism'). In brief the working class is conceived to be *the* agent of 'real', read progressive, radical, social(ist) change; successful economic strategy is considered to produce determinate political effects; and extending the role of the state is believed to be the solution to all significant social problems. To counter the problems of essentialism and metaphysical necessity Laclau and Mouffe employ discourse theory, and argue for the contingent character or 'radical historicity of being', and thus display a 'commitment to show the world for what it is : an entirely social construction of human beings' (1987, p. 106).

It is indisputable that the social analyses conventionally generated from within a Marxist paradigm have provided a degree of understanding of aspects of the dynamic of development internal to the capitalist mode of production, as well as of the effects, antagonisms, and dislocations to which the latter has given rise. But, in so far as such analyses have largely been derived from a nineteenth-century European frame of reference it is necessary 'to radicalise and transform . . . Marx's conception of the social agent and of social antagonisms' (1987, p. 106). This does not mean, as Gorz (1982) implies, withdrawing the privilege accorded to the proletariat and presenting it to a 'non-class of non-workers', but rather of recognising that antagonisms may be constituted in a plurality of discursive forms, and that the forms in which an antagonism is articulated are not predetermined but 'the result of a hegemonic struggle' (Laclau and Mouffe 1985, p. 168). In other words there is no privileged agent of social(ist) change, rather a plurality of social agents exists within an extended field of diverse social conflicts. Furthermore there can be no final end to antagonism and struggle.

The existence of new forms of antagonism and struggle, new social movements, and the corollary, an erosion of remaining vestiges of a 'politics based solely on class interests and class perception' make it necessary for us to face up to the fact that 'trends and upheavals in

217

today's politics simply cannot be understood in modernist-class categories' (Heller and Feher 1988, p. 3). In turn the classic Marxist conception of 'revolution' leading to a centralised reorganisation of a 'higher' form of social life, free from antagonisms and conflicts, cannot be sustained. Social transformation is processual in character, never complete(d), and synonymous with the presence of a plurality of political subjects and spaces. In such circumstances the notion of socialism as the immediate focus or sole objective of radical politics is vulnerable to challenge. The challenge which I have been analysing comes not from a move to the 'right' but from critical reflections on modernity and associated deliberations on postmodernity. The project of modernity has sought to fabricate order, cultivate certainty, and engineer progress. A condition of postmodernity materialises with the realisation that the modern quest for order, certainty, and perpetual progress simultaneously promotes ambivalence, contingency, dissatisfaction, and restlessness. As Bauman (1987) suggests, it is not that modernity has been displaced by postmodernity, but rather that postmodernity represents a coming to terms with the limits and limitations of modernity. Postmodernity involves facing up to the fact that 'certainty is not to be', that 'the growth of knowledge expands the field of ignorance', and that 'our journey has no clear destination' (Bauman 1991, p. 244). However, 'facing up' does not mean 'giving up'; it means proceeding differently without the promises, hopes, and guarantees ascribed to modernity.

Recognition of the 'virtually complete reliance of socialism on the programme set by modernity' (Bauman 1991, p. 263) has meant that as the project of modernity has been subjected to question, criticism, and doubt, so has the related programme of socialism. The crisis of socialism is 'a reflection of the crisis of the modern project as such' (Bauman 1991, p. 266). It is in this context that discussion of radical political strategy has returned to the question of socialism and democracy. Under postmodern political conditions, the focus of debate has shifted from socialism to democracy. Emphasis has been placed upon a project of radical and plural democracy, of which socialism is one prominent dimension, 'necessary to put an end to capitalist relations of production, which are at the root of numerous relations of subordination' (1985, p. 178); radicalised democracy as 'the absolute precondition of articulating social issues, as a *conditio sine qua non* of the various types of socialism' (Heller and Feher 1988, p. 117); and upon a regeneration of democratic politics as the sole vehicle for the implementation of the values of liberty, diversity, tolerance, and solidarity which alone offer 'a chance of a better society' (Bauman 1991, p. 276).

The absence of analytical and political guarantees, privileged political positions and agents, necessary links between antagonisms and struggles, and a determinate end to politics is symptomatic of postmodern conditions. The postmodern condition of politics is plurality, a plurality of subjects, political spaces, and social logics through which various forms of social and political identity are constituted. The implication is of an open and precarious system, one in which identity and relations of equivalence between the plurality of social and political constituencies, antagonisms, and struggles are hegemonically articulated, rather than of a closed, fixed, and potentially stable totality. And in the absence of guarantees such articulations are necessarily relatively unstable, partial, open to contest, and in consequence transformation.[7]

The modern task, namely achieving mastery over both nature and the organisation of social life, in order to be able to redesign or refashion the world in accordance with a blueprint derived from reason, has been in question for some time. The emergence of postmodern conditions has cast further doubt on the prospect, if not the point, of attempting to complete the project of modernity. The modern assumption of a close correspondence between increasing rationalisation and increases in freedom, autonomy, and happiness has long been a contested matter (Horkheimer and Adorno 1973; Wright Mills 1970; Lyotard 1988). But if in present circumstances 'all old and prospective blueprints for a "good society" seem embarrassingly unreal and naive' (Bauman 1987, p. 194), that should not be taken to mean that there is no place for conceptions of alternative social futures, or reconstituted utopian forms within the political field.

Increasing rationality cannot guarantee increases in freedom, and to that extent the 'utopian' modern project is in trouble. But that should not give rise to disillusionment and despair, nostalgia, frustration or panic. Little has actually been lost, beyond excessive faith, misplaced hope, and unrealistic expectations. The radical modern project has all along been a political project, one without either certainty or security, one whose outcome could not be technocratically programmed, or guaranteed by reason. But too often it has appeared otherwise, has been presented as predetermined, if not predestined. The possible articulation between 'democracy' and 'socialism' can only be a political project, the result, as Laclau and Mouffe caution, 'of a long and complex hegemonic construction

219

which is permanently under threat and thus needs to be continuously redefined' (1987, p. 101). It is a project which requires a reconstruction of utopian forms within the political field, by which I do not mean forms of life that are to be considered directly realisable, nor for that matter a return to emancipatory figures formed within resurrected grand narratives. Rather, I mean utopian forms as critical resources for challenging prevailing forms of social life and as contributions to the complex process of realising possible alternatives, if of necessity in forms that are always, to a degree, unintended or not according to our designs. Given the circularity of social knowledge, envisaging alternatives plays an important part in the complex process of transforming the present (Giddens 1990, pp. 154–5), one important implication of which is that changing the world cannot be divorced from the unavoidable necessity of continuing to (re)interpret it.

Radical democratic 'postmodern' politics is open, precarious and incomplete. There is no place for privileged agents of political struggle, or subjects with privileged access to 'the truth'. The open and indeterminate character of the social, and the constitutive character of social divisions and antagonisms means that a radical democratic politics is necessarily located in a political field of articulatory and hegemonic practices, in brief, that radical democracy involves a political game of hegemony, a game currently being played under postmodern conditions. New social and political conditions make necessary new forms of analysis and understanding and, in the case of social action and political conduct, new forms of judgment. Under postmodern conditions Marxism constitutes merely one possible form of critical analysis, one point of reference within a reconstructed critical tradition. It is not a situation which is recommended, but it is one to which Marxism needs to accommodate if it is to continue to contribute to our understanding of present conditions and future prospects.

All that once seemed so solid and secure does indeed now appear quite different, increasingly fragile and uncertain. Conditions are not as once we expected, or anticipated, they might be(come). We are not able to predict, control, or design our future, but that should not occasion surprise or stop us continuing to attempt to influence the course of events. As Foucault optimistically reminds us, 'things can be changed, fragile as they are, held together more by contingencies than by necessities, more by the arbitrary than by the obvious, more by complex but transitory historical contingency than by inevitable anthropological constraints' (1982, p. 35). We know that social futures are not predetermined, that they cannot be simply engineered or designed. The problems associated with the discredited techno-scientific, instrumental–rational, legislative model of social change make it necessary for us not only to continue to envisage possible alternative social futures, but also to think differently about questions of actualisation, about the complex processes through which social realities are constituted. Understanding the reasons why the complex conditions within which we live are bound to remain, in significant respects, beyond our control, parodoxically provides us with the opportunity of contributing more effectively to the shaping of social futures.

NOTES

1 REFLECTIONS ON CHANGE

1 At the foundation of Parsons's evolutionary schema is a conception of a developmental societal trend towards 'greater generalised adaptive capacity'. It is this criterion which constitutes the basis for the observation that 'intermediate societies are more advanced than primitive societies, and modern societies are more advanced than intermediate societies' (Parsons 1977, p. 231).
The conception of 'generalised adaptive capacity' introduced by Parsons is, as Giddens comments, 'as vague and all-embracing as any in the literature' (1984, p. 270).

2 In particular Parsons refers to the following as conducive to the 'restoration' of integration:
(i)   the legal system
(ii) the extension of citizenship
(iii) market systems
(iv) bureaucratic organisations
(v)   associational organisations (Parsons 1977, pp. 174–81).

3 There are a number of possible parallels that might be explored here with Baudrillard's comparative observations on Europe and America. I have in mind Baudrillard's comment that all-out modernity is beyond Europe because it will never be able to rid itself of its residues of tradition. In contrast, in America radical modernity is said to have been realised, to have been made possible by the historical and cultural conditions of formation peculiar to the United States (Baudrillard 1988c; Smart 1991).

4 As Giddens remarks, 'the modern West [is] the highest evolutionary form in Parsons's scheme . . . Which society is farthest along the evolutionary route today? Why, the United States! A comforting, if not especially original conclusion for an American sociologist to reach after a grand survey of human evolution as a whole. This sounds like the sort of thing that gets sociology a bad name – at least in the remainder of the world' (1984, pp. 268–9).

5 This is a reference to a video-debate on modernity and its discontents between Gellner and Charles Taylor entitled 'The Tough and The Tender', London, Brook Productions.

6   To the contrary, Giddens (1984) identifies five concepts relevant to the development of generalisations about forms of social change. These are as follows:
    (i)   structural principles
    (ii) episodic characterisations
    (iii) intersocietal systems
    (iv) time–space edges
    (v)   world time.

7   It has been suggested that traces of a postmodern position may be found in Foucault's work, notably in *The Order of Things*, specifically the enigmatic comments offered there on the possible end of the modern *episteme*. However, when Foucault was called upon to respond to questions about the 'postmodern' he invariably expressed bewilderment and opposition to the idea, and argued that his work belonged within a 'modern' critical tradition of inquiry. But had he lived longer perhaps, as David Hoy suggests, he would have had to 'address the question of postmodernity in detail' (1988, p. 13).

8   Additional factors include differential access to knowledge; the role of values; design faults; and operator failure (Giddens 1990, pp. 44–5: 151–3).

2   QUESTIONS CONCERNING TECHNOLOGY AND (POST)INDUSTRIAL SOCIETY

1   As Heidegger remarks, 'Everywhere we remain unfree and chained to technology, whether we passionately affirm or deny it. But we are delivered over to it in the worst possible way when we regard it as something neutral; for this conception of it, to which today we particularly like to do homage, makes us utterly blind to the essence of technology' (1977, p. 4).

2   See Heidegger (1977) for a discussion of the limitations of the prevailing instrumental definition of technology.

3   ALTERNATIVE FUTURES

1   See for example the documentary *The Third Wave* which was transmitted to television audiences around the world, involved the cooperation of a range of international communications companies, and received an international television award. Also Toffler 1984, pp. 1:62 and Toffler and Toffler 1985.

2   For a discussion of the forces in conflict and the emerging struggle between 'Second' and 'Third' wave political forces see Toffler 1983, pp. 446–9; 1984, pp. 86–7: pp. 132–3.

3   See also Bell's comment that 'By the end of the century, the United States, Japan, Western Europe, and the Soviet Union will take on aspects of the post-industrial society and have to confront the management of

these new dimensions. How this is done will vary from country to country' (1973, p. 483).

4 Bahro at this stage refers to the 'capitalist mode of reproduction' as central to the crisis confronting our whole system and, in turn, identifies a communist perspective, albeit ecologically sensitised, as the key to any resolution (1984, ch. 4).

5 'Social costs' include the infrastructures, networks and public services which allow the production system to function. They include education and training; urban development and transport programmes; communications, health, recreation and sanitation services; legal and welfare provision (Gorz 1985, pp. 13–18).

6 See, for example, Illich's discussion of the need to invert existing institutions and substitute 'convivial' for 'industrial' tools (1985, pp. 10–14).

7 Subsequently Gorz articulates a third level of 'micro-social activity' involving forms of communal action, mutual aid, and cooperation. (1985, pp. 62–3).

8 See also Toffler's comments on 'reversionism' in *The Third Wave*, pp. 148:162:368.

9 In some respects Bahro's conception of an alternative to industrial capitalism replicates elements of Penty's (1917: 1922) idea of postindustrialism (see chapter 2).

10 Roszak comments:

> where everything — *everything* — has been staked out as somebody's specialised field of knowledge, what is the thinking of ordinary people worth? Precisely zero. For what do they know about anything that some expert does not know better? They are even experts on *their* sex life, *their* dreams, *their* relations with their children, *their* voting habits, *their* morals and manners, *their* tastes, *their* needs (1972, p. 258).

11 Roszak's critique of the 'world of experts' parallels features of both Illich's criticisms of the disabling effects of professionals and Foucault's critical concern about professionals and intellectuals.

4 ART, WORK AND ANALYSIS IN AN AGE OF ELECTRONIC SIMULATION

1 McLuhan's general view is that,

> If a technology is introduced either from within or from without a culture, and if it gives new stress or ascendancy to one or another of our senses, the ratio among all of our senses is altered. We no longer feel the same, nor do our eyes and ears and other senses remain the same (1967, p. 24).

2 See for example J.F.Lyotard's discussion of the condition of knowledge in *The Postmodern Condition* (1986).

3 McLuhan states that:

Archimedes once said, 'Give me a place to stand and I will move the world'. Today he would have pointed to our electric media and said, 'I will stand on your eyes, your ears, your nerves, and your brain, and the world will move in any tempo or pattern I choose'. *We have leased these 'places to stand' to private corporations* (1973, pp. 79–80: emphasis added).

4   For McLuhan the fact that jobs disappear with automation seems to present relatively few problems. See 'Automation: Learning a Living' in *Understanding Media* (1973).
5   The two most significant texts are *The Mirror of Production* (1975) and *For a Critique of the Political Economy of the Sign* (1981).
6   See for example the analyses provided by Gorz (1982:1985).
7   Baudrillard comments that:

It is directly at the level of the production of social relations that capitalism is vulnerable and en route to perdition. Its fatal malady is not its incapacity to reproduce itself economically and politically, but its incapacity to reproduce itself *symbolically* . . .
    It is this fatality of symbolic disintegration under the sign of economic rationality that capitalism cannot escape (1975, p. 143).

8   See my discussion in chapters 2 and 3.
9   A criticism of Baudrillard's work on this score is provided by Hall (1986).
10 See Laclau and Mouffe (1985).
11 See for example Kellner (1987); Morris (1988); Poster (1988); Hebdige (1988); and Smart (1990).

5   THE POSTMODERN PARADOX

1   Toynbee states that:

'From the Modern West's own point of view, its modernity had begun at the moment when Western Man had thanked, not God, but himself that he was as different a being from his 'medieval' predecessor as the Pharisee claimed to be from the publican in the parable (1954a, p. 114).

See also 1954a, pp. 110–11.
2   It is argued by Calinescu that the new contrast between antiquity and the modern age probably derives from the work of Francis Bacon. However, an earlier theological use of the simile, which broadly anticipates aspects of Bacon's 'secular paradox about modernity's ancientness', is to be found in Augustine's *The City of God* (Calinescu 1977 p. 26).
3   See for example Bell's reference to the work of modernist poet Octavio Paz. Bell cites Paz's comment that 'Today modern art is beginning to lose its powers of negation . . . Negation is no longer creative . . . we are living the end of the *idea of modern art*'. Bell remarks that his only qualification would be 'with the word "today". I believe that modernism lost its power 50 years ago' (1976, p. 20, n. 20).
4   Specifically Foucault states:

I've never clearly understood what was meant in France by the word 'modernity'. In the case of Baudelaire, yes, but thereafter I think the sense begins to get lost. I do not know what Germans mean by modernity. The Americans were planning a kind of seminar with Habermas and myself. Habermas had suggested the theme of 'modernity' for the seminar. I feel troubled here because I do not grasp clearly what that might mean, though the word itself is unimportant; we can always use any arbitrary label. But neither do I grasp the kind of problems intended by this term — or how they would be common to people thought of as being 'post-modern' (1983, p. 205).

5 Toynbee's view of the predicament confronting Western civilisation is summarised as follows:

The challenge of War and Class-Conflict had now been raised to a pitch of intensity at which the choice with which Mankind found itself confronted was the extreme choice of kill or cure. A latter-day Western Civilisation's technological *tours de force* had, in fact, made War intolerable by making it manifestly suicidal, and made Class-Conflict intolerable by making it apparently remediable (1954b, p. 468).

6 Another related event, not noted by Toynbee in this context, is the Holocaust, the employment of modern technology and rational forms of organisation in the extermination of European Jewry (Bauman 1989). This is equally a manifestation of the dark side of the dialectic of Enlightenment, of the contradictory character of the 'civilising process' of modernity.

7 The 'exotic' initiatives in French social and philosophical thought, exemplified by the respective works of Baudrillard, Barthes, Foucault, Deleuze, Derrida, Guattari, Laçan, and Lyotard have been described as contributions to 'poststructuralism' (Giddens 1987; Dews 1987; Poster 1990). As different as the analyses of the aforementioned figures are in a number of important respects, they are each considered to call attention and to contribute to the 'crisis of representation' evident in epistemological, artistic, and political contexts (Boyne and Rattansi 1990, p. 13); to 'deny us any access to an independent reality' (Callinicos 1990, p. 101); and to present the subject as 'fragmented and decentred in the social field', thereby undermining the notion of 'identity as a fixed and unified phenomenon' (Sawicki 1988, p. 174). As such the collection of positions and analyses brought together under the appellation 'poststructuralism' have made an important contribution to the current debate over the question of postmodern conditions (Lash 1990). However, whilst 'poststructuralist' forms of thought constitute a frequently identified element in deliberations over the question of the postmodern and, in turn, contribute to our understanding of present conditions, 'postmodernism' and 'poststructuralism' are not equivalent (Huyssen 1984a; Jay 1988).

8 There are a number of important parallels that might be drawn between Lyotard's position and the analysis of the present developed by Foucault,

notably a mutual antipathy towards totalising forms of thought and analysis, criticism of the universalising pretensions of (post)modern intellectuals, and an associated scepticism about the appropriateness and the adequacy of grand metanarratives of emancipation (Smart 1983).

9 A comparison might be made here with Harvey's (1989) analysis of the condition of postmodernity as the cultural corollary of the post-1973 transition in the capitalist mode of production towards 'flexible accumulation'.

6 MARXISM AND POSTMODERNISM

1 The developments concerned encompass the deployment of information technologies in production, a parallel proliferation of new electronic media of communication and representation, and, in particular, associated transformations in the conduct of knowledge, (re)production of information, and role or responsibility of intellectuals. Implied in the latter series of transformations are an increasing tendency for knowledge to be conceived in terms of the technical values and interests of business, industry, and the market, to the detriment of the humanities and moral forms of knowledge; transformations in the role of the university as a 'crucial intermediary between knowledge and culture' (Scott 1989); changes in the status and condition(s) of intellectual work; and associated changes in analytic assumptions and practices.

2 See for example *The Postmodern Condition: A Report on Knowledge* (1986) pp. 5:38–9:45.

3 It is equally inappropriate to attribute 'some pristine and unsullied concept of justice' (Harvey 1989, p. 358) to Lyotard. For example see Lyotard and Thébaud (1985).

4 The four stages or phases of modernisation distinguished by Soja (1989, pp. 3–4:183–8) are as follows:
   (i)   the classical era of competitive industrial capitalism (1830–70)
   (ii) an age of empire and corporate oligopolistic capitalism (1870–1920)
   (iii) Fordist and bureaucratic state capitalism (1920 to late 1960s)
   (iv) postmodern capitalism (1970 to the present).

5 For example Lyotard comments that:

> the complexification due to new technologies in both everyday life and the work process . . . makes this traditional province of Marxism *more and more important and serious*. It is obvious for example that the level of unemployment foreseen by Marx . . . is today a reality. And we have no solution to that. I think this will be the main problem for the next century because it's impossible to consider a mankind in which only one person in ten is working. It's *perfectly possible to elaborate this problem in Marxist terms* (1989, p. 21, emphasis added).

6 The idea of a 'crisis in marxism' was first introduced in 1898 by Thomas Masaryk (cf. Laclau and Mouffe 1985; Jay 1988).

7 Laclau and Mouffe note that:

A situation of hegemony would be one in which the management of the positivity of the social and the articulation of the diverse democratic demands had achieved a maximum of integration — the opposite situation, in which social negativity brings about the disintegration of every stable system of differences, would correspond to an organic crisis . . .

Every hegemonic position is based, therefore, on an unstable equilibrium; construction starts from negativity, but is only consolidated to the extent that it succeeds in constituting the positivity of the social (1985, p. 189).

BIBLIOGRAPHY

Anderson, P. (1984) 'Modernity and Revolution', *New Left Review*, No 144.

Arac, J. (1989) *Critical Genealogies: Historical Situations for Postmodern Literary Studies*, New York, Columbia University Press.

Aron, R. (1967) *The Industrial Society: Three Essays on Ideology and Development*, London, Weidenfeld and Nicolson.

Aron, R. (1972) *Progress and Disillusion: The Dialectics of Modern Society*, Harmondsworth, Penguin.

Aronowitz, R. (1987/88) 'Postmodernism and Politics', *Social Text*, 18.

Augustine, A. (1931) *The City of God*, London, Dent.

Bacon, F. (1855) *The Novum Organon, or a true guide to the interpretation of nature*, Oxford, Oxford University Press.

Badham, R. (1986) *Theories of Industrial Society*, London, Croom Helm.

Bahro, R. (1978) *The Alternative in Eastern Europe*, London, New Left Books.

Bahro, R. (1984) *From Red to Green*, London, Verso.

Bahro, R. (1986) *Building the Green Movement*, London, Heretic Books.

Baudrillard, J. (1975) *The Mirror of Production*, St Louis, Telos Press.

Baudrillard, J. (1981) *For a Critique of the Political Economy of the Sign*, St Louis, Telos Press.

Baudrillard, J. (1983a) *Simulations*, New York, Semiotext(e).

Baudrillard, J. (1983b) *In the Shadow of the Silent Majorities*, New York, Semiotext(e).

Baudrillard, J. (1984a) 'Games with Vestiges', *On the Beach*, 5.

Baudrillard, J. (1984b) 'On Nihilism', *On the Beach*, 6.

Baudrillard, J. (1988a) *The Ecstasy of Communication*, New York, Semiotext(e).

Baudrillard, J. (1988b) *The Evil Demon of Images*, Sydney, Power Institute Publications.

Baudrillard, J. (1988c) *America*, London, Verso.

Baudrillard, J. (1989) 'The Anorexic Ruins' in D. Kamper and C. Wulf (eds) *Looking Back on the End of the World*, New York, Semiotext(e).

Baudrillard, J. (1990) *Seduction*, New York, St Martin's Press

Bauman, Z. (1987) *Legislators and Interpreters: On Modernity, Post-modernity and Intellectuals*, Cambridge, Polity Press.

Bauman, Z. (1988a) 'Is there a postmodern sociology?', *Theory, Culture and Society*, Vol 5, Nos 2–3.

Bauman, Z. (1988b) 'Sociology and Postmodernity', *The Sociological Review*, Vol 36, No 4.

Bauman, Z. (1989) *Modernity and the Holocaust*, Cambridge, Polity Press.

Bauman, Z. (1991) *Modernity and Ambivalence*, Cambridge, Polity Press.

Bell, D. (1973) *The Coming of Post-Industrial Society: A Venture in Social Forecasting*, New York, Basic Books.

Bell, D. (1976) *The Cultural Contradictions of Capitalism*, New York, Basic Books.

Bell, D. (1979) 'The Social Framework of the Information Society' in M.L. Dertouzos, and J. Moses, (eds) *The Computer Age: A Twenty Year View*, London, MIT Press.

Bell, D. (1980) *Sociological Journeys: Essays 1960–1980*, London, Heinemann.

Bendix, R. (1967) 'Tradition and Modernity Reconsidered', *Comparative Studies in Society and History*, Vol 9, No 3.

Benjamin, W. (1973) *Illuminations*, London, Fontana.

Berger, P. (1979) *The Heretical Imperative: Contemporary Possibilities of Religious Affirmation*, New York, Doubleday.

Berger, P. (1987) *The Capitalist Revolution*, Aldershot, Wildwood House.

Berman, M. (1983) *All That Is Solid Melts Into Air*, London, Verso.

Bierstedt, R. (1979) 'Sociological Thought in the Eighteenth Century', in T. Bottomore and R. Nisbet (eds) *A History of Sociological Analysis*, London, Heinemann.

Bock, K. (1979) 'Theories of Progress, Development Evolution' in T. Bottomore and R. Nisbet (eds) *A History of Sociological Analysis*, London, Heinemann.

Boyne, R. and Rattansi, A. (eds) (1990) *Postmodernism and Society*, London, Macmillan.

Burawoy, M. (1989) 'Marxism, Philosophy and Science', *Berkeley Journal of Sociology*, 34.

Burger, P. (1984/85) 'The Decline of the Modern Age', *Telos*, 62.

Burgin, V. (1986) *The End of Art Theory: Criticism and Postmodernity*, London, Macmillan.

Burnham, J. (1962) *The Managerial Revolution*, Harmondsworth, Penguin.

Bury, J.B. (1921) *The Idea of Progress: An Inquiry into its Origin and Growth*, London, Macmillan.

Calinescu, M. (1977) *Faces of Modernity*, London, Indiana University Press.

Callinicos, A. (1989) *Against Postmodernism: A Marxist Critique*, Cambridge, Polity Press.

Callinicos, A. (1990) 'Reactionary Postmodernism?' in Boyne, R. and Rattansi, A. (eds) *Postmodernism and Society*, London, Macmillan.

Chatwin, B. (1987) *The Songlines*, London, Jonathan Cape.

Kuan-Hsing Chen. (1987) 'The Masses and the Media: Baudrillard's Implosive Postmodernism', *Theory, Culture and Society*, Vol 4, No 1.

Dahrendorf, R. (1975) *The New Liberty: Survival and Justice in a Changing World*, London, Routledge.

D'Amico, R. (1986) 'Going Relativist', *Telos*, 67.

Davis, M. (1985) 'Urban Renaissance and the Spirit of Postmodernism', *New Left Review*, 151.

Derrida, J. (1981) *Positions*, Chicago, University of Chicago Press.

Dertouzos, M.L. and Moses, J. (eds) (1979) *The Computer Age: A Twenty Year View*, London, MIT Press.

Dews, P. (1987) *Logics of Disintegration: Post-structuralist Thought and the Claims of Critical Theory*, London, Verso.

Durkheim, E. (1964) *The Rules of Sociological Method*, New York, Free Press.

Durkheim, E. (1984) *The Division of Labour in Society*, London, Macmillan.

Eco, U. (1978) 'Requiem for the Media' in P. Foss and M. Morris (eds) *Language, Sexuality and Subversion*, Sydney, Feral Publications.

Eco, U. (1987) *Travels in Hyperreality*, London, Picador.

Emmison, M., Boreham, P. and Clegg, S. (1987/88) 'Against Antinomies: For a Post-Marxist Politics', *Thesis Eleven*, 18/19.

Featherstone, M. (1988) 'In Pursuit of the Postmodern', *Theory, Culture and Society*, Vol 5, Nos 2–3.

Fekete, J. (1988) *Life After Postmodernism: Essays on Value and Culture*, London, Macmillan.

Fletcher, R. (ed) (1974) *The Crisis of Industrial Civilisation: The Early Essays of August Comte*, London, Heinemann.

Focillon, H. (1970) *The Year 1000*, New York, F. Unger Publication Co.

Foster, H. (ed.) (1985) *Postmodern Culture*, London, Pluto Press.

Foucault, M. (1973) *The Order of Things: An Archaeology of the Human Sciences*, New York, Vintage Books.

Foucault, M. (1979) *Discipline and Punish: The Birth of the Prison*, London, Allen Lane.

Foucault, M. (1981) 'Questions of Method: An Interview', *I and C*, No 8.

Foucault, M. (1982) 'Is it really important to think?', *Philosophy and Social Criticism*, Vol 9, No 1.

Foucault, M. (1983) 'Structuralism and Post-Structuralism: An Interview', *Telos*, 55.

Foucault, M. (1986) 'What is Enlightenment?' in P. Rabinow (ed.) *The Foucault Reader*, Harmondsworth, Penguin.

Frankel, B. (1987) *The Post-Industrial Utopians*, Cambridge, Polity Press.

Fukuyama, F. (1989) 'The End of History?', *The National Interest* 16 (Summer).

Furbank, P.N. (1988) 'A definite article debagged', *The Times Higher Education Supplement*, No 839.

Galbraith, J.K. (1969) *The New Industrial State*, Harmondsworth, Penguin.

Galtung, J. (1984) 'On the Dialectic Between Crisis and Crisis Perception' *International Journal of Comparative Sociology*, Vol 25, Nos 1–2.

Gardner, J. (1989) 'Postmodernist Blues', *Commentary*, Vol 87, No 1.

Gellner, E. (1964) *Thought and Change*, London, Weidenfeld and Nicolson.

Geras, N. (1987) 'Post-Marxism?', *New Left Review*, 187.

Geras, N. (1988) 'Post-Marxism: A Rejoinder', *New Left Review*, 188.

Gershuny, J I. (1987) 'The Leisure Principle', *New Society*, Vol 79, No 1259.

Gershuny, J.I. and Miles, I.(1983) *The New Service Economy: The Transformation of Employment in Industrial Societies*, London, Frances Pinter.

Ghirardo, D. (1984/85) 'Past or post modern in architectural fashion', *Telos*, 62.

Giddens, A. (1984) *The Constitution of Society*, Cambridge, Polity Press.

Giddens, A. (1985) *The Nation-State and Violence*, Cambridge, Polity Press.

Giddens, A. (1987) *Social Theory and Modern Sociology*, Cambridge, Polity Press.

Giddens, A. (1990) *The Consequences of Modernity*, Cambridge, Polity Press.

Golding, P. and Middleton, S. (1982) *Images of Welfare: Press and Public Attitudes to Poverty*, Oxford, Martin Robertson.

Gorz, A. (1976) 'On the Class Character of Science and Scientists' in H. Rose and S. Rose (eds) *The Political Economy of Science*, London, Macmillan.

Gorz, A. (1980) *Ecology as Politics*, London, Pluto Press.

Gorz, A. (1982) *Farewell to the Working Class: An Essay on Post-Industrial Socialism*, London, Pluto Press.

Gorz, A. (1985) *Paths to Paradise: On the Liberation from Work*, London, Pluto Press.

Gouldner, A. (1971) *The Coming Crisis of Western Sociology*, London, Heinemann.

Graff, G. (1973) 'The Myth of the Postmodernist Breakthrough', *Triquarterly*, 26.

Gramsci, A. (1976) *Selections from the Prison Notebooks*, (ed.) Q. Hoare and G. Nowell Smith, London, Lawrence and Wishart.

Habermas, J. (1981) 'Modernity versus Postmodernity', *New German Critique*, No 22.

Habermas, J. (1984) *The Theory of Communicative Action, Vol 1, Reason and the Rationalisation of Society*, London, Heinemann.

Habermas, J. (1986) *Autonomy and Solidarity Interviews* (ed.) P. Dews, London, Verso.

Habermas, J. (1987) *The Philosophical Discourse of Modernity*, Cambridge, Polity Press.

Hall, S. (1986) 'On Postmodernism and Articulation: An Interview', *Journal of Communication Inquiry*, Vol 10, No 2.

Hall, S. (1988) 'The Toad in the Garden: Thatcherism among the theorists'; and 'Discussion' in C. Nelson, and L. Grossberg (eds) *Marxism and the Interpretation of Culture*, London, Macmillan.

Harvey, D. (1989) *The Condition of Postmodernity*, Oxford, Blackwell.

Hassan, I. (1985) 'The Culture of Postmodernism', *Theory, Culture and Society*, Vol 2, No 3.

Hebdige, D. (1988) *Hiding in the Light: On Images and Things*, London, Routledge.

Heidegger, M. (1977) *The Question Concerning Technology and Other Essays*, London, Garland Publishing Inc.

Heilbroner, R.L. (1961) *The Future as History*, New York, Grove Press.

Heilbroner, R.L. (1976) *Business Civilization in Decline*, London, Marion Boyars.

Heller, A. and Feher, F. (1988) *The Postmodern Political Condition*, Cambridge, Polity Press.

Horkheimer, M. and Adorno T. (1973) *Dialectic of Enlightenment*, London, Allen Lane.

Howe, I. (1971) *The Decline of the New*, London, Victor Gollancz.

Hoy, D. (1988) 'Foucault: Modern or Postmodern?' in J. Arac, (ed.) *After Foucault: Humanistic Knowledge, Postmodern Challenges*, London, Rutgers University Press.

Huyssen, A. (1981) 'The Search for Tradition: avante-garde and postmodernism in the 1970s, *New German Critique*, 22.

Huyssen, A. (1984a) 'Mapping the postmodern', *New German Critique*, 33.

Huyssen, A. (1984b) 'From counter-culture to neo-conservativism and beyond: stages of the postmodern', *Social Science Information*, Vol 23, No 3.

Illich, I. (1978) *The Right to Useful Unemployment: and its professional enemies*, London, Marion Boyars.

Illich, I. (1985) *Tools for Conviviality*, London, Marion Boyars.

Jameson, F. (1984a) 'The politics of theory: ideological positions in the postmodern debate', *New German Critique*, 32.

Jameson, F. (1984b) 'Postmodernism or the cultural logic of late capitalism', *New Left Review*, 146.

Jameson, F. (1985) 'Postmodernism and consumer society', in H. Foster (ed.) *Postmodern Culture*, Pluto, London.

Jameson, F. (1988) 'Cognitive Mapping' in C. Nelson and I. Grossberg (eds), *Marxism and the Interpretation of Culture*, Macmillan, London.

Jameson, F. (1989) 'Marxism and Postmodernism', *New Left Review*, 176.

Jay, M. (1988) *Fin-De-Siècle Socialism: and other essays*, Routledge, London.

Karatani, K. (1989) 'One Spirit, Two Nineteenth Centuries' in M. Miyoshi and H.D. Harootunian (eds) *Postmodernism and Japan*, London, Duke University Press.

Keane J. and Owens, J. (1986) *After Full Employment*, London, Hutchinson.

Kellner, D. (1987) 'Baudrillard, Semiurgy and Death', *Theory, Culture and Society*, Vol 4, No 1.

Kellner, D. (1988) 'Postmodernism as Social Theory: Some Challenges and Problems', *Theory, Culture and Society*, Vol 5, Nos 2–3.

Kerr, C., Dunlop, T., Harbison, F. and Myers, C.A. (1960) *Industrialism and Industrial Man*, Cambridge, Harvard University Press.

Kroker, A. and Cook, D. (1988) *The Postmodern Scene: Excremental Culture and Hyper-Aesthetics*, London, Macmillan.

Kroker, A., Kroker, M. and Cook, D. (1989) *Panic Encyclopedia. the definitive guide to the postmodern scene*, London, Macmillan.

Kuhn, T. (1970) *The Structure of Scientific Revolutions*, London, University of Chicago Press.

Kumar, K. (1978) *Prophecy and Progress: The Sociology of Industrial and Post-Industrial Society*, Harmondsworth, Penguin.

Kumar, K. (1987) *Utopia and Anti-Utopia in Modern Times*, Oxford, Blackwell.

Kumar, K. (1988) *The Rise of Modern Society: Aspects of the Social and Political Development of the West*, Oxford, Blackwell.

Laclau, E. (1988) 'Politics and the limits of modernity', in Ross, A. (ed.)

Universal Abandon? The Politics of Postmodernism, Minneapolis, University of Minnesota Press.

Laclau, E. and Mouffe, C. (1985) *Hegemony and Socialist Strategy: Towards a Radical Democratic Politics*, London, Verso.

Laclau, E. and Mouffe, C. (1987) 'Post-Marxism without apologies', *New Left Review*, 166.

Lash, S. (1987) 'Modernity or Modernism? Weber and Contemporary Social Theory', in S. Whimster and S. Lash (eds) *Max Weber, Rationality and Modernity*, London, Allen and Unwin.

Lash, S. (1990) *Sociology of Postmodernism*, London, Routledge.

Lash, S. and Urry, J. (1987) *The End of Organised Capitalism*, Cambridge, Polity Press.

Lyon, D. (1988) *The Information Society: Issues and Illusions*, Cambridge, Polity Press.

Lyotard, J.F. (1986) *The Postmodern Condition: A Report on Knowledge*, Manchester, Manchester University Press.

Lyotard, J.F. (1988) 'An Interview', *Theory, Culture and Society*, Vol 5, Nos 2–3.

Lyotard, J.F. (1989) 'Defining the Postmodern' and 'Complexity and the Sublime' in L. Appignanesi (ed.) *Postmodernism: ICA Documents*, London, Free Association Books.

Lyotard, J.F. and Thébaud, J.L. (1985) *Just Gaming*, Manchester, Manchester University Press.

McLuhan, M. (1967) *The Gutenberg Galaxy*, London, Routledge and Kegan Paul.

McLuhan, M. (1973) *Understanding Media*, London, Abacus.

Mandel, E. (1980) *Late Capitalism*, London, Verso.

Manuel, F.E. (1965) *The Prophets of Paris*, New York, Harper Torchbooks.

Marx, K. (1964) *Pre-Capitalist Economic Formations*, London, Lawrence and Wishart.

Marx, K. (1973a) *Grundrisse*, Harmondsworth, Penguin.

Marx, K. (1973b) *Economic and Philosophic Manuscripts of 1844*, London, Lawrence and Wishart.

Marx, K. (1974) *Capital, Volume One*, London, Lawrence and Wishart.

Marx, K. (1976) *Preface and Introduction to 'A Contribution to the Critique of Political Economy'*, Peking, Foreign Language Press.

Marx, K. and Engels, F. (1968) *The Communist Manifesto*, Harmondsworth, Penguin.

Marx, K. and Engels, F. (1975) *Selected Correspondence*, Moscow, Progress Publishers.

Marx, K. and Engels, F. (1976) *The German Ideology, Collected Works*, Vol 5, London, Lawrence and Wishart.

Miyoshi, M. and Harootunian, H.D. (eds) (1989) *Postmodernism and Japan*, London, Duke University Press.

Moore, W. E. (1974) *Social Change*, Englewood Cliffs, Prentice Hall Inc.

Morris, M. (1988) *The Pirate's Fiancée: Feminism, reading postmodernism*, London, Verso.

Morris-Suzuki, T. (1984) 'Robots and Capitalism', *New Left Review*, 147.

Nietzsche, F. (1968) *The Will to Power*, New York, Vintage Books.

Nisbet, R. (1979) 'Conservatism' in T. Bottomore and R. Nisbet (eds) *A History of Sociological Analysis*, London, Heinemann.

Nisbet, R. (1980) *A History of the Idea of Progress*, New York, Basic Books.

Noble, D. (1983) 'Present Tense Technology', *Democracy*, Vol 3, Nos 2–4.

Noble, D. (1984) *Forces of Production: A Social History of Industrial Automation*, New York, A. Knopf.

Norris, C. (1982) *Deconstruction: Theory and Practice*, London, Methuen.

Offe, C. (1985) *Disorganised Capitalism*, Cambridge, Polity Press.

Parsons, T. (1951) *The Social System*, New York, Free Press.

Parsons, T. (1977) *The Evolution of Societies*, Englewood Cliffs, Prentice Hall Inc.

Penty, A. (1917) *Old Worlds For New: A Study of the Post-Industrial State*, London, Allen and Unwin.

Penty, A. (1922) *Post-industrialism*, London, Allen and Unwin.

Polak, F. (1973) *The Image of the Future*, London, Elsevier.

Poster, M. (1984) *Foucault, Marxism and History: Mode of Production versus Mode of Information*, Cambridge, Polity Press.

Poster, M. (ed.) (1988) *Jean Baudrillard: Selected Writings*, Stanford, Stanford University Press.

Poster, M. (1990) *The Mode of Information: Poststructuralism and Social Context*, Cambridge, Polity Press.

Raulet, G. (1986) 'Marxism and the Post-Modern Condition', *Telos*, 67.

Riesman, D. (1958) *Mass Leisure*, Illinois, Glencoe.

Robertson, R. (1990) 'Mapping the Global Condition: Globalization as the Central Concept', *Theory, Culture and Society*, Vol 7, Nos 2-3.

Robertson, R. and Lechner, F. (1985) 'Modernisation, Globalization and the Problem of Culture in World-Systems Theory', *Theory, Culture and Society*, Vol 2, No 3.

Robins, K. and Webster, F. (1989) *The Technical Fix: Education, Computers and Industry*, London, Macmillan.

Rocher, G. (1974) *Talcott Parsons and American Sociology*, London, Nelson.

Rose, R. (1988) *The Postmodern President: The White House meets the World*, London, Chatham House Publishers.

Roszak, T. (1972) *Where the Wasteland Ends. Politics and Transcendence in Postindustrial Society*, New York, Doubleday.

Roszak, T. (1986) *The Cult of Information: The Folklore of Computers and the True Art of Thinking*, Cambridge, Lutterworth Press.

Roth, G. (1987) 'Rationalization in Max Weber's Developmental History', in S. Whimster and S. Lash (eds) *Max Weber, Rationality and Modernity*, London, Allen and Unwin.

Rubin M. R. and Huber M. T. (1986) *The Knowledge Industry in the United States 1960–1980*, Princeton, Princeton University Press.

Saint-Simon, H. (1964) *Social Organisation, the Science of Man, and Other Writings*, edited and translated by Felix Markham, New York, Harper Row.

Sawicki, J. (1988) 'Feminism and the Power of Foucaldian Discourse', in Arac, J. (ed.), *After Foucault: Humanistic Knowledge, Postmodern Challenges*, London, Rutgers University Press.

Sayer, D. (1991) *Capitalism and Modernity: An Excursus on Marx and Weber*, London, Routledge.

Scott, P. (1989) 'Knowledge, Culture and the Modern University', *The Times Higher Educational Supplement*, No 875.

Smart, B. (1982) 'Foucault, Sociology and the Problem of Human Agency', *Theory and Society*, Vol 2, No 2.

Smart, B. (1983) *Foucault, Marxism and Critique*, London, Routledge.

Smart, B. (1988) 'Workfare or Unfair?', *Economic Affairs*, Vol 8, No 4.

Smart, B. (1990) 'On the Disorder of Things: Sociology, Postmodernity and the "End of the Social"', *Sociology*, Vol 24, No 3.

Smart, B. (1991) 'Europe Today and the Postmodern Paradox' in B. Nelson, (ed.) *The Idea of Europe: Problems of National and Transnational Identity*, Berg European Studies Series.

Smith, D. (1973) *The Concept of Social Change: A Critique of the Functionalist Theory of Social Change*, London, Routledge.

Soja, E.W. (1989) *Postmodern Geographies: The Reassertion of Space in Critical Social Theory*, London, Verso.

Sommer, T. (1991) 'A world beyond order and control', *The Guardian Weekly*, Vol 144, No 17.

Stonier, T. (1983) *The Wealth of Information*, London, Methuen.

Toffler, A. (1971) *Future Shock*, London, Pan Books.

Toffler, A. (1983) *The Third Wave*, London, Pan Books.

Toffler, A. (1984) *Previews and Premises: An Interview*, London, Pan Books.

Toffler, A. and Toffler, H. (1985) 'An Appointment with the Future', *The Sunday Times*, 17/2/1985.

Touraine, A. (1971) *The Post-Industrial Society*, New York, Random House.

Touraine, A. (1982) 'Triumph or downfall of civil society' *Humanities in Review*, Vol 1, Cambridge, Cambridge University Press.

Touraine, A. (1984) 'The Waning Sociological Image of Social Life', *International Journal of Comparative Sociology*, Vol 25, Nos 1–2.

Touraine, A. (1989) 'Is Sociology Still the Study of Society?', *Thesis Eleven*, No 23.

Toynbee, A. (1954a) *A Study of History*, Vol 8, London, Oxford University Press.

Toynbee, A. (1954b) *A Study of History*, Vol 9, London, Oxford University Press.

Vattimo, G. (1988) *The End of Modernity: Nihilism and Hermeneutics in Post-modern Culture*, Cambridge, Polity Press.

Weber, M. (1970) *From Max Weber: Essays in Sociology*, (eds) H.H. Gerth and C. Wright Mills, London, Routledge and Kegan Paul.

Weber, M. (1976) *The Protestant Ethic and the Spirit of Capitalism*, London, Allen and Unwin.

Weber, M. (1978) 'Anticritical Last Word on *The Spirit of Capitalism,*' *The American Journal of Sociology*, Vol 83, No 5.

Webster, F. (1986) 'The Politics of New Technology' in R. Miliband *et al.* (eds) *The Socialist Register 1985/86*, London, The Merlin Press.

Webster, F. and Robins, K. (1986) *Information Technology: A Luddite Analysis*, New Jersey, Ablex.

Weizenbaum, J. (1979) 'Once more: the computer revolution', in M.L. Dertouzos and J. Moses, (eds), *The Computer Age: A Twenty Year View*, London, MIT Press.

Weizenbaum, J. (1984) *Computer Power and Human Reason*, Harmondsworth, Penguin.

Whimster, S. and Lash, S. (eds) (1987) *Max Weber, Rationality and Modernity*, London, Allen and Unwin.

Wilkinson, B. (1983) *The Shopfloor Politics of New Technology*, London, Heinemann.

Williams, R. (1974) *Television, Technology and Cultural Form*, London, Fontana.

Williams, R. (1985) *Towards 2000*, Harmondsworth, Penguin.

Williams, R. (1989) *The Politics of Modernism: Against the New Conformists*, Verso, London.

Wright Mills, C. (1970) *The Sociological Imagination*, Harmondsworth, Penguin.

NAME INDEX

SUBJECT INDEX